JCMS

VOLUME 61 • ISSUE 3 • SPRING 2022

THE JOURNAL OF CINEMA AND MEDIA STUDIES IS PUBLISHED FOR
THE SOCIETY FOR CINEMA AND MEDIA STUDIES
BY MICHIGAN PUBLISHING

JCMS: Journal of Cinema and Media Studies (ISSN 2578-4900, e-ISSN 2578-4919) is published quarterly in Fall (November), Winter (February), Spring (May), and Summer (August) by Michigan Publishing, Michigan Publishing Services, 839 Greene Street, Ann Arbor, MI 48104-3200. Please visit https://www.cmstudies.org/page/MembershipRates for current subscription rates. PERIODICALS POSTAGE PAID at Ann Arbor, Michigan, and additional mailing offices. POSTMASTER: Send address changes to Society for Cinema and Media Studies, 640 Parrington Oval, Wallace Old Science Hall, Room 300, Norman, OK 73019.

Journal design by Finchfinger.

JCMS is published in cooperation with the Society for Cinema and Media Studies; members of the society receive the journal as one of the benefits of membership. For further information on membership, see the inside back cover of this issue. All business inquiries (subscriptions, advertisements, and change-of-address notices) should be addressed to the Society for Cinema and Media Studies at scms-office@ou.edu. All views or conclusions are those of the authors of the articles and not necessarily those of the editorial staff, Michigan Publishing, the University of Michigan, or the Society for Cinema and Media Studies. For ordering information, visit: https://www.cmstudies.org/general/custom.asp?page=jcmsnonmembers. Domestic and non-US claims for missing issues must be received within 90 days of the publication date. To process a claim, please contact mpub-help@umich.edu.

This journal is a member of CELJ, the Conference of Editors of Learned Journals. It is indexed in *Academic Search Premier*, *Arts and Humanities Citation Index*, *Film Literature Index*, *IBR (International Bibliography of Book Reviews)*, *IBZ (International Bibliography of Periodical Literature)*, *International Index to Film Periodicals*, and *MLA Bibliography* and abstracted in *Academic Search Premier* and *Extended Academic Abstracts*.

JCMS is available electronically: current content through Project Muse, a full archive through JSTOR, and back issues through ProQuest, EBSCO, and Gale/Cengage Inc.

Sarah Hamblin and Christopher Robé,
SIG Co-chairs

Spotlight: Activist and Revolutionary Film and Media Scholarly Interest Group

HOW DID THE SIG ORIGINATE?

The Activist and Revolutionary Film and Media scholarly interest group (SIG) emerged from a desire for community. There are lots of people invested in radical political film and media, but since the 1980s, this research has become increasingly factionalized. Although we both knew people working in this area, things felt pretty disconnected. We wanted to develop a SIG that would reconnect scholars and practitioners working across these subfields and forge a scholarly community that would help formalize and legitimize this area of study. Interdisciplinarity remains central; we didn't want to create a group around a singular definition of activism or that privileged a particular type of media or methodology. We work in quite different areas ourselves—Sarah is interested in aesthetics and tends to focus on more traditional conceptions of cinema, whereas Chris takes a more ethnographic approach that centers community media—and we wanted to draw on these complementary investments as a way to bring in scholars and practitioners working across a variety of historical periods, geographical contexts, theoretical perspectives, and methodological approaches.

Creating the SIG in 2019 felt timely as well; we're facing an exponential series of socio-political and environmental crises that have coupled with the emergence of new forms of digital media and major transformations in the structures of production, distribution, and exhibition to spark a profound

Sarah Hamblin and Christopher Robé, "Spotlight: Activist and Revolutionary Film and Media Scholarly Interest Group," *JCMS* 61, no. 3 (Spring 2022): 1–4.

reinvestment in activist and revolutionary film and media of all kinds. We wanted to build a SIG that would connect people working on these urgent contemporary issues.

HOW DO YOU SEE THE SIG IN RELATION TO THE SOCIETY FOR CINEMA AND MEDIA STUDIES (SCMS) AS AN ORGANIZATION AND FILM AND MEDIA STUDIES AS A FIELD?

The SIG is an extension of our investment in the politicization of both the organization and the field more broadly. This is a vital task in the current climate, which includes frequent attacks on academic freedom; the infiltration of well-funded far-right groups like Campus Reform and Turning Point USA onto campuses; the evisceration of humanities funding; and the increasing neoliberalization of the university and the precarization of academic labor. Making political work and the engaged analysis of it more visible is important; it provides a support system for those of us who teach and research material that might put us at risk from these attacks while also affirming the significance of this approach and the wide range of politically engaged media we study.

We also want to push SCMS as an organization to take a more active stance on these issues and to dedicate itself more explicitly to offering guidance and support around politically engaged teaching and research. We're hoping we can work with the Executive Committee and other SIGs and caucuses to develop resources for advice and assistance when a faculty member is targeted by Campus Reform or is attacked for teaching critical race theory, for example. We'd also like to encourage SCMS to engage in institutional advocacy and activism around professional issues that affect those working in cinema and media studies.

Overall, we see the SIG as more than a means to connect scholars around shared research interests, although this is central. The conditions of academic work need to be addressed just as much as the movements, filmmakers, and artists that we write about. After all, thoughtful and engaged research requires substantive resources. In light of this, we want to engage with other SIGs and caucuses working at these intersections to help make SCMS more inclusive and inviting to non-white, non-middle-class scholars.

HOW DOES THE SIG RESONATE WITH THE CURRENT MOMENT OF ONLINE AND OFFLINE ACTIVISM?

We see the current wave of protests as a partial extension of grassroots resistance to the Great Recession of 2007–2009, which included global student movements against tuition hikes and reduced funding; Take Back the Land and other land reclamation movements influenced by the Brazilian Landless Workers' Movement and Indigenous activism; copwatching and community organizing against the murder of Oscar Grant in 2009 and others; climate justice movements like Extinction Rebellion; and Antifa and other antiauthoritarian activists. A massive dispossession has launched many into precarious living positions and further dispossessed those already on the absolute margins of the social safety net. The rise of social media and platform capitalism plays a central role in much activism and collective organizing with both positive and negative consequences; sites provide activists with an expansive reach but create tenuous senses of solidarity. So examining these new manifestations of resistance and thinking through the relations between on-the-ground organizing and media activism is of the utmost importance in order to understand how successful social movements work and where others fall short.

WHAT DOES THE FIELD OF RADICAL POLITICAL FILM AND MEDIA LOOK LIKE CURRENTLY? WHAT TRENDS ARE YOU MOST EXCITED ABOUT?

The 1960s is often held up as the pinnacle of revolutionary filmmaking, and a lot of contemporary scholarship is revisiting this period to recover new possibilities for radical political cinema and media. Many of these new histories challenge the Eurocentrism of existing scholarship by focusing on movements and filmmakers from other regions or comparatively tracing the global circulation and development of radical cinema at that time. The canon of films for this period has radically expanded as a result, as have our ways of defining revolutionary film in terms of both its form and its production, distribution, and exhibition. This work has impacted the way we understand the relationships between art cinema, documentary film, and the avant-garde while also connecting activist film to the emergence of world cinema in really compelling ways.

Another dynamic trend in current scholarship is the focus on right-wing media. Film and media scholars have long seen left and progressive political cinema and media as their sole purview. But the mainstreaming of far-right ideologies over the past decade has made it increasingly important to understand how conservative activists have so effectively mobilized film and media. As a result, the SIG's first event was a discussion of Scott Krzych's book, *Beyond Bias*, to highlight and support research in this area.[1]

HOW DO YOU WANT TO SEE THE SIG FURTHER DEVELOP?

We're a new SIG, and because of the pandemic, we have only been able to meet virtually. So the key thing for us at the moment is to keep growing and stay active. We don't want the SIG to only generate activity around the annual conference. Rather, we'd like to see the SIG become a dynamic hub for engagement year-round so that scholars and practitioners feel more connected and supported. To this end, we've already hosted a virtual talk, as mentioned above, and discussed plans for other possible research forums, a website to share teaching resources, and writing groups. We're still learning about our members' interests, though, so it's important that our actions grow organically from the needs of our community. If anyone has an idea for an event or activity, we encourage them to reach out to us. We'll help mobilize and organize however we can.

1 Scott Krzych, *Beyond Bias: Conservative Media, Documentary Form, and the Politics of Hysteria* (Oxford: Oxford University Press, 2021).

Editor's Note: In the spirit of emphasizing the collective nature and approach of the Activist and Revolutionary Film and Media Scholarly Interest Group (SIG), the co-chairs asked and answered their own questions for this spotlight.

Sarah Hamblin is an associate professor of cinema studies and English at the University of Massachusetts Boston. Her research focuses on global art cinema, emphasizing the relationships between aesthetics, affect, and radical politics.

Christopher Robé is a professor of film and media studies at Florida Atlantic University and studies the intersections of media activism and social movements.

Interview by Samantha N. Sheppard

Spotlight: Lakshmi Padmanabhan

Samantha N. Sheppard: *Can you explain how your research in experimental cinema and new media intersects with postcolonial theory, critical race theory, and queer feminisms?*

Figure 1. Lakshmi Padmanabhan. Photograph by Aaron Kovalchik.

Lakshmi Padmanabhan: I'm broadly interested in the way images mediate our sense of ourselves and structure our sense of belonging in the world. When I first started writing academically about film, I wrote about mainstream Bollywood cinema and its limited visual vocabulary for addressing queer life in India at a time when there was a growing national LGBTQ movement and ongoing fights for women's rights. But I became tired of writing critiques of films with bad politics and wanted to focus on work by artists and filmmakers who are committed to queer minoritarian life and to exploring the formal possibilities of moving images for building more inhabitable worlds for us. To me, that is a fundamental question posed by postcolonial theory: How do we build livable worlds for ourselves out of the violent structures of coloniality that we have inherited? I find that same

---

Samantha N. Sheppard, "Spotlight: Lakshmi Padmanabhan," *JCMS* 61, no. 3 (Spring 2022): 5–8.

question posed by a lot of independent filmmakers and visual artists working in experimental or documentary practices who see film and visual art as modes of worldmaking.

Sheppard: *What is compelling about how films imagine the end of the world, and how does your work intervene in ecocritical discourses?*

Padmanabhan: There has been some debate in the humanistic disciplines recently about how to create adequate representations of the climate crisis, an event that seems both too abstract and too far in the future to capture through novels, films, and so on. In film, some scholars have turned to writing about Hollywood's apocalyptic cinema and its figuring of future climate catastrophe. My frustration with this future-oriented understanding of the climate crisis is the actuarial logic that underpins it. The climate crisis is obviously already here and unfolding through existing structures of racial violence, labor exploitation, gendered and sexual discrimination, and so on. The debates about the Anthropocene might be new, but the experiences of environmental racism and the long colonial history of land and labor exploitation that are detrimental to the planet are not. This is the point I take from Christina Sharpe's discussion of "weather" as the stochastic yet inexorable atmosphere of racial violence, which is lived as the attrition of bodily capacity and slow death for certain populations.[1] Or, to put it more simply: there is no universal subject of climate change.[2]

So I'm interested in how postcolonial filmmakers are already utilizing the language of film to capture the disjunctive experience of colonial violence as an ongoing structural relation rather than a unified event. For example, the first five minutes of *Xala* (Ousmane Sembène, 1975) provide a very clear picture of the relations between the erstwhile colonizer and the newly decolonized, along with a sharp critique of the economic dependence of newly postcolonial countries on their former rulers, all without any dialogue. *West Indies: The Fugitive Slaves of Liberty* (Med Hondo, 1979) likewise dramatizes centuries of colonialism through the form of a musical, without any conventional focalizing character narratives. These are not new films. Film, particularly Third Cinema and non-Western cinema, has long been inventing a visual language for thinking structural violence. In my current writing, I'm discussing these ideas through the work of Tsai Ming-liang, whose films are all set in intense and difficult urban environments—incessant rain, smog, polluted rivers—where the characters of these films, usually underemployed, homeless drifters, have to make a home. The weather is simply the environment they operate within, which formally works through the kind of banal anxieties and difficulties of survival in the midst of ongoing catastrophe.

1 See Christina Sharpe, *In the Wake: On Blackness and Being* (Durham, NC: Duke University Press, 2016), 102–134. On slow death, see Lauren Berlant, *Cruel Optimism* (Durham, NC: Duke University Press, 2011), 95–119.

2 Ajay Singh Chaudhary provides a clear working-through of this logic in relation to right-wing climate realism in a recent essay. See Ajay Singh Chaudhary, "We're Not in This Together," *The Baffler*, 51 (April 2020), https://thebaffler.com/salvos/were-not-in-this-together-chaudhary.

Sheppard: *How does your research influence or inspire how you approach your role as co-chair of the Society for Cinema and Media Studies' (SCMS) Caucus Coordinating Committee?*

Padmanabhan: The most basic yet difficult ethical work we in the humanities have to do is to practice thinking across categories of social difference. For example: What can postcolonial theory learn from Black feminism and vice versa? In my professional service and administrative roles, I'm drawn to work that raises related ethical questions. This is my first year working with the Caucus Coordinating Committee, and in our last meeting, we discussed the difficulty of developing shared working definitions of equity, diversity, and inclusion that adequately account for precariously employed, minoritarian scholars in the United States and Canada and that also address the very different issues scholars from non-Western countries face regarding hierarchies of academic labor and racial or ethnic difference. These are urgent questions for us today, because we are all aware that academic jobs are scarce, that the pandemic has caused an unknown amount of damage to our profession, and that the weight of these crises falls most heavily on underrepresented minority scholars, graduate students, and untenured faculty. The caucuses are one place within SCMS where we can have explicit conversations about how to make SCMS and the larger academic community of film and media studies a more livable place for minoritarian scholarship.

Sheppard: *Since academic work often fuses the pleasurable with the productive, either intentionally and overtly or not, can you reflect on the complicated dynamics of pleasure and joy between teaching, researching, and writing?*

Padmanabhan: I've spent much of the last year reflecting on this question, particularly because teaching virtually felt really isolating for me and for students of mine who were trying to learn without the right technology or under terrible conditions while a crisis of world historical proportions raged around us. Even then, though, there were days when students would talk through some complicated idea and I'd learn something meaningful that changed my own views about the text, and it was such a joy to help facilitate that kind of theoretical insight. This also happens in spaces beyond the classroom; for example, I just spent ten days at the Flaherty Film Seminar, watching and discussing a range of brilliant films curated by Janaína Oliveira around the theme of opacity. It was generative to think with hundreds of people from around the world who shared my enthusiasm for the films but didn't often agree with what I thought about them. So there can be a lot of heated debate, especially when we're meeting in person. Similarly, it's a lovely feeling to hear from someone who finds my writing changed their thinking about something, like when I co-edited a special issue of *Women & Performance* and had intense conversations with my friend and colleague Lily Mengesha across our different approaches: hers from Indigenous studies and mine from postcolonial theory.[3] Those moments of collective thought across difference make this work feel worth it.

Lakshmi Padmanabhan is an assistant professor of global media studies in the Department of Radio/Television/Film at Northwestern University. Her teaching and research focus on world cinema and experimental film, postcolonial theory, queer theory, and feminist theory. Her current book project, "The Untimely Image: Cinematic Form and Postcolonial Refusal," explores the relationship between cinematic form and the history of feminist struggle in Indian experimental film.

3 See Lilian Mengesha and Lakshmi Padmanabhan, eds., "Performing Refusal/Refusing to Perform," special issue, *Women & Performance: A Journal of Feminist Theory* 29, no. 1 (Spring 2019). The introduction is available open access at https://www.womenandperformance.org/bonus-articles-1/29-1/intro.

Megan Boyd

"A Ripple of Mirth, Feminine in Sound": Female Audiences and the Rise of Feature Comedy

ABSTRACT
This article examines how female audiences shaped the development of feature-length comedy in the American film industry during the 1910s. Worrying that women were alienated by forms of humor thriving in shorts, producers redesigned comedy for the feature. I argue that female audiences' centrality as a commercial force helped determine the direction of feature-length comedy. I also call into question standard histories of silent comedy that either ignore the shift or dismiss it as an acquiescence to genteel tastes. Such a characterization overlooks the degree to which comedies designed to appeal to women reflected and contributed to modern popular culture.

Reviewers of actress Marguerite Clark's feature comedy *Mice and Men* (J. Searle Dawley, 1916) stressed women in the audience as the main sources of laughter during the film's screenings. One reviewer was struck by "the ripple of mirth, feminine in sound, that passed over the big house in the Strand."[1] Exhibitors likewise observed that feature comedies went over well with female patrons. A theater owner from Carrollton, Illinois, discerned that Madge Kennedy's *Baby Mine* (John S. Robertson and Hugo Ballin, 1917) was "especially pleasing to the women; the house was full of giggles."[2] Sometimes

1 George Blaisdell, "Mice and Men," *Moving Picture World*, January 15, 1916, 440.
2 "What the Picture Did for Me," *Motography*, June 22, 1918, 1157.

Megan Boyd, "'A Ripple of Mirth, Feminine in Sound': Female Audiences and the Rise of Feature Comedy," *JCMS* 61, no. 3 (Spring 2022): 9–35.

exhibitors even suggested that feature comedies played to feminine tastes at the expense of male customers. Reporting that Olive Thomas's *Limousine Life* (John F. Dillon, 1918) did "big business," several exhibitors opined that the film "appeals to the ladies—not so much to the men."[3] By 1918, exhibitors in the United States maintained that five-reel comedy features were their most popular offerings and that women made up over 60 percent of audiences.[4]

Such reports point to a curious gap in prevailing accounts of silent American cinema. Scholars who affirm the importance of female audiences make virtually no mention of comedy, while those who study silent comedy almost entirely overlook female audiences. Although film historians spotlight the effects women had on the silent industry, the films they point to in this regard tend to be serials, problem plays, or other types of dramatic fare.[5] Conversely, accounts of silent comedy prioritize slapstick, a form of humor that the industry strongly associated with male patrons and performers.[6]

This article revises our understanding of silent comedy by presenting evidence that women were a crucial audience for feature comedy, one that had a profound impact on its development. With the rise of the feature film, trade articles, exhibitor reports, and advertising consistently linked female patrons to comedy in ways they had not for comedy shorts. As the industry sought to lure more women to film showings in the early 1910s, the trade press inferred that trends in comedy shorts discouraged their attendance.[7] Feature producers thus made concerted efforts to craft comedies that appealed to women. They began to rely on adaptations of plays already known to attract female audiences and adopted stories from publications with primarily female readership. More generally, producers reoriented content in ways that accorded with cultural perceptions of feminine tastes.

I also suggest here that scholars have misinterpreted the influence of

3 "Exhibitors Box Office Reports," *Motion Picture News*, March 30, 1918, 1872.

4 "Cut Out the Sobs, Exhibitors Say," *Motography*, March 2, 1918, 393.

5 See Diana Anselmo, "Screen-Struck: The Invention of the Movie Girl Fan," *Cinema Journal* 55, no. 1 (Fall 2015): 1–28; Miriam Hansen, *Babel and Babylon: Spectatorship in American Silent Film* (Cambridge, MA: Harvard University Press, 1991); Lauren Rabinovitz, *For the Love of Pleasure: Women, Movies, and Culture in Turn-of-the-Century Chicago* (New Brunswick, NJ: Rutgers University Press, 1998); and Shelley Stamp, *Movie-Struck Girls: Women and Motion Picture Culture after the Nickelodeon* (Princeton, NJ: Princeton University Press, 2000).

6 Gerald Mast's *The Comic Mind: Comedy and the Movies*, 2nd ed. (Chicago: University of Chicago Press, 1978), characterizes silent comedy as ruled by male, slapstick comedians. More recent works still present slapstick as the most influential approach and acknowledge the industry's presumptions about its appeal to working-class, male patrons, such as Alan Dale's *Comedy Is a Man in Trouble: Slapstick in American Movies* (Minneapolis: University of Minnesota Press, 2000) or Rob King's *The Fun Factory: The Keystone Film Company and the Emergence of Mass Culture* (Berkeley: University of California Press, 2008). The form's prioritization carries over into accounts of women in silent comedy. See Maggie Hennefeld, *Specters of Slapstick and Silent Film Comediennes* (New York: Columbia University Press, 2018).

7 Though scholars don't dissect female audiences' relationship with comedy shorts, they note how slapstick ran afoul of industry hopes for respectability. Respectability discourse was gendered, with many reformers being middle-class women and society aligning them with respectability. See Eileen Bowser, *The Transformation of Cinema, 1907–1915* (Berkeley: University of California Press, 1990), 179–180; Lee Grieveson, *Policing Cinema: Movies and Censorship in Early-Twentieth-Century America* (Berkeley: University of California Press, 2004), 104; or Alison M. Parker, *Purifying America: Women, Cultural Reform and Pro-Censorship Activism, 1873–1933* (Urbana: University of Illinois Press, 1997).

female audiences on comedy by characterizing the feature transition as having led to more *genteel* humor.[8] Scholars use the term *genteel* to describe a shift toward humor that relies more on narrative situations, such as domestic misunderstandings, than on eccentric costuming or physical gags (e.g., slapstick).[9] They interpret narratively driven humor as genteel due to its presumed palatability to higher-class tastes. While the feature's longer format and prestige certainly held class connotations, notions of gentility point toward gender as well due to women's cultural connections to respectable entertainments and genteel culture's cult of domesticity. However, the term is pejorative as well as inadequate. Modernist critics and intellectuals often framed gentility as a feminization that restrained art and entertainment forms. Such framing of gentility denigrates women's humor and impedes the adequate recognition of their imprint on film comedy. In fact, the industry's attempts to cater to female audiences diverged significantly from genteel culture. The following analysis seeks to add to the contributions of recent scholars, such as Maggie Hennefeld and Kristen Anderson Wagner, who have aided our understanding of the intersections of gender and silent comedy through the analysis of female performers.[10] My focus is somewhat different, as I consider the centrality of female audiences as a commercial force that helped determine the development and direction of feature-length comedy.

To advance the argument that producers constructed feature comedies to engage female consumers, the simplest path would be to analyze production memos as evidence of producer intent. Internal memos or studio correspondence from the 1910s are rare, but I address those documents where available. Other evidence more consistently indicates that film producers designed feature comedies to satisfy female patrons. Articles in the trade press, exhibitor reports, reviews, and advertisements all explicitly cited women as the target audience for many feature comedies. We can also look at the sources the filmmakers drew from. Finally, we can identify certain shifts in the films' production planning and actual content. Feature comedies largely utilized performers and modes of humor that contemporary observers believed would please women.

While producers responded to audience feedback, it is crucial to acknowledge that their conceptions of feminine taste did not necessarily

8 For references to comedy becoming more genteel due to the transition, see Geoff King's *Film Comedy* (London: Wallflower Press, 2002), 23; Steve Neale and Frank Krutnik, "The Case of Silent Slapstick," in *Hollywood Comedians, the Film Reader*, ed. Frank Krutnik (London: Routledge, 2003), 60; Frank Scheide, "The Mark of the Ridiculous and Silent Celluloid: Some Trends in American and European Film Comedy from 1894 to 1929," in *A Companion to Film Comedy*, ed. Andrew Horton and Joanna E. Rapf (Malden, MA: Wiley-Blackwell, 2013), 29–33; and Kristen Anderson Wagner, *Comic Venus: Women and Comedy in American Silent Film* (Detroit: Wayne State University Press, 2018), 38.

9 See Scheide, "Mark of the Ridiculous"; and Wagner, *Comic Venus*. Other scholars also place emphasis on clearer cause-and-effect structures or realism. Steve Neale and Frank Krutnik touch on all three when discussing slapstick's incorporation of genteel components for features in *Popular Film and Television Comedy* (London: Routledge, 1990), 96–131.

10 See Hennefeld, *Specters of Slapstick*; and Wagner, *Comic Venus*, 34–38. Wagner does helpfully mention that the industry conceived of feminine tastes in humor as "refined," but unpacking female audiences' relationship to feature comedy lies beyond her study's aim to analyze the contributions of silent film comediennes.

reflect how individual female patrons actually felt.[11] Even columns and fan letters in magazines may not offer an accurate representation of female columnists' or fans' feelings. For instance, the power of male editors potentially affected women's self-presentation. Wagner rightfully shows how women were encouraged at the end of the nineteenth century to partake in less bawdy, gentler forms of humor, so written assessments of feminine taste were undoubtedly influenced by social norms.[12] But while cultural biases do inflect the evidence concerning female audiences, these factors should not lead us to regard the industry's gauging of audiences as worthless. The industry was concerned with profit, and it behooved them to accurately discern audiences' preferences. Moreover, my main goal in this article is not to pinpoint the individual responses of female spectators. Rather, this article explores how the industry's efforts to attract them altered feature-length comedies. What the industry *thought* female audiences wanted shaped their strategies for production.

WOMEN AND FILM HUMOR BEFORE FEATURE COMEDY

Before feature comedies appeared regularly on release schedules in the second half of the 1910s, female audiences' relationship to comedy was nearly invisible in trade commentaries.[13] The sparse references to women in advertising, reviews, or exhibitor reports for comedy shorts in the early 1910s likely stemmed from two factors. First, women were not yet seen as the major body of moviegoers they would become by the end of the decade. Second, the types of broad farce popular in shorts were seldom associated with female consumers. The industry sought female patronage prior to the rise of features, but their efforts showed signs of yielding limited results when compared to their presence after the transition.[14] A 1911 academic study compared the class, age, and gender makeup of standard (or legitimate) theaters versus popular priced theaters (which included film as well as both big- and small-time vaudeville). For film audiences, it found that "the boys outnumber the girls two to one, and among the adults the men exceed the women by about the same ratio."[15] As Shelley Stamp and Kathy Peiss have discussed, even as women were becoming more of a presence in nickelodeons and early

11 M. Alison Kibler, *Rank Ladies: Gender and Cultural Hierarchy in American Vaudeville* (Chapel Hill: University of North Carolina Press, 1999), 5. Other studies also consider how entertainment industries promote certain tastes as appropriate for female consumers: see Lynn Spigel, *Make Room for TV: Television and the Family Ideal in Postwar America* (Chicago: University of Chicago Press, 1992); and Allison McCracken, *Real Men Don't Sing: Crooning in American Culture* (Durham, NC: Duke University Press, 2015).

12 Wagner, *Comic Venus*, 34.

13 While 1914 only saw thirty-three comedy releases of three reels or longer and multiple months without a release, by 1915, ninety-five feature comedies were released with several released every month. These numbers stem from the comedy and comedy drama listings in AFI's feature catalog cross-checked with analysis of the trade press between 1913 and 1920. This cross-checking is useful, as there were some where AFI included a two-reel comedy. See the "AFI Catalog of Feature Films," American Film Institute, https://aficatalog.afi.com.

14 See Robert C. Allen's "Motion Picture Exhibition in Manhattan 1906–1912: Beyond the Nickelodeon," *Cinema Journal* 18, no. 2 (Spring 1979): 2–15, https://doi.org/10.2307/1225438; or Stamp, *Movie-Struck Girls*, chap. 1.

15 "Economics of Amusements," *New York Times*, May 28, 1911, xii.

picture theaters, they were still a definite minority.[16] Audience makeup varied from theater to theater, but nevertheless, the imbalance was prominent enough for the film industry to openly express concerns about their ability to draw women.[17]

In the early 1910s, trade press columns, reviews, exhibitor comments, and recorded reactions from female viewers all illustrated concern that major trends in comedy shorts failed to please female patrons, especially middle-class women. The general consensus was that women liked light comedies, yet broad farces predominated film shorts. Edward Dillon, a producer of comedy shorts, asserted, "slapstick comedy is all right for a certain element of people, but the clean minded young girl, the faithful wife, and the intelligent class of motion picture attendants in general, are more in favor of the clean, refined, light comedy than the riff-raff or slap-stick comedy."[18] Female exhibitors also claimed women wanted comic forms that they considered higher class than broad farce. An announcement for a motion picture theater in Los Angeles owned and operated by women proposed that its program would be "of special interest to the feminine sex," which only allowed for "a few high class comedies."[19] This perception of feminine taste was at odds with the industry's characterization of most comedic shorts. *Moving Picture World* advised scenario writers in 1914, "It cannot be said too often that the present demand for comedy is almost wholly 'rough stuff' . . . a broad farce or travesty."[20] Light and romantic comedies certainly existed in shorts, but industry observers presented broad farce as the most common approach.[21] Even producers seen today as more concerned with cultural respectability, such as Vitagraph Studios, typically requested farce scenarios.[22]

In accordance with industry opinions that film producers relied on forms of broad farce that did not interest female consumers, exhibitors, reviewers, and advertisements rarely mentioned women as fans of comedy in the early 1910s. Instead, trade articles mainly referenced boys or men. A column in *Moving Picture News* opined that while the department store girl's favorite star was romantic lead Maurice Costello, the office boy preferred comedian John Bunny.[23] Publicity also seemed crafted for male subjects by proffering the

16 See Stamp, *Movie-Struck Girls*, 195; and Kathy Peiss, *Cheap Amusements: Working Women and Leisure in Turn-of-the-Century New York* (Philadelphia: Temple University Press, 1986), 148. Stamp cites articles from the early 1910s that express an interest in female patrons but admit that men are the majority. Peiss puts the percentage of working-class women at the nickelodeon at 40 percent of a 75 percent working-class audience, which is around 30 percent of film audiences.

17 See F. H. Richardson, "Women and Children," *Moving Picture World*, February 21, 1914, 962.

18 Dillon is quoted as claiming this in Bennie Zeidman's article, "What Is Comedy and Why?," *Picture-Play Weekly*, July 10, 1915, 29.

19 "Los Angeles News," *Moving Picture World*, April 1912, 641.

20 "Comedy," *Moving Picture World*, January 1, 1914, 41.

21 Though the terms *light comedy*, *romantic comedy*, and *comedy drama* appear before the rise of the feature, the references pale numerically compared to *farce*. Prior to 1913, romantic comedy yields no more than twenty-one references per year, light comedy no more than 135 references per year, and comedy drama no more than 235 per year, while farce had up to 864 references and never fell below 367. See Project Arclight, http://search.projectarclight.org.

22 "The Photoplay Mart," *Photo Playwright*, May 1912, 26.

23 "Current Comment," *Moving Picture News*, August 2, 1913, 22.

films as an escape from feminine authority or financial woes—both cultural anxieties still typically associated with men. Advertisements for Vitagraph shorts urged the viewer to see them "if you possess a proverbial mother-in-law" or "owe money you can't pay."[24] If women were mentioned, the trade press fretted over comedy's ability to drive them away. Some writers indicated that women would dislike the films' immorality, which columnists repeatedly posited as a rampant problem.[25] William Lord Wright of *Moving Picture News* insisted, "Slap-stick comedy, and suggestive songs and monologue have no place in a refined moving picture show, catering to women and children."[26] Other writers reported that women disliked the unsympathetic or unkind humor of comedy shorts.[27] While one might wonder if the trade press over-estimated the delicacy of women's tastes, their concerns overlapped with female commentators' complaints about the immorality, physical violence, and illogic of some comedy shorts.[28] Even by 1915, one female fan griped in *Motion Picture Magazine* that "if it is to be comedy, let it be good comedy, and not such ridiculous piffle as is given the public by Keystone Company. What is there funny about seeing Roscoe hit by a brick or Mabel fall into the lake, or the Keystone policemen, who do such meaningless stunts. There is no discoverable plot to their pictures, and to me they are nothing more or less than torture."[29]

Thus, discourse around comedy shorts in the first half of the decade stressed their potential liabilities rather than their attractions for female fans. Although it is almost certain that some comedy shorts found female followings prior to the feature, trade columnist, exhibitor, and viewer comments portrayed the films as impediments for female attendance. Overt outreach to female viewers in publicity for comedy shorts also remained sparse in comparison to producers' and exhibitors' later conspicuous efforts to target women through the feature comedy.

FEMALE AUDIENCES AND FEATURE COMEDY

Producers and trade commentators viewed the longer feature as an opportunity to expand film audiences to include further legitimate theatergoers, and that expansion held both class and gender implications for feature comedies.[30] The trade press repeatedly conveyed that while shorts represented a

24 "Goodness, Gracious," *Janesville Daily Gazette*, August 8, 1914, 4; and "Love, Luck and Gasoline," *Hutchinson News*, August 24, 1914, 6.

25 W. Stephen Bush, "Just Complaints of Exhibitors," *Moving Picture World*, February 14, 1914, 784.

26 William Lord Wright, "William Lord Wright's Page," *Motion Picture News*, April 20, 1912, 23.

27 "For Those Who Worry O'er Plots and Plays," *Motion Picture News*, January 22, 1913, 13.

28 See Richard Abel, *Menus for Movieland: Newspapers and the Emergence of American Film Culture, 1913–1916* (Oakland: University of California Press, 2015), 92, 188, 200, 222. Sample complaints include "vulgarity" in Keystone and Chaplin shorts; the female columnists praise feature comedies such as Edwin S. Porter and Hugh Ford's *Such a Little Queen* (1914) or Cecil B. DeMille's *Chimmie Fadden* (1915).

29 "Letters to the Editor," *Motion Picture Magazine*, August 1915, 167. I include this later source because feature comedy still had not been established as a stable market until around 1917 to 1918.

30 "Economics of Amusements," *New York Times*, May 28, 1911, X2.

"motographic vaudeville," the "long subject" would serve as a "motographic legitimate."[31] The term *legitimate theater* came to describe Broadway playhouses that showed a single production of an hour or longer as an evening's entertainment.[32] This contrasted them from lower-priced, variety venues such as burlesque or vaudeville theaters. Writers for the film trade press repeatedly expressed the opinion that lengthier features would draw the better audiences who had previously shunned filmgoing in favor of legitimate entertainment.[33] At the time, attendees of legitimate theater were reported to have not just a higher-class makeup than film or vaudeville audiences but a more feminine makeup.

As the film industry transitioned to features in the early 1910s, magazine and newspaper articles simultaneously attested to the feminized nature of legitimate audiences. Historian Richard Butsch recognizes that legitimate theaters foregrounded their female clientele in part to prove the shows were safe and respectable.[34] However, Butsch also identifies an *actual* increase of female patrons at these theaters over the second half of the nineteenth century.[35] As the film industry solidified its efforts to entice playgoers through feature films in the early 1910s, women were variously estimated to make up three-fourths to four-fifths of legitimate theaters' audiences.[36] While one might be skeptical of these numbers, the theatrical publications *The Green Book Magazine* and *The Theatre* included advertisements for feminine products such as corsets, garters, and maternity care items. These magazines also foregrounded the personal lives and fashions of female stars in a manner very similar to later film magazines aimed toward female fans (see Figure 1). They contained full articles on the "matinee girl" and her tastes in plays.[37] One finds no corresponding articles discussing male theatergoers.

Articles covering the theater throughout the 1910s avowed that women determined the success of legitimate plays, whether they saw this as a benefit or detriment to the drama. A 1910 article for *Woman's Home Companion* entitled "Women as Theater-Goers" considered them the main audience and aligned men with vaudeville and musical comedies instead. The author contends that for appraising legitimate audiences, "It is not necessary to mention the American man at all." He quotes a theater manager saying, "Women not only form the main support of the drama, but half of the men who do come to see plays would, if left to themselves, either go to their club or drop in on a vaudeville show or a musical comedy. They come because their wives or sweethearts want to. Cut out the women from the audiences, and four fifths of the dramas in the country would shut up shop."[38] Thus, the film industry's

31 "The Backbone of the Business," *Motography*, September 30, 1913, 191.

32 See Richard Butsch's distinctions between legitimate theater and other theatrical spaces in *The Making of American Audiences: From Stage to Television, 1750–1990* (Cambridge: Cambridge University Press, 2000), 121–138.

33 The Goat Man, "On the Outside Looking In," *Motography*, March 15, 1913, 194.

34 See Butsch, *Making of American Audiences*, 66–80.

35 Butsch, 66–80.

36 "Plays and Players," *The Theatre*, August 1913, 38.

37 See, for example, Julia Dean, "What Women Like Best in Plays of Today," *The Green Book Magazine*, July 1914, 961–965.

38 Walter Prichard Eaton, "Women as Theater-Goers," *Woman's Home Companion*, October 1910, 13. Eaton does not provide the name of this manager but calls them

HOW A RED-HAIRED WOMAN SHOULD DRESS 25

gold, for instance. How would you frame it? In bright gold? A thousand times no. It would destroy the luster of the painting itself. In a shining black frame? That would be almost as bad. The sheen of the frame would reduce the shine of the painting. The unique artist shows his appreciation of the problem by doing his metal paintings on a background of black velvet, or on screens that are papered with dull colors. The frame of the red-haired woman is as important as it is for the showing of the metal paintings. Hair and paintings have one preeminent quality in common, a high grade of brilliance.

A woman I know whose hair is red had her automobile lined with the palest shade of ecru, practically a cream, the most negative of colors. The background does precisely what she chose it for. it

Figure 1. Billie Burke discussing how the redheaded woman should dress in *The Green Book Magazine,* July 1914. HathiTrust Digital Library.

hope that feature adaptations of stage plays would lure legitimate audiences to film theaters represented an effort to attract not just higher-class patrons but *female* patrons.

When the number of feature comedies grew significantly after 1915, the trade press presented the films as catering to women.[39] It should be noted that the industry often distinguished these feature-length comedies from shorts with the term *comedy drama.* Comedy drama today tends to signify a genre hybrid of half-humorous and half-serious content. However, in the 1910s, the industry used the term to demarcate feature comedies from shorts, applying it to almost every humorous feature from romantic comedies to farces.[40]

Many humorous features exploited the same performers or plays that drew women to legitimate theaters. This connection dominated feature comedy's first few years of development. In 1914, 70 percent of comedy features (21 out of 30) were adaptations of plays.[41] By 1915, the percentage was around 66 percent (63 out of 95).[42] While original scenarios increased in 1916, over 60 percent of features (64 out of 105) still either directly adapted a play or

"one of the oldest and shrewdest managers in New York."

39 Ninety-five feature comedies were released in 1915, 106 in 1916, and a jump up to 233 in 1918 and 222 in 1919. See the AFI catalog.

40 See Frances Taylor Patterson, *Cinema Craftsmanship: A Book for Photoplaywrights* (New York: Harcourt, Brace and Howe, 1920), 135.

41 See AFI catalog.

42 AFI catalog.

Figure 2. Advertisement seeking out female patrons for *Peggy* (1916). *South Bend News-Times*, April 14, 1916, 13.

starred a player from legitimate theater.[43] Trade commentators observed how these legitimate connections would carry over female fans. A review for *The Mysterious Miss Terry* (J. Searle Dawley, 1917) characterized Billie Burke's following from theater as "consisting largely of matinee girls."[44] An advertisement for her debut feature film, *Peggy* (Thomas Ince and Charles Giblyn, 1916), announced, "ladies, make up your Matinee Parties now" (see Figure 2).[45] Douglas Fairbanks also had been considered a matinee idol in light comedies on the legitimate stage before achieving stardom in feature comedies.[46] Though producers became less reliant on direct adaptations or theater stars by the end of the decade—recognizing that not all proved equally amenable to the screen—they continued to copy character types and strategies from legitimate theater. A review for Dorothy Dalton's *The Homebreaker* (Victor Schertzinger, 1919) remarked that the film's "saleswoman who matches her brains against men and altogether gets the best of the argument" was a character type "popular on the stage in plays such as 'Maggie Pepper.'"[47]

Feature comedies released later in the decade not only adapted plays but also adopted material from other sources that targeted female consumers. Feature comedies lifted stories and novelettes from women's magazines such as *Woman's Home Companion*, *Ladies' Home Journal*, and *Ainslee's*.[48] Producers

43 The year provides a mixture of play adaptations, such as *Mice and Men*, or films that starred players with reputations from legitimate theater, such as Billie Burke, Douglas Fairbanks, Vivian Martin, and Mary Miles Minter.

44 Peter Milne, "The Mysterious Miss Terry," *Motion Picture News*, September 8, 1917, 1665.

45 "Auditorium—Today," *South Bend News-Times*, April 14, 1916, 13.

46 "A Gentleman of Leisure," *Variety*, January 2, 1911, 24.

47 "The Homebreaker," *Film Daily*, May 4, 1919, 5.

48 See Helen Damon-Moore, *Magazines for the Millions: Gender and Commerce in the* Ladies' Home Journal *and the* Saturday Evening Post, *1880–1910* (Albany: State

also hired female screenwriters for feature comedies and touted their ability to reflect a feminine perspective. A publicity piece for Clara S. Beranger, who primarily wrote light comedies for World and Paramount, claimed that women enjoyed motion pictures more than men, which necessitated female screenwriters. "To appeal to the female patrons," Beranger argued, "the photoplay must display the feminine point of view and no one is better able to project this angle than women writers."[49]

Reviews and advertisements stressed that women would like these feature comedies and that exhibitors should play to them. A review for actress Margarita Fischer's *Charge It to Me* (Roy William Neill, 1919) recommended that exhibitors use the line "Did you ever try to earn your own spending money without confiding in your husband? Margarita Fisher does in her most amusing comedy."[50] Similarly, *The Film Daily* pushed exhibitors to sell Viola Dana's *The Gold Cure* (John H. Collins, 1919) with the question "Girls, did you ever get into a romantic tangle with your girl friend?"[51] When feature comedies did not succeed, exhibitors often blamed it on the film's inability to satisfy women. For instance, John Barrymore's farce *On the Quiet* (Chester Withey, 1918) received the critique that it "does not appeal to women," while Ethel Clayton's *The Man Hunt* (Travers Vale, 1918) prompted the complaint that "no woman picturegoer will accept [it] as a bona fide entertainment."[52]

By the end of the 1910s, fan magazines and exhibitor reports broadly suggested ties between female fans and feature-length humor. Fan magazine polls by the decade's end consistently ranked performers who appeared regularly in feature comedies within the top twenty most popular stars. Regulars on these lists included Marguerite Clark, Viola Dana, Douglas Fairbanks, Harold Lockwood, Mary Miles Minter, Tom Moore, Charles Ray, Wallace Reid, Constance Talmadge, and Olive Thomas.[53] Except for Charles Chaplin, no comic associated with shorts was listed among the available polls' top twenty stars between 1917 and 1920.[54] Exhibitors also affirmed the popularity of comedy features with a female-dominated audience. A 1918 article titled "Cut Out the Sobs, Exhibitors Say" conveyed exhibitors' opinion that women made up 60 percent of their audiences. The piece echoed earlier comments about female attendees of legitimate theater by asserting, "It is the

University of New York Press, 1994); Jennifer Scanlon, *Inarticulate Longings: The* Ladies' Home Journal, *Gender, and the Promises of Consumer Culture* (New York: Routledge, 1995); or Richard Ohmann, *Selling Culture: Magazines, Markets, and Class at the Turn of the Century* (London: Verso, 1996).

49 "Are Women the Better Script Writers?," *Moving Picture World*, August 24, 1918, 1128.

50 "Charge It to Me," *Film Daily*, April 23, 1919. The trade press dropped the c from the actress's name during World War I.

51 "The Gold Cure," *Film Daily*, January 12, 1919, 8.

52 "Exhibitors Box Office Reports," *Motion Picture News*, November 2, 1918, 2765; and "Exhibitor to Exhibitor Service," *Motion Picture News*, June 22, 1918, 3689.

53 My most consistent source was contests in *Motion Picture Magazine* between 1915 and 1920. Editions are available on Lantern, Media History Digital Library, https://mediahistoryproject.org. I also considered results from national popularity contests: see "Star Popularity Contests Are Arousing the Nation," *Moving Picture World*, January 1, 1921, 32–33; and "Duluth Paper Stirs New Interest by Contests," *Motion Picture News*, June 22, 1918, 3696.

54 Chaplin came in seventeenth for male performers in *Motion Picture Magazine*'s 1918 contest and rose to tenth in their 1920 contest.

fair sex who bring the men out evenings to see the movie plays. They study our weekly programs, and it is they who generally are the ones who pick the nights he and she will attend our theater."[55] The article also tied this feminized audience to feature-length comedies as opposed to humorous shorts. It opined that these audiences did not want "these cheap two-reel so-called comedy subjects," reporting an exhibitor's comment "just at present I find the comedy-drama with a pleasing climax, of five to seven reels, best suited" as representative.[56]

Over the course of the 1910s, discussions of film comedy displayed a striking increase in references to female audiences once comedy features became industry fixtures. Whereas producers had been concerned about women's objections to comedy shorts, many of their feature comedies relied upon the support of female patrons. Legitimate theater and other source materials had strong ties with female consumers; reviews and advertising also foregrounded women. By the late 1910s, when over 60 percent of audiences were believed to be female, five-reel comedies proved very popular. The remarkable rise in industry references to female viewers once comedy transitioned to features should prompt consideration of how producers' efforts to please feminine tastes influenced silent comedy.

FEATURE COMEDIES, FEMININE HUMOR, AND GENTILITY

The existing literature has largely overlooked the importance of women as a key audience for feature-length comedy. The main reason for this oversight, I argue, is that scholars consistently view the film industry's transition to feature comedies as a capitulation to a genteel mode of humor. I will now summarize prior accounts and then use the films themselves to complicate this characterization.

Studies of silent humor tend to skim over feature comedy's development in the 1910s. When it is discussed, most authors refer vaguely to a shift toward genteel, or higher-class, humor.[57] The sparse attention likely reflects scholars' predilection for the anarchic vitality of slapstick and their view of genteel comedy as its stuffy adversary. The term *genteel* harkens back to a critique of the genteel tradition by George Santayana, Van Wyck Brooks, and other modernist critics and academics in the 1910s. They coined the phrase to describe a cadre of New England literary tastemakers in the mid- and late 1800s who sought to establish a high culture in the United States.[58] The modernists deployed the phrase to denounce Victorian-era bourgeois constraints on art. Some historians also use the term more broadly to denote a prevailing system of polite manners, moral conservatism, and refined tastes that ostensibly signal higher-class status.[59] Assimilating this conception, film scholars apply the term

55 "Cut Out the Sobs, Exhibitors Say," *Motography*, March 2, 1918, 393.

56 "Cut Out the Sobs," 393.

57 For references to comedy becoming more genteel due to the transition, see King's *Film Comedy*, 23; Neale and Krutnik, "Case of Silent Slapstick," 60; Scheide, "Mark of the Ridiculous," 29–33; and Wagner, *Comic Venus*, 38.

58 Alan Trachtenberg, ed., *Critics of Culture: Literature and Society in the Early Twentieth Century* (New York: John Wiley and Sons, 1976). This debate is summarized well on pages 1–13.

59 See Ann Douglas, *The Feminization of American Culture* (New York: Knopf, 1977);

to narratively driven comedies seen as suiting the tastes of higher classes.[60] Echoing the earlier modernist critics, contemporary scholars typically apply the term negatively, either implicitly or explicitly presenting genteel comedy as a tame, unfunny, and repressive imposition of elite tastes on a less receptive general public.[61] This perception may be why an interesting contradiction pervades the literature. While scholars remark in passing that genteel, respectable humor numerically dominated features, they still present slapstick as the culturally relevant form and largely ignore comedy features until the films start integrating slapstick comedians. In his analysis of the Keystone Company, Rob King presents the Mack Sennett cohort as triumphant over a "genteel assault on laughter" in producing comedy for mass audiences.[62] He connects slapstick to more modern forms of New Humor at the turn of the century that crucially shaped popular culture. He argues that a sudden rise in comic amusements at the turn of the century stemmed "not from the drawing rooms of the genteel elite, but from an audience of laborers, recent immigrants, working-class families . . . attuned to a new, urban world of popular amusement."[63] Given the negative view of genteel humor in studies of silent comedy, scholars may avoid the transition because of the belief that it resulted in films that were culturally stagnant, elitist, and less influential.

When scholars mention genteel modes of humor, they hint at the presence of female audiences even if they do not explicitly address them. Some historians have called the genteel movement the "feminization of culture," with many genteel publishers targeting middle-class women and encouraging a cult of domesticity.[64] Though scholars of American history usually focus on genteel expectations for middle-class women, Stamp's work on female film spectators in the 1910s notes that "refined filmgoing promoted to middle-class women" did not exclude working-class or immigrant women hoping to experience "upward mobility through leisure."[65] In fact, the trade press often effaced class difference, instead treating women's supposed preference for respectable humor as somewhat monolithic.[66] Dismissing film humor for supposedly genteel characteristics thus indirectly marginalizes women's general engagement

---

John Tomsich, *A Genteel Endeavor: American Culture and Politics in the Gilded Age* (Stanford, CA: Stanford University Press, 1971); or Dorothy C. Broaddus, *Genteel Rhetoric: Writing High Culture in Nineteenth-Century Boston* (Columbia: University of South Carolina Press, 1999).

60 For references to narratively driven comedies as "genteel," see King, *Film Comedy*, 23; King, *Fun Factory*, 40–41; Neale and Krutnik, "Case of Silent Slapstick," 60; Scheide, "Mark of the Ridiculous," 29–33; and Wagner, *Comic Venus*, 38.

61 This characterization would apply to all of the works in the footnote above except Scheide, who describes the shift neutrally.

62 King, *Fun Factory*, 4.

63 King, 3.

64 See Douglas, *Feminization of American Culture*, or Tomsich, *Genteel Endeavor*, 15, for more on American feminization. Work connecting gentility to femininity extends past American culture in works such as Dianne Lawrence's *Genteel Women: Empire and Domestic Material Culture, 1840–1910* (Manchester: Manchester University Press, 2012).

65 Stamp, *Movie-Struck Girls*, 15.

66 For instance, a review for the feature comedy *His Official Fiancée* (Robert G. Vignola, 1919) only directed exhibitors to "go after the women as hard as you can" without specifying class, age, or regional subsets. See Laurence Reid, "His Official Fiancée," *Motion Picture News*, October 18, 1919, 3045.

with and influence upon film comedy. In addition, the idea of gentility does not fully encapsulate how feature comedies were shaped by the producers' desire to cater to women. In certain respects, feature comedies' debt to legitimate theater and their initial ties to higher-class audiences did overlap with the class component of gentility. However, simply calling the transition to feature comedies *genteel* does not fully capture the relationship of female audiences with the form. Female protagonists in comedy features of the 1910s complicate historical narratives that have cast polite comedies targeting women as genteel opponents to slapstick's modernity. Features increasingly relied upon female stars and their cult of personality in contrast to genteel critics' emphasis on story merits. In addition, while these actresses' vehicles did tend toward the gentler humor sometimes associated with genteel tastes, that humor often stemmed from character behaviors at odds with genteel womanhood.

FEMALE STARDOM AND THE COMEDY FEATURE

Although scholars call attention to the narrative nature of genteel humor, the film industry believed female audiences cared more about appealing stars in feature comedies. With *appealing*, I refer not only to leads who were seen as either beautiful or fashionable but also to those who projected amiable personalities. While scholars have attended to the centrality of female fans to the rise of the star system, they do not typically examine how producers' attempts to appeal to women encouraged a notable move in comedy features toward conventionally congenial male and female leading characters, particularly further female leads.[67] I will first detail these changes before explaining their relationship to assumptions about female consumers. To consider differences between typical leads in comedy shorts versus comedy features, I examined reviews and synopses for 1,388 shorts released by American companies in 1913 immediately prior to the release of comedy dramas over four reels (using schedules from *Moving Picture World*) as well as those for the 992 comedies over four reels released between 1913 and 1920 (along with viewing 150 of the 212 extant films).[68] Approximately 76 percent of the comedy shorts had leads whose appearances were depicted unflatteringly in reviews and synopses, and 86 percent had personality deficiencies foregrounded.[69] In contrast, by 1917, 94 percent of leads in comedy features were praised for physical or personal appeal in written coverage.[70]

67 See Kathryn H. Fuller's analysis of film fans becoming increasingly feminized through an emphasis on stars, in *At the Picture Show: Small-Town Audiences and the Creation of Movie Fan Culture* (Charlottesville: University of Virginia Press, 2001). Gaylyn Studlar discusses how female audiences drove the star system in both theater and film, in chapter 2 of *This Mad Masquerade: Stardom and Masculinity in the Jazz Age* (New York: Columbia University Press, 1996).

68 The earliest evidence that I could locate of four- or five-reelers being referred to as "comedy drama" or "comedy" is *Checkers* (Augustus Thomas, November 1913) and *Caprice* (J. Searle Dawley, November 1913). This comes from reviewing *Moving Picture World*, *Moving Picture News*, and *Motography* from 1909–1920 (available through Media History Digital Library).

69 The shorts were determined by checking release schedules in *Moving Picture World* and examining plot synopses and reviews (discussed further in chapter 1 of my dissertation, "Legitimizing Laughter: Class, Gender and the Rise of Feature Comedy," University of Wisconsin–Madison, 2021).

70 See appendix III of "Legitimizing Laughter: Class, Gender and the Rise of Feature

A shift to appealing stars motivated a meteoric rise of female protagonists from short to feature comedies. While only roughly 10 percent of comedy shorts released by American manufacturers in 1913 had a clear female lead, by 1918, women starred in about 68 percent of feature comedies.[71] As Wagner duly notes the difficulties of reconciling society's emphasis on women's physical or moral virtues with broad comedy's dependency upon unusual appearances and embarrassment in her study on silent comediennes, it is logical that more women could be included in comic narratives where sacrificing social notions of beauty or morality was unnecessary.[72] A theater columnist for *Variety* reported that attractive women rarely anchored broad comedies. They posited, "character comediennes have achieved something of a success in broad comedy, women like May Irwin, Florence Moore, Marie Dressler, or Elizabeth Murray, but no young, pretty, girlish looking creature."[73] In contrast, many young women had anchored light comedy plays and now did so in comedy features. Producers openly communicated the need for feature comedies to have female stars. In 1917, George Kleine lamented about the failure of his earlier feature comedies. These had been group farces emphasizing men, and Kleine now identified the exigency for a female lead. In a letter to Edison's distributor, Kleine advised producing future comedies with theatrical star Marie Doro based on exhibitor advice. He urged, "It is increasingly impressed upon us that we must have female stars."[74] The feature comedies with female leads became financially vital to the American film industry. Clark's comedy *Miss George Washington* (J. Searle Dawley, 1916) proved to be one of the major hits of the 1910s, holding the US box office record for eighteen months.[75] By the end of the decade, when the trade press surmised that women made up a majority of patrons, exhibitor surveys declared comedies with female leads to be the safest bet with moviegoers. In 1920, *Moving Picture World* announced, "light society comedy starring a woman is voted most popular of all features."[76]

The increased use of appealing, young female leads for feature comedies accorded with the theatrical and film industries' conceptions of feminine tastes in entertainment. Theatrical publications already attributed productions' reliance on appealing actresses to female audiences prior to the rise of the feature film. Certainly, critics assumed that women's preference for attractive leads included male matinee idols as well. However, most coverage in *The Theater* and other magazines intended for middle-class women devoted

Comedy." That appendix also evaluates affirmative traits in all feature comedies for the years 1918 and 1919, and these traits remain dominant.

71 See the AFI catalog. I cross-checked with trade publications to see who received first billing, as AFI sometimes lists casts in an order that does not accord with their original billing.

72 See the entirety of chapter 2 in Wagner, *Comic Venus*.

73 "Opinion," *Variety*, November 1, 1912, 44.

74 "Letter from George Kleine to Leo McChesney," July 24, 1917, box 16, George Kleine Papers, Library of Congress, Washington, DC.

75 "Notes on Motion Picture Record of J. Searle Dawley," folder 18, J. Searle Dawley Papers, Margaret Herrick Library, Academy of Motion Pictures Arts and Sciences, Beverly Hills, CA.

76 "Light Society Comedy Starring a Woman Is Voted Most Popular of All Features," *Moving Picture World*, October 23, 1920, 1068.

articles to female performers such as Billie Burke or Marie Doro.[77] These magazines regularly prioritized female leads and presumed female readers wanted information about an actress's private life and style. A weekly column for female readers in *Variety* provided an overview of actresses and their costuming while scarcely mentioning the men in their productions.[78]

While some theater critics supposed that women merely wanted to see clotheshorses, others felt that such patrons enjoyed female leads because they hoped to see cute and likable role models. Critics commented on how young women responded to the personality of Laurette Taylor in the smash comedy play *Peg O' My Heart* (J. Hartley Manners, 1912–1914) despite its meager narrative. *Variety* opened its review of the theatrical production by quoting a matinee girl standing outside the theater. The reviewer recounts how the girl, despite admitting there wasn't much to the show's story, still looked lovingly at Taylor's photographs, murmuring "but the star is a dar-r-rling."[79] As opposed to replicating genteel expectations about edifying content, theatrical discourse purported that female fans prioritized stars' charms over narrative structure. Critic Walter Prichard Eaton surmised that this interest stemmed from women's desire to see themselves depicted positively, that female patrons wanted to "go to see something that will please and flatter them."[80] He critiqued Charles Frohman for refusing to put on plays if "it is not complimentary to their sex." Theater critics likewise repeatedly blamed female theatergoers for the light comedies of Maude Adams or Ethel Barrymore, which were seen as excuses to showcase their personae.[81]

An association between female viewers and appealing role models carried over into the film industry. Richard Abel discerns that coverage of moving picture stars in newspapers, which increased at the time of the feature transition, were located in the sections aimed at female readers. As he notes, columnists emphasized female stars' personal lives, their role as advice givers, and their function as conduits for fantasies about women leading active, independent lives.[82] The trade press also consistently connected comedies with female leads to a feminine audience. One reviewer pegged Clara Kimball Young's *Marrying Money* (James Young, 1915) as "a very girly picture," while another called Vivian Martin's *Her Father's Son*

77 For instance, *The Green Book Magazine* (July 1914) contains detailed probes about Maude Adams's family and Billie Burke's fashion, along with four extended articles about female performers, with only two, briefer articles about a male matinee idol and a character actor. Women were also seen as primary buyers of biographies about theatrical stars. See "New Dramatic and Musical Books," *The Theatre*, November 1903, ii.

78 Between 1913 and 1915, *Variety* ran a column titled "All for the Ladies," authored by "Plain Mary," that commented on female performers and their costumes, largely from the legitimate stage.

79 "Peg O' My Heart," *Variety*, December 27, 1912, 20.

80 Eaton, "Women as Theater-Goers," 13.

81 See Ethan Mordden, *The American Theatre* (Oxford: Oxford University Press, 1981), 27; and Sherry Engle, "New Women Dramatists in American Theater, 1890–1920: Martha Morton and Madeleine Lucette Ryley" (PhD diss., University of Texas at Austin, 1996), 10.

82 Abel, "'Film Girls' and Their Fans in Front of the Screen," in *Menus for Movieland*, 182–256.

(William Desmond Taylor, 1916) "a picture for young women."[83] Among the female stars who had female fans mentioned frequently in reviews, publicity, or exhibitor reports for their comedy features were Marguerite Clark, Vivian Martin, and Mary Pickford for Paramount Pictures; Constance Talmadge and Olive Thomas for Select Pictures; Madge Kennedy for Goldwyn Pictures; May Allison and Viola Dana for Metro Pictures Corporation; Jackie Saunders and Margarita Fischer for American Film Company; and June Caprice and Peggy Hyland for Fox Film. Like theater critics, exhibitors and reviewers ascribed women's penchant for female stars to aesthetic admiration and the stars' engaging personalities. To wit, a 1918 exhibitor report on the general popularity of comedy dramas made an overt connection between female leads and fans, declaring, "Girl stars are bigger box office attractions than the men because the women like to see the pretty clothes they wear."[84] Beyond wardrobe, commenters also cited female fans' appreciation for the lovability of a star as opposed to comedians' eccentricities. A reviewer of *Mice and Men* noted that "there are women who carry their market baskets on Saturday night to revel in the delights of Miss Clark's 'cuteness.'"[85] Similarly, a review for Talmadge's *Sauce for the Goose* (Walter Edwards, 1918) predicted "this will hit the women strong" due to "the pleasing personality of the star."[86]

While previous accounts of silent comedy would likely classify these comedies as genteel due to their presentation of role models, in contrast to the scholarship's emphasis on genteel humor's narrative structure, film critics felt that comedy features targeting women often succeeded because of the stars as opposed to the films' narrative merits. One critic suggested that "the substance of the story is almost negligible" in *A Girl of Yesterday* (Allan Dwan, 1915) and that it was "constructed explicitly for the charms of Mary Pickford."[87] Another similarly complained that *Satan Junior* (Herbert Blaché and John H. Collins, 1919) was "ridiculously inconsistent" but noted incredulously that "the audience howled with delight over the hoydenish antics of Viola Dana."[88] Though very different from slapstick, feature comedies that sought female patronage prioritized female performers and their charisma in ways that the label *genteel* does not capture. These star vehicles moved women's tastes in comedy past gentility toward the emerging mass celebrity culture. Viewers' support for the star system can be seen as part of a larger cultural shift from nineteenth-century discourses that highlighted internal virtues to twentieth-century discourses that praised external projections of personality.[89] Sumiko Higashi has already recognized such shifts in the industry's appeals to middle-class, female audiences, and we can usefully nuance

83 Hugh Hoffman, "Marrying Money," *Motography*, August, 7, 1915, 258; and Hanford C. Judson, "Her Father's Son," *Moving Picture World*, August 21, 1916, 380.

84 "Cut Out the Sobs, Exhibitors Say," *Motography*, March 2, 1918, 394.

85 Sime, "Mice and Men," *Variety*, January 14, 1916, 19.

86 P. S. Harrison, "Sauce for the Goose," *Motion Picture News*, September 7, 1918, 1595.

87 Peter Milne, "A Girl of Yesterday," *Motion Picture News*, Ocober 23, 1915, 82.

88 Jolo, "Satan Jr.," *Variety*, March 7, 1919, 66.

89 See Warren I. Susman, *Culture as History: The Transformation of American Society in the Twentieth Century* (New York: Pantheon Books, 1973), 271–285.

studies of silent comedy by not subsuming the comedies marketed to women under a monolithic, genteel category.[90]

SYMPATHETIC HUMOR AND THE COMEDY FEATURE

Not only did comedy features often emphasize star spectacle over genteel narrative coherence, but the films also targeted female fans through types of *sympathetic humor* that cannot be completely conflated with genteel culture. While the concept of *sympathetic humor* overlapped with genteel culture's recommendations for higher-class consumers, the films can also be distinguished from gentility through the ways in which their female leads generated that humor. Comedy features' supposedly sympathetic humor (very much predicated on a subjective, white and middle-class framework) often stemmed from the leads engaging in behavior that actually defied genteel prescriptions for proper femininity. *Genteel* implies a cultural stasis that is not to be found in these films. Historians note that women were already strongly associated with sentimental currents in nineteenth-century literature. Women's presumed roles as empathetic civilizers tempering society's more aggressive instincts encouraged this association.[91]

Following this line of thought, theatrical circles associated female consumers with what they deemed sympathetic humor, wherein the audience laughs with likable, humanized leads as opposed to laughing at characters' inferiority. For instance, a review of the light comedy *Why Smith Left Home* (1899) contrasted it from William Collier's previous work in farces by claiming his move to more a "sympathetic role" would appeal to the "feminine portion of the playgoing public."[92] All-women theater troupes also advertised themselves as offering sympathetic humor to female consumers.[93] Some directors and performers framed female patrons' desire for less cruel, good-natured comedy as a sign of their good taste. The French actor Benoît-Constant Coquelin defended American women from the notion that they did not have a sense of humor but used adjectives highlighting their sympathy toward characters, such as "gentle," "sensitive," or "magnanimous."[94] Women's supposedly gentle or optimistic humor, however, was not always regarded as artistically beneficial. Observers often blamed women for what they deemed escapist fluff dominating the legitimate stage. Critic Walter Prichard Eaton griped in 1910 that female audiences only judged and enjoyed theater "according as it tells a pretty story, with sufficient 'love interest,' and prefer-

90 Sumiko Higashi, *Cecil B. DeMille and American Culture: The Silent Era* (Berkeley: University of California Press, 1994).

91 Women, especially middle-class women, had already been associated with gentle humor and attachment to characters in genteel and sentimental literature of the nineteenth century. See Mary G. De Jong, ed., *Sentimentalism in Nineteenth-Century America: Literary and Cultural Practices* (Lanham, MD: Fairleigh Dickinson University Press, 2013), 3–4; and Tomsich, *Genteel Endeavor*, 15.

92 "Willie Collier in Congenial Role at the Manhattan Theatre," *New York Times*, September 3, 1899, 7.

93 "Plays and Players," *The Theatre*, August 1913, 38.

94 Constant Coquelin, "Have Women a Sense of Humor?," *Harper's Bazaar*, January 12, 1901, 2.

ably a happy ending."[95] Wagner usefully observes that presumptions about women's gentler humor carried over into the film industry's coverage of female performers.[96]

Corresponding with popular conceptions of feminized humor, reviews, advertisements, and production documents for feature comedies increasingly stressed sympathetic humor. A review for *The Heir to the Hoorah* (William C. deMille, 1916) specified that the feature was "comedy of the sympathetic kind, where you don't laugh at but with the hero."[97] In a similar vein, a review for *The Social Secretary* (John Emerson, 1916) claimed the comic heroine "makes an irresistible bid for the affection and sympathy of the spectator."[98] Behind the scenes, continuity scripts and correspondence about feature comedies also display a shift toward gentle and flattering descriptions of characters, such as "hard working," "vivacious," and "timid but with potential."[99] Production documents convey that the young leads in these features needed to remain in the audience's good graces despite the film's humor. When adapting Ann Murdock and her play *The Impostor* (Dell Henderson, 1918) to the screen, notes on earlier script drafts fretted that her part "would have no chance whatever to gain the sympathy of an audience. She should not be a shrew nor should she be a liar."[100] While these descriptions are somewhat vague, there are quantifiable shifts in the story structures from many comedy shorts emphasizing character humiliation earlier in the decade compared to the lead characters' enjoyment or innocent misunderstandings in most comedy features. In contrast to 84 percent of 1913 comedy shorts released prior to the rise of feature comedies foregrounding character embarrassment and anti-social behavior, by 1917, 90 percent of comedy features contained plots centered on beneficial adventures and well-intentioned misunderstandings.[101]

Trade publications linked this promotion of good-natured humor to feminine taste. In an assessment of Gladys Leslie's *A Stitch in Time* (Ralph Ince, 1919), the reviewer opined, "Women and children are certain to respond to the sympathetic qualities of Miss Leslie's personality."[102] Another review called *Persuasive Peggy* (Charles Brabin, 1917) "light and human" and stressed it would go well in "matinee houses where women predominate."[103] These commentaries were seconded by female writers commenting in fan magazines and newspaper columns, who often praised feature comedies with sympathetic characters and expressed discontent when this component was

95 Eaton, "Women as Theater-Goers," 13.

96 Wagner, *Comic Venus*, 34.

97 George N. Shorey, "The Heir to the Hoorah," *Motion Picture News*, November 11, 1916, 3017.

98 Thomas C. Kennedy, "The Social Secretary," *Motography*, September 16, 1916, 671.

99 "The Clodhopper," scenario 1, box 2, Harry and Roy Aitken Papers, Wisconsin Center for Film and Theater Research. His character is described as "hard working" and "timid" but "with potential." In "Madcap Madge," the title character is called "vivacious" and an "idol of the school girls." See "Madcap Madge," continuity script, box 7, folder 3, scene 11, Aitken Papers.

100 "The Imposter," undated, box 68, R. H. Burnside Papers, New York Public Library.

101 See Boyd, "Legitimizing Laughter." The shorts data is unpacked further in chapter 1, while chapter 4 discusses the data for feature comedies.

102 "A Stitch in Time," *Film Daily*, April 24, 1919.

103 Peter Milne, "Persuasive Peggy," *Motion Picture News*, November 17, 1917, 3485.

missing. A female newspaper critic praised *Betty of Greystone* (Allan Dwan, 1916) for being a "charming comedy of character," while another female writer for *Motion Picture Magazine* felt disappointed that Fairbanks's *When the Clouds Roll By* (Victor Fleming and Theodore Reed, 1919) "no more touches your emotions or heart than an ordinary two-reel slapstick comedy."[104]

While sympathetic and sentimental humor have been characterized as genteel in discussions of silent comedy, the female leads producing this type of humor in feature comedies differed vastly from the nineteenth century's cult of domesticity.[105] In fact, the films' heroines often behave in ways that overlap with contemporaneous notions of the New Woman. The New Woman emerged as a cultural concept in the late nineteenth century to describe women who contradicted genteel prescriptions for separate spheres. Early uses of the term by Henry James and Sarah Grand describe women seeking careers, pursuing education, or adopting changes in dress to move outside of the domestic domain.[106] Though it is almost impossible to avoid this term in studies of women's representation in silent cinema, few scholars addressed New Womanhood in film comedy until recent examinations of silent comediennes.[107] However, period critics noted that women in the audience responded enthusiastically to so-called modern women in feature-length comedies. A *Film Daily* reviewer pronounced of *Peggy Does Her Darndest* (George D. Baker, 1919), "Many of your women folk will term it a 'cute' story and they are sure to like May Allison in another interpretation of the ultra-modern and resourceful girl."[108] Sometimes the focus on characters who defied gender strictures irritated male critics and exhibitors. In *All of a Sudden Norma* (Howard C. Hickman, 1919), Bessie Barriscale played a successful gambler, which caused one male exhibitor to deprecate that "it was too much of a picture showing what women can do and showing man as her inferior."[109]

Reviews and publicity highlighted the modern and unconventional behaviors of the female leads in feature comedies. Much of the humor in the films actually came from the characters' revolt against older, genteel patricians. Rebellious types ranged from uncouth hoydens to wealthy madcaps, baby vamps, and young wives hoping to gain new rights within their marriages. One common plot type placed a rural or working-class hoyden into high society to let her wreak havoc. Typically, the narratives validated the leads' less socialized demeanor. In Elsie Janis's *Nearly a Lady* (Hobart Bosworth, 1915), a Western ranch girl becomes engaged to an English lord

104 Abel, *Menus for Movieland*, 231; and Hazel Simpson Naylor, "Across the Silver Sheet," *Motion Picture Magazine*, April–May 1920, 74–75.

105 See King, *Fun Factory*, 227–233; and Wagner, *Comic Venus*, 34–38.

106 Martha H. Patterson, ed., *The American New Woman Revisited: A Reader, 1894–1930* (New Brunswick, NJ: Rutgers University Press, 2008), 1–25.

107 For more on chorus girls as New Women, see Linda Mizejewski, *Ziegfeld Girl: Image and Icon in Culture and Cinema* (Durham, NC: Duke University Press, 1999). On working girls in sex trafficking films, see Janet Staiger, *Bad Women: Regulating Sexuality in Early American Cinema* (Minneapolis: University of Minnesota Press, 1995). Ben Singer also links the serial queen to the New Woman in *Melodrama and Modernity: Early Sensational Cinema and Its Contexts* (New York: Columbia University Press, 2001), 221–262. For recent examinations of silent comediennes, see Wagner, *Comic Venus*, 183–231.

108 "Peggy Does Her Darndest," *Film Daily*, February 23, 1919, 13.

109 "What the Picture Did for Me," *Exhibitors Herald*, December 13, 1919, 98.

and travels with him to the East where she "is disgusted by the general artificiality of life."[110] Other films showcase the hoyden bringing pigs and other inappropriate animals into genteel parlor spaces, sliding down bannisters, wearing men's clothes to society events, and trying to cover up playing poker by pretending to gather coins for a church service.[111] The opposition of hoydens to genteel, parlor room activities is encapsulated by a line from *Put Up Your Hands!* (Edward Sloman, 1919) in which Olive Barton (Margarita Fischer) declares, "I prefer boxing to tea" (see Figure 3).

Extant comedy features of this era show how the hoyden character type created humor from defying parlor manners. In *The Demon* (George D. Baker, 1918), Edith Storey plays a tomboyish "gypsy" (Romani characters in feature comedies were often referred to by this pejorative label) who shakes up her wealthy guardian's social circle. She sticks out her tongue, throws rocks at the nuns in her convent, and repeatedly mocks the snobbish friends of her guardian. In one particular scene, she grows annoyed that a wealthy woman in the front seat of the car will not move to make room for an older friend. She forcefully yanks the woman out of the front seat and throws her from the vehicle so the old woman can take her place. Films like *The Demon* create humor out of the inability of these young women to fit genteel notions of womanhood; they reward the hoyden with romance or fortune and present her informal behavior as more desirable than that of overly mannered upper-class women.

The wealthy, teenaged madcap also defied genteel strictures in feature comedies of this era. While the hoyden defied society manners due to an ignorance about protocols, the madcap grew up in high society but purposefully disrupted her environment with pranks. Plot formulae often brought the sophisticated madcap to a provincial town to modernize it. Hence a review for Vivian Martin's *The Fair Barbarian* (Robert Thornby, 1917) aligned her with modern femininity as the "slangy American cousin who drops like a bomb in the midst of the impossible quiet of an old English village" where she "rubs against the old-fashioned aristocracy."[112] Other films had the wealthy madcap defy a restrictive upbringing by running away from home or adopting another identity. Those disguises included "wild" mountain women, boys, cabaret dancers, chorus girls, and vamps.[113]

In Olive Thomas's *Madcap Madge* (Raymond B. West, 1917), the college-aged Madge visits her mother and sister in Florida after getting kicked out of school. The rest of the film follows her as she engages in pranks and wears various disguises. To prevent her from competing with her older sister for suitors, her mother and sister bribe Madge to disguise herself as a fourteen-year-old girl. She uses the innocent disguise as an excuse to borrow a car for a joyride

110 W. Stephen Bush, "Nearly a Lady," *Moving Picture World*, August 21, 1915, 1325.

111 The hoyden insists on having her pet pig in *The Little Terror* (Rex Ingram, 1917), shoots craps in *Bab the Fixer* (Sherwood MacDonald, 1917), and wears boys' clothing in *Muggsy* (Sherwood MacDonald, 1919).

112 Peter Milne, "The Fair Barbarian," *Motion Picture News*, December 29, 1917, 4590.

113 As some examples, the gypsy disguise can be found in *The Caprices of Kitty* (Phillips Smalley, 1915) and *The Madcap* (William C. Dowlan, 1916), the cabaret dancer and vamp in *Indiscreet Corinne* (John Francis Dillon, 1917), the chorus girl in *Betty in Search of a Thrill* (Phillips Smalley and Lois Weber, 1915), and the young man in *Peggy* (Charles Giblyn and Thomas H. Ince, 1916) and *The Antics of Ann* (Edward Dillon, 1917).

Figure 3. Advertisement for *Put Up Your Hands!* (1919). *The Moving Picture World*, March 15, 1919, 1423.

Figure 4. Madge (Olive Thomas) races into a ball on roller skates in *Madcap Madge* (Triangle Distributing, 1917). Image courtesy of the Wisconsin Center for Film and Theater Research.

and spend time unchaperoned with a male companion. A masked ball scene provides just one notable instance of the film contrasting Madge from stodgy, outdated gatekeepers of high society. She races into the ballroom on roller skates wearing a loose, Grecian robe, in contrast with everyone else's formal attire (see Figure 4). When an older man leads Madge in a slow waltz, she turns to the camera with a bored expression. She then bursts into quicker, looser movements, engaging in fast kick steps around him in a circle before abandoning him. While critics praised the madcap's escapades as delightful, some commentary hinted that the madcap's rebellion against authority could lead to trouble. Whereas genteel culture valued women's sexual purity, advertisements for madcap films stressed the risqué aspects of the madcap's quest for independence. Publicity for *The Madcap* (William C. Dowlan, 1916) proclaimed, "It's a dangerous thing for a girl as pretty as Flora to throw conventions to the wind, no matter how innocent her intentions might be."[114]

Romantic comedies in this period also exhibited non-genteel behaviors from their female leads. Remarriage plots regularly explored how couples

114 "Universal's Programs," *Moving Picture World*, May 27, 1916, 1434.

could adapt to make their marriages more companionate. The films reflected changing public perceptions of marriage resulting from mid-nineteenth-century marital reformers' critiques of women's financial dependence and sexual dissatisfaction.[115] In *Persuasive Peggy*, Peggy tricks her old-fashioned, farmer husband into granting her an equal say in the household, from refurnishing their home to receiving a separate checking account.[116] Other female characters modeled more radical notions of marital reform. In *Experimental Marriage* (Robert G. Vignola, 1919), for instance, Constance Talmadge's character openly identifies as a feminist and insists upon only spending weekdays with her husband while enjoying weekends separately.[117]

Single women in romantic comedies also deviated from genteel notions of demure femininity. The pursuing woman trope appeared in many romantic comedies of the 1910s in response to changing courtship protocols.[118] Anticipating 1930s screwball comedies such as *My Man Godfrey* (Gregory La Cava, 1936) or *Bringing Up Baby* (Howard Hawks, 1938), these young women chased a resistant love interest until he submitted. *Satan Junior* follows heroine Diana (Viola Dana) who keeps breaking into a playwright's home since she has heard he is a "wicked" New Yorker. Despite the playwright's efforts to get rid of her, she eventually tricks him into letting her drive him to a secluded location (see Figure 5). Once there, she informs him, "When you get back—they'll ask you about your bride. The papers have been notified we've eloped. Aunt Emmeline knows it by this time—so you're *beautifully* compromised." Fortunately for these characters, the men had already fallen for them. *Photoplay* affirmed that the success of films like *Satan Junior* came from the female leads performing an updated style of sexual assertiveness. "Gone is the brooding little sad-eyed thing of the regular Dana photoplay. Gone is the meekness," one review raved. "In their place appears a silk-stockinged whirlwind, a total of adolescent and healthy girl, a suave practical joker, a cunning and altogether modern master of men."[119] Exhibitors were told to advertise these irrepressible leads to women. A catchline for *Satan Junior* advised, "To all the girls . . . you don't have to wait for him to take the initiative after all."[120]

It thus oversimplifies the feature comedies that targeted women to conflate them with genteel culture. The films foregrounded female performers' star personae and women's shifting social roles in ways that deviate notably from nineteenth-century conceptions of genteel behaviors.

DENIGRATION OF WOMEN'S HUMOR

It becomes even more troublesome to classify female audiences as genteel when one considers how critics regarded feminine humor by the end of the 1910s. Though reviewers originally discussed female audiences as holding higher or refined tastes in humor, as the decade progressed, they increasingly

115 See Clare Virginia Eby, *Until Choice Do Us Part: Marriage Reform in the Progressive Era* (Chicago: University of Chicago Press, 2014).

116 "Persuasive Peggy," *Variety*, November 9, 1917, 54.

117 "Experimental Marriage," *Film Daily*, March 30, 1919, 16.

118 See Beth L. Bailey, *From Front Porch to Back Seat: Courtship in Twentieth-Century America* (Baltimore: Johns Hopkins University Press, 1989), 13–25.

119 "The Shadow Stage," *Photoplay*, June 1919, 72.

120 "Satan Junior," *Film Daily*, March 9, 1919, 3.

Figure 5. Diana (Viola Dana) speeding at her lover's expense in *Satan Junior* (Metro, 1919). Image courtesy of The BFI National Archive.

framed women as a demographic regardless of class. While entertainment industries in the late nineteenth and early twentieth centuries often sought female audiences to improve their reputations, industry rhetoric typically became more dismissive, bordering on resentful, once female consumers achieved considerable presence.[121]

To that end, some film critics bemoaned women's penchant for gentle humor as over-domesticating the potential action of comedy features, even if the extant films do show vigorous physicality. A review for Alice Brady's *The Indestructible Wife* (Charles Maigne, 1919) decried, "Women, and those men who abhor 'vile' rapid action, or sternly object to having their slumbering emotions disturbed, may enjoy it immensely; but for anybody who looks for life and vigor in photoplays may beg and pray for the Sennett comedy that might be next on the bill."[122] Critics also grumbled about female fans encouraging overly sentimental humor. The *Moving Picture World* reviewer for *Mice and Men* sniped, "To borrow an expression from the women, and those women who see the picture very likely unhesitatingly will loan it—it is a 'sweet' picture; it is satisfying."[123] A review for *Variety* seconded this disparaging conception of women's taste, saying women would "revel in the delights of Miss Clark's 'cuteness'" and that "being [a Famous Players film] of the mushy kind, you know what to expect before you see it."[124] Critics also held women

121 See Kibler, *Rank Ladies*, 1–22; and Butsch, *Making of American Audiences*, 80.
122 P. S. Harrison, "The Indestructible Wife," *Motion Picture News*, March 1, 1919, 1387.
123 Thomas C. Kennedy, "Mice and Men," *Moving Picture World*, January 22, 1916, 196.
124 Sime, "Mice and Men," *Variety*, January 14, 1916, 19.

accountable when dismissing the wish fulfillment structures of many feature comedies. Writer Joshua Lowitke later noted in a *Variety* review that *Thirty a Week* (Harry Beaumont, 1918) would please female audiences, especially lower-class women, due to the positive trajectory of a working girl experiencing raised fortunes. The reviewer quipped, "The sentimental shopgirls and 'kitchen mechanics' who enjoy novels where the rich young man marries the poor working girl, vice versa, will revel in the development of 'Thirty a Week.'"[125] Critics' irritation with women's tastes reveals that the discourses surrounding female audiences and comedy moved beyond the bounds of respectability rhetoric. In fact, by the end of the 1910s, critics saw feminized humor to be nearly as problematic as slapstick.

Unfortunately, the denigration of women's effect on humor continues in current histories of silent comedy. When scholars simply categorize comedy features that played to women as genteel, they accept the pejorative premise that these films were culturally pernicious and distanced from the modern. Lea Jacobs astutely notes that film scholars have often unconsciously carried forward gendered tastes from earlier cultural critics. She observes that critic Gilbert Seldes's early elevation of slapstick at the expense of supposedly genteel forms in the 1920s exhibited "misogyny attendant upon the simultaneous rejection of sentimentality and celebration of the vulgate."[126] Indeed, Seldes often lauded slapstick for not being "prettified" or the absence of "sentiment," phrases associated with the comedies crafted for women.[127] Literary scholars share Jacobs's observation that modernist intellectuals, including those who disparaged gentility in the 1910s, often indicated distaste for middlebrow forms associated with female consumers.[128] While scholars of film comedy often employ the adjective *genteel* to mark the class of audiences, Rob King acknowledges how the idea also encompasses a "feminized concept of culture."[129] The way literature frames non-slapstick comedies as genteel, and even as assaults on laughter, fixes the tastes of female audiences statically in the nineteenth century and positions them as impediments to film comedy's development.

Beyond silent comedy, it is worth considering how the investments of comedy studies more broadly promote a disinterest in the kinds of comedies the film industry crafted for female patrons. Scholars' interest in slapstick and dispassion for other forms of silent humor is a microcosm of the manner in which comedy analyses often downplay films intended for women. While female audiences have long been associated with sentimental entertainment, comedy scholars still cite Henri Bergson's belief that "sentiment is the enemy of humor" and emphasize comedy's emotional distance.[130] Studies of film

125 "Thirty a Week," *Variety*, October 18, 1918, 39.

126 Lea Jacobs, *The Decline of Sentiment: American Film in the 1920s* (Berkeley: University of California Press, 2008), 16.

127 Gilbert Seldes, *The Seven Lively Arts* (New York: Harper and Brothers, 1924), 12.

128 See Rita Felski, *The Gender of Modernity* (Cambridge, MA: Harvard University Press, 1995); and Diana Holmes, *Middlebrow Matters: Women's Reading and the Literary Canon in France since the Belle Époque* (Liverpool: Liverpool University Press, 2018).

129 King, *Fun Factory*, 10.

130 Bergson's notion of emotional distance is repeated in Andrew Horton's introduction to *Comedy/Cinema/Theory* (Berkeley: University of California Press, 1991), 9. Linda Mizejewski and Victoria Sturtevant note that Bergson's view of comedy

comedy also foreground social disruption, drawing on Mikhail Bakhtin's theory of the carnivalesque, but feature comedies aimed at women promoted more socially conciliatory forms of humor.[131] Female audiences usually remain isolated within studies of romantic comedy as opposed to having their broader consumption of comedy films explored.[132] Such assessments of comedy can discourage a more thorough examination of female audiences' relationship to film humor. By better understanding the influence of female audiences on feature-length comedy, and complicating the perspective that this influence was simply tame or old fashioned, we can create more space for examining their relationship to film comedy and its evolution.

CONCLUSION

Despite the muted role accorded to female audiences in histories of silent comedy, the US film industry gauged the tastes of women when designing comedy features. This article moves past the valuable recognition of comediennes toward delineating how the perceived tastes of female audiences impacted the production of comedy films. The industry's respectability goals for the feature, and their desire for more legitimate patrons, gave producers a strong impetus to consider the preferences of female audiences. Though female viewers had rarely been mentioned in connection to comedy shorts in the early 1910s, trade writers saw them as a crucial audience for feature comedies. Exhibitors likewise believed certain forms of humor succeeded with women, and producers' strategies for comedy features increasingly accorded with their conceptions of feminine taste.

Though the feature transition is generally described as genteel, the industry's attempts to entice female viewers did not result in a straightforward replication of genteel culture's principles. Producers and trade writers' presumption that female fans wanted appealing stars in comedy features, especially female stars, expands feminine taste in humor past gentility to the rise of mass celebrity culture. Moreover, producers' incorporation of sympathetic and polite humor for female audiences also did not simply reflect the nineteenth century's genteel elitism. The leads in these features engaged in behaviors at odds with genteel manners. In fact, by the end of the decade, feminine humor hardly represented cultural refinement. Critics placed feminine tastes in conflict with admirable film comedy once women achieved a

would indirectly exclude women due to its unsympathetic aggression, in the introduction to their edited collection *Hysterical! Women in American Comedy* (Austin: University of Texas Press, 2017), 13.

131 Mikhail Bakhtin's concept of carnivalesque is used to discuss comedy's disruptive nature in regard to many aspects, including class, gender, or narrative structure. See Christopher Beach, *Class, Language, and American Film Comedy* (Cambridge: Cambridge University Press, 2002); Henry Jenkins, *What Made Pistachio Nuts? Early Sound Comedy and the Vaudeville Aesthetic* (New York: Columbia University Press, 1992); and Kathleen Rowe, *The Unruly Woman: Gender and the Genres of Laughter* (Austin: University of Texas Press, 1995).

132 Neale and Krutnik's overview of comedy in film and television brings up female viewers in relation to romantic comedy; see Neale and Krutnik, *Popular Film*, 133. This is tricky, as the form's gender politics are often stressed over its humor. Leger Grindon notes that many studies of romantic comedy actually neglect what makes the films funny. See Leger Grindon, *The Hollywood Romantic Comedy: Conventions, History, Controversies* (Malden, MA: Wiley-Blackwell, 2011), 70.

strong market presence. Contemporary accounts of film comedy that characterize non-slapstick comedies as genteel, including most comedy features, risk generating an inaccurate narrative that female audiences were obstacles for, as opposed to contributors to, popular film humor.

The perceived tastes of female patrons molded feature-length comedy, the form that would come to surpass short film economically. The attempts of producers to gratify women's tastes laid groundwork for the engaging protagonists and sentimentality of later landmark feature comedies starring Chaplin, Buster Keaton, and Harold Lloyd.[133] Focusing on slapstick, or other types of comedy less associated with female audiences, may unintentionally erase women's larger historical impact on film humor. The feature comedy as we know it *would not exist* without feminine taste cultures.

I would like to warmly thank Ben Singer for reading drafts and helping me wrestle with such copious amounts of material. Additional thanks to Maria Belodubrovskaya, A. Henderson Boyd, Thomas Brami, and Eric Hoyt for their valuable insights.

Megan Boyd is a visiting assistant professor of film studies at Lawrence University. She received her PhD from the University of Wisconsin–Madison. Her current book project, "Legitimizing Laughter: Female Audiences and the Rise of Feature Comedy," details the ways in which female audiences profoundly shaped the development of feature-length comedy in the American film industry.

133 For one analysis of Chaplin, Keaton, and Lloyd's integration of respectability elements to befit the feature market, see Neale and Krutnik, *Popular Film*, 96–131.

Elyce Rae Helford

Racialized Darkness and *Ace in the Hole*

ABSTRACT

Limited scholarly attention has been devoted to Billy Wilder's *Ace in the Hole* (1951), at least in part because of limited availability before its 2007 DVD release. While Wilder biographies and available criticism focus primarily on the film's critique of tabloid journalism, this study explores the film's engagement with racialized darkness, figured in Native American imagery and engagement with Jewishness and Holocaust survivor guilt. I argue that seemingly superficial markers of racial and cultural difference in the film, particularly when read through film noir anxiety, reveal significant cultural concerns of the immediate postwar era, including those of its émigré writer, producer, and director.

THE RUNT OF THE LITTER

Ace in the Hole (1951) is the first Hollywood film for which Austrian-Jewish émigré Billy Wilder served as producer, director, and head screenwriter. It was also his first box office flop. The work came on the heels of *Sunset Boulevard* (1950) and Wilder's breakup with writing partner Charles Brackett. With new, younger writers who would follow his lead and whims, Wilder used his film to treat the tabloids and thrill-chasing midcentury audiences as cynically as he and Brackett had treated Hollywood and the media in *Sunset Boulevard*.

The picture follows the exploits of sneering, ambitious reporter Chuck Tatum (Kirk Douglas), who has been banished from New York to New Mexico as punishment for journalistic misdeeds. In Albuquerque, he plots his return to acclaim by manipulating a story about a man from the nearby town of Escudero, Leo Minosa (Richard Benedict), who has become trapped in a mine while searching for Indian pottery to sell at his family's trading post.

Elyce Rae Helford, "Racialized Darkness and *Ace in the Hole*," *JCMS* 61, no. 3 (Spring 2022): 36–58.

Tatum convinces local authorities to take a circuitous route in their rescue of Minosa, giving the reporter time to work the story up to one of national interest. He seduces his victim's wife, Lorraine (Jan Sterling), and attempts to use her to increase the public's sympathy, then turns the accident site into a literal carnival of paying bystanders. The plan ultimately results in Leo Minosa's death in the cave. Soon after, Tatum also dies after having been stabbed by Lorraine for his brutal behavior toward her.

Wilder drew on personal experience for the film, having been a tabloid journalist in his European youth to avoid a career as the lawyer his father wanted him to be.[1] *Ace in the Hole* included research into tragedies that received ample newspaper coverage, including that of ill-fated Kentucky caver Floyd Collins, who was trapped underground until his death in 1925, and three-year-old Californian Kathy Fiscus, who fell into and died in a San Marino well in 1949. This emphasis on suffering and death meant that *Ace in the Hole* found fewer opportunities for humor, however bleak, than several of Wilder's previous directorial efforts. Its commentary was aimed not only at the popular press but also at moviegoing audiences. Critique and even ridicule of Hollywood's aging stars and greedy young writers in *Sunset Boulevard* did not implicate the average viewer, but viewers may have found *Ace in the Hole*'s attack far closer to home, as it depicted a voracious public feeding on spectacle—no matter how gruesome or fantastic—to pep up daily life in the wake of World War II.

Contrasting audience and critical responses to the two pictures illustrates this issue of spectator proximity. The Hollywood elite loved *Sunset Boulevard*; for example, "Barbara Stanwyck was so impressed that she reportedly knelt down and kissed the hem of Gloria Swanson's silver lamé gown."[2] The Hollywood press also praised the film mightily, even as some reviewers found it disturbing. The *Hollywood Reporter*, for instance, gushed, "You want to applaud *Sunset Boulevard* frame by frame."[3] Film critic Andrew Sarris claimed to have seen it at least twenty-five times.[4] Audiences also drove the film to unqualified box office success. Even the Academy of Motion Pictures Arts and Sciences (of which Brackett was president at the time) bestowed its endorsement, as *Sunset Boulevard* received eleven Academy Award nominations, including Best Picture and Best Director.

Similar praise might have been heaped on *Ace in the Hole* but generally was not. Direction and acting were commended, and the film won an International Award at the Venice Film Festival. A few magazines sang its praises, including *Newsweek* and the *Saturday Review*.[5] More common, however, were mixed reviews, in which critics expressed a combination of admiration and disapprobation, at times with unacknowledged self-interest. Bosley Crowther's *New York Times* review, for example, applauded Wilder's "spectac-

1 Noah Isenberg, introduction to *Billy Wilder on Assignment: Dispatches from Weimar Berlin and Interwar Vienna* (Princeton, NJ: Princeton University Press, 2021), 3.

2 Ed Sikov, *On Sunset Boulevard: The Life and Times of Billy Wilder* (New York: Hyperion, 1998), 303.

3 Sikov, 104.

4 Sikov, 104.

5 See Tom Wood, *The Bright Side of Billy Wilder, Primarily* (New York: Doubleday, 1970), 105.

ular job" in bringing a "sordid and cynical drama" to the screen. Crowther lauded the film as "masterly" for showing "revolting" truths about the "monstrous vulgarity of mob behavior." Yet he decried a "poorly constructed plot" based "upon assumptions that are not only naïve but absurd."[6] Specifically, he referenced the portrayal of the newsroom, arguing that his fellow newspapermen would have stopped protagonist Tatum before his dangerous, self-aggrandizing actions became lethal, and Crowther also rejected what he saw as Tatum's remorse in the film's final moments. In projecting "shame in his heart" onto what most reviewers read as an unrepentant Tatum and describing reporters as a strong, ethical community, Crowther's review displays a noteworthy defensiveness. As director Guy Maddin noted decades later, "most critics considered themselves newspapermen and therefore within the target range of the movie's furious contempt."[7] Rather than consider the possibility of a passive or craven newspaper staff, Crowther proclaimed the success of Tatum's poisonous plan as "simply incredible," for "Mr. Wilder's exclusive machinator would have [had] his head knocked off within two days."[8] One might call this wishful thinking.

Such a perspective also tints, or perhaps taints, Crowther's perspective on the technical elements of the film, such as the reflexive "bold shot," as Wilder called it, of Tatum's death fall directly into the lens of the camera—a shot that required digging a hole in front of the set.[9] While Maddin dubs it "the best fall in movie history," Crowther did not praise this or any other shot.[10] Perhaps Crowther was not impressed because Orson Welles dug a hole in the floor to get his extreme low-angle shot of Charles Foster Kane after his election loss in *Citizen Kane* (1941), or because this shot in *Ace in the Hole* can be read as reminiscent of Norma Desmond's close-up as she blurs into the screen at the end of *Sunset Boulevard*. Instead, Crowther read the shot's significance as being the moment when "the whole yarn collapses limply and depressingly at the audience's feet."[11] Crowther's review, full of both high praise and great disappointment, exemplifies the film's complex impact.

For Wilder, *Ace in the Hole* was the biggest economic and popular failure of his storied career. Over time, he would occasionally defend it, but he more frequently acknowledged its limitations. A reluctant fondness led him to label it, at best, "the runt of my litter."[12] Audiences were indeed overwhelmed by the film's bleakness and cynicism, perhaps because Brackett's "restraining, civilizing influence" was no longer tempering Wilder's "disenchanted views of sordid human frailty," in Sarris's words, or the director's response to the postwar paranoias that drove the House Un-American Activities Committee

6 Bosley Crowther, "The Screen in Review: *Ace in the Hole*," *New York Times*, June 30, 1951, 8.

7 Guy Maddin, "*Ace in the Hole*: Chin up for Mother," Criterion.com, May 5, 2014, https://www.criterion.com/current/posts/590-ace-in-the-hole-chin-up-for-mother.

8 Crowther, "Screen in Review," 8.

9 Gene D. Phillips, *Some Like It Wilder: The Life and Controversial Films of Billy Wilder* (Lexington: University Press of Kentucky, 2010), 138.

10 Maddin, "Chin up for Mother."

11 Crowther, "Screen in Review," 8.

12 Wood, *Bright Side*, 29.

hearings and subsequent industry blacklists.[13] To some, the film may have seemed dangerously unpatriotic. Only after several decades passed and the accuracy of Wilder's prophetic media critique became undeniable did *Ace in the Hole* begin to find a larger, more appreciative audience. The new millennium even brought public accolades. The American Film Institute, for example, presented a special screening of the "overlooked masterpiece" in 2002. Five years later, the newly restored picture received a DVD release from the Criterion Collection along with a week's run at New York's Film Forum.[14] The Criterion release included articles by Molly Haskell and Guy Maddin and a video afterword by Spike Lee, all of which testify to the film's ongoing cultural importance. In 2015, the BBC even named it one of the top one hundred American films of all time.[15]

Academic study has not entirely followed this popular reevaluation, however. Relatively few scholarly articles on the film have been published to date. Within books on film noir, *Ace in the Hole* earns some attention for its femme fatale, hard-boiled protagonist, documentary-style elements, and unexpected setting. In a 2011 edited collection on Wilder's films, by contrast, only two of fourteen chapters deal directly with the film.[16] Sustained attention to issues of race and ethnicity within the film and its production context has been largely absent.

Within such context, this study considers *Ace in the Hole*'s engagement with racialized darkness as it is evoked and figured in Native American imagery and engagement with Jewishness and issues of Holocaust survivor guilt. I argue that seemingly superficial markers of racial and cultural difference in the film reveal important social anxieties of the immediate postwar era, particularly ongoing nativism alongside the mistreatment of Native Americans and reluctance to address the details and implications of the Nazi genocide. I find biographer Tom Wood's claim that *Ace in the Hole* is a "ferocious black parable on man's inhumanity to his fellow man" persuasive, to which I add that darkness is figured through cultural or racial othering, specifically of Native American figures and symbols, while "inhumanity" is addressed through metaphorized images of Jewish trauma, from biblical allusions to Holocaust imagery.[17] Within a postwar America rife with recent

13 Andrew Sarris, "Billy Wilder, Closet Romanticist," *Film Comment* 12, no. 4 (July–August 1976): 8, https://www.jstor.org/stable/43753071; and Gerd Gemünden, *A Foreign Affair: Billy Wilder's American Films* (New York: Berghahn Books, 2008), 3.

14 Phillips, *Some Like It Wilder*, 141.

15 BBC Culture Staff, "The 100 Greatest American Films," BBC.com, July 20, 2015, https://www.bbc.com/culture/article/20150720-the-100-greatest-american-films.

16 See Lance Duerfahrd, "What Exposure Is the World? The Desert Noir of *Ace in the Hole*," in *Billy Wilder, Movie-Maker: Critical Essays on the Films*, ed. Karen McNally (Jefferson, NC: McFarland, 2011), 11–25; and Nancy Steffen-Fluhr, "Palimpsest: The Double Vision of Exile," in McNally, *Billy Wilder, Movie-Maker*, 178–192. Brief coverage related to film noir also appears, for example, in Vincent Brook, *Driven to Darkness: Jewish Émigré Directors and the Rise of Film Noir* (New Brunswick, NJ: Rutgers University Press, 2009); Foster Hirsch, *The Dark Side of the Screen: Film Noir* (Boston: Da Capo Press, 1981); Mark Osteen, *Nightmare Alley: Film Noir and the American Dream* (Baltimore: Johns Hopkins University Press, 2013); Alain Silver and Elizabeth Ward, eds., *Film Noir: An Encyclopedic Reference to the American Style* (Woodstock, NY: Overlook Press, 1979); and Imogen Sara Smith, *In Lonely Places: Film Noir Beyond the City* (Jefferson, NC: McFarland, 2011).

17 Wood, *Bright Side*, 44.

and long-standing racism and antisemitism, *Ace in the Hole* emerges as what critic Nancy Steffen-Fluhr vividly calls "a textual fabric of guilt and grief."[18] From the Navajo rugs sold as souvenirs to a corrupt, ethnocentric sheriff who carries around a snake in a box, Wilder provides a tightly woven vision that deserves greater critical unwinding.

NATIVE AMERICAN IMAGERY

Because *Ace in the Hole* is set in New Mexico, its primary marker of racial otherness is the figure of the disenfranchised Native American (and the Native Mexican) of the post–World War II Southwest. This setting is made plain from the first moments of the film. The harsh horns of the soundtrack behind the opening credits give way to a more lighthearted, jaunty melody on the strings. A medium shot captures the side of a moving truck with "Chico's Garage" in large letters. The camera allows the truck to pass, revealing a convertible in tow in which a man sits in the driver's seat, reading a newspaper. A close-up reveals his relaxed pose. This is newspaperman Chuck Tatum. Soon, he rises out of his seat and yells to the driver to pull over at the corner, where we see "Albuquerque Sun-Bulletin" printed on the side of a stucco building with rounded arches. Tatum's white privilege is clearly shown in this scene. The city, we will soon learn, is alien to Tatum, but he is in no danger, for he is in the driver's seat, literally and symbolically. Moreover, he and his car are pulled by a generically named "chico," or "boy" in Spanish. When he jumps down out of his car, Tatum condescendingly tells the tow truck driver to wait, as if this is his personal taxi service or chauffeur.

Beside the doorway to the local paper, we see two women, wearing long skirts and multiple strands of beads, their long black hair rolled and tied. They casually observe the loud, brash Tatum, functioning via framing and silence as scene decoration rather than characters. Upon entering the newspaper office, Tatum is greeted by a tall, dark man wearing silver bracelets and also with long, bound black hair.[19] The man is an employee, cutting paper clippings at a counter on which sits an ornately glazed ceramic pot. The contrast in portrayals between the women and the male employee illustrates postwar changes occurring across the cultural landscape of America. A 1952 *Christian Science Monitor* article, quoted by Roberta E. Pearson in a study of classic Hollywood representations of Native Americans, expresses the opposition vividly: "The picturesque, beaded, feathered, and quaint American Indian has just about vanished from the lands of his ancestors. In his place stands Mr. Indian, modern American citizen. Clad in a business suit, his keen black eyes view the passing scene with growing understanding and appreciation of his rights

18 Steffen-Fluhr, "Palimpsest," 189.

19 The character is played by Iron Eyes Cody. Cody was not Native but Italian American, born Espera Oscar de Corti. He became famous for his Native media portrayals, however, particularly as the Indian with a tear in his eye in the "Keep America Beautiful" PSA of the early 1970s. Such an example reveals how the absent presence of Native Americans in the film is extended by whitewashed casting, further hollowing out an already prop-like role, though we know this only in retrospect. There is no reason to believe Cody/de Corti did anything other than identify as Native American and was taken as such by central casting.

and obligations."[20] The "quaint" women vanish after the camera offers us a quick glimpse, and, although the newspaper worker wears a shirt and trousers rather than a suit, "Mr. Indian" seems an apt descriptor for this individual, what Pearson identifies as a "positive, but assimilationist, representation."[21] Tatum's response to the employee, however, shows that assimilation into a white-dominated workplace will not necessarily bring respect. "How!" Tatum exclaims. "Good afternoon, sir," replies the man, whose name we never learn but whom Tatum will later nickname "Geronimo." And while we will see this man again during the film, he will become Tatum's errand-runner and speak to almost no other characters. Tatum's relationship to the city and its Indigenous inhabitants is thus quickly established: he wields power by presuming racial superiority and regards Indigenous Americans as objects to be condescended to or ignored based on their value to him.[22]

A less-assimilated Native family appears later in the film, at the cliffside where the film's central victim, Leo Minosa, is trapped in a cave. We do not know why the family has gathered there. They do not assist Leo or take any other action. Like the two women outside the newspaper office, the five individuals mostly stand together and form a stereotypical tableau. They, too, are unnamed and undeveloped background characters. Their diegetic purpose emerges when the father of the family is asked to assist in retrieving the entombed man. A policeman wonders aloud, "How about those Indians?" suggesting to the white characters in the scene that the family might go into the cave to help. The implication may be that they would know the cave because they are Native American. The officer turns to the silent father, "What do you say, Chief?" Leo's father, known in the film only as Papa Minosa (John Berkes), is the one to reply. "They won't go in. They never do. Bad spirits," he remarks. The cop scoffs, asking the Indigenous father, "What are you holding out for? A couple of bucks?" At last, the man speaks, but not in English.[23] Papa Minosa translates: "He said it's their Holy Mountain. The Mountain of the Seven Vultures." I read the Indigenous man's refusal to use English and his stiff-legged stance with his arms folded across his chest as a signifier of resistance to white, Anglo-European dominance, as is his unwillingness to risk his life to save the treasure-hunting man in the sacred cave. In their silent gaze, the Native family symbolizes opposition to the greed and presumption of those who have taken their land and continue to exploit and misuse it. Of course, the family is also disempowered in visual terms; they are dressed humbly, and their ability to stand by and witness the rescue effort

20 Roberta E. Pearson, "Indianism? Classical Hollywood's Representation of Native Americans," in *Classic Hollywood, Classic Whiteness*, ed. Daniel Bernardi (Minneapolis: University of Minnesota Press, 2001), 251.

21 Pearson, 251.

22 Tatum's cynicism also extends to biases against the Southwest compared to the Northeast, small towns versus big cities, and provincial versus urban whites.

23 Pearson, "Indianism?," 245–246. Whether the actor speaks Navajo (as would be appropriate given the setting) or any actual (Indigenous) language is unclear. Given the standard of Native American representation in Hollywood at the time of filming—a standard Wilder does not challenge—it is perhaps most accurate to say that the audience is encouraged to believe the man speaks a Native American language, which, as Pearson argues, "amounts to much the same thing for the Euro-American viewer" of the era of release.

shows the parents do not seem to have jobs. Moreover, they are never seen or heard from again in the film. I thus interpret the figures as static icons, reflecting the destructiveness of whites who have claimed Native American land and discarded their traditions.

Taken together, the Native American characters in *Ace in the Hole* reveal what Dan Flory calls "divided allegiances" toward race and ethnic relations within film noir of the postwar era.[24] On the level of representation, the figures are symbols rather than characters. On the level of social critique, however, they point to the destructiveness of the white male gaze that dominates the film. Thus, aligned with Matthias Konzett's study of whiteness in film noir, I find that Wilder left industry standards for racial representation mostly unchallenged, with people of color functioning primarily as props reflecting white supremacy.[25] For example, Konzett's conclusions about the African American garage attendant Charlie (Sam McDaniel) in *Double Indemnity* (Billy Wilder, 1944) extend well to the unnamed Native American copyperson of *Ace in the Hole*: such men are isolated from community or power, reduced to their "flat semiotic function of reliability, invisibility, and social death."[26] Such reductive objectification reifies white supremacy, doing violence to already violated peoples even as the film critiques such bigotry. Lance Duerfahrd clarifies, "*Ace in the Hole* presents history as an endless layering of violence. Stealing from an Indian burial site as old as the settlement of America, Leo believes the Indian dead have trapped him. These fears are both assuaged and replicated by Tatum, who steals Leo's story for his own purposes and ensures Leo's doom."[27] As this quotation suggests, the film's most scathing critique is reserved for the hubris of Tatum, a representative of white privilege.

In a larger historical context, the film's Native American imagery reflects the political climate of a postwar era, when the US government worked to settle claims to land and then relinquish its control over reservations.[28] Indigenous Americans were encouraged to assimilate without "special handicaps or special advantages," in the words of then president Harry S. Truman.[29] Poverty, isolation, and loss of culture—a process begun in the earliest days of white colonization of what is now North America—continued in new and devastating ways. *Ace in the Hole* thus exemplifies the settler colonialist ideology of its day for the purposes of social critique. During World War II, New Mexico had the highest volunteer rate and the highest casualty rate of

24 Dan Flory, "Ethnicity and Race in American Film Noir," in *A Companion to Film Noir*, ed. Andrew Spicer and Helen Hanson (Malden, MA: Wiley-Blackwell, 2013), 388.

25 Matthias Konzett, "The Egotistical Sublime: Film Noir and Whiteness," in *Hollywood at the Intersection of Race and Identity*, ed. Delia Malia Caparoso Konzett (New Brunswick, NJ: Rutgers University Press, 2020), 160.

26 Konzett, 162.

27 Duerfahrd, "What Exposure," 11–25.

28 Native Americans were officially legal "wards" of the US government until 1953, when the House of Representatives formally initiated a series of "termination" laws that cut federal benefits and attempted relocation from reservations. Pearson, "Indianism?," 250.

29 Andrew Boxer, "Native Americans and the Federal Government," *History Review* 64 (2009), https://www.historytoday.com/archive/native-americans-and-federal-government.

the forty-eight states then in the Union. Among New Mexico's Native American population, at least 540 Navajos served in the Marine Corps, 400 trained as code talkers. These individuals saved countless lives. Their code, the Navajo language itself, was never broken.[30] Such contributions did not result in improved social or economic status after the war, however, nor did the representation of Native Americans in Hollywood cinema shift much because of such service.[31] *Ace in the Hole* illustrates such injustice even as it critiques racism and white privilege by relegating Indigenous characters to static background roles.

Certainly, there is no attempt to present Tatum as a sympathetic figure, and his aforementioned racist wisecracks to the Native American newspaper employee say more about white privilege than about Indigenous culture. The grasping journalist's inability to show the slightest sympathy toward any other human being is central to the film's message that presumptions of superiority can be lethal—to oneself and to others. Nonetheless, we should not ignore the fact that, to illustrate Tatum's offensiveness, the film's Native American characters are reduced to stereotypes or dehumanized props. Even material objects serve to point up this double bind, such as when we see a *molcajete de Piedra Negra* (a Mexican black stone mortar) on the desk of white paper editor Jacob Q. Boot (Porter Hall). Boot displays it rather than using this practical cooking vessel, and Tatum shows further disrespect for Indigenous life and traditions (as well as his superior) when he casually flicks his cigarette ash into it.

RACIALIZED NOIR ANXIETY

Racial difference also operates metaphorically in *Ace in the Hole*. Film noir tropes and style help to reveal the process by which stylistic darkness can carry the connotation of racial otherness. The film is clearly a drama: taut, tense, and bleak. As a film noir, however, it further features criminality as a centerpiece, morally ambiguous characters, a femme fatale, and chiaroscuro lighting in indoor scenes. Certain staples of the noir mode are missing, such as the private eye, although Chuck Tatum is as hard-boiled a character in as cutthroat a business as the toughest noir detective. Similarly, *Ace in the Hole* does not employ the urban setting typical of most noir films.[32] However, Tatum's banishment from New York renders the city a constant referent: a lost, if grimy, paradise and a world Tatum is desperate to return to.[33] As noir critic Foster Hirsch puts it, "*Ace in the Hole* simply brings the mean streets to

30 Boxer.

31 For an exception, one might consider *Broken Arrow* (Delmer Daves, 1950). That white actors play the central Apache characters (Jeff Chandler as Cochise and Debra Paget as Sonseeahray), however, reflects ongoing ambivalence regarding race in Hollywood.

32 For details about the central tropes of film noir, see the "Seminal Essays" section of Alain Silver and James Ursini's *Film Noir Reader* (New York: Limelight, 1996) or Hirsch's *Dark Side*.

33 See Smith, *In Lonely Places*, 3. Smith rightly notes that many a noir takes place beyond urban confines. While she identifies the city as "film noir's most elaborate visual metaphor," its importance is primarily thematic, related to incarceration or entrapment. She argues we can find equal resonance in the suffocating suburban home or the enforced conformity of the small town.

the country."[34] Through his unscrupulous and ultimately lethal stratagems, Tatum turns the lonely outpost of Escudero into a massive carnival site, as full of thrill-seekers as Coney Island and as full of cars and campers as any big city auto dealership—at least until the announcement of Leo Minosa's death in the cave renders it suddenly empty after the mass of gawking visitors leaves in a rush. The "mean streets" turn out to be the massive lot outside the cave, from which tourists flee the tragedy and its implications—including their participation in turning Leo's suffering into a spectacle.[35]

The positioning of Native American characters in *Ace in the Hole* renders them an absent presence, significant as they make visible the specter of race, or what Eric Lott calls the "racial unconscious" of noir.[36] The genre, he posits, "is replete with characters of color who populate and signify the shadows of white American life."[37] An important function of this symbolic haunting is its "merciless exposure of white pathology."[38] Certainly, Tatum displays a supremacist pathology, although he shares this tendency with all the white middle-class members of the media circus that come to surround the cave and its suffering inhabitant. Everyone wants to see Leo Minosa, the victim of the so-called Indian Curse of the Seven Vultures, though the "vultures" turn out to be not Native American spirits but white, middle-class Americans.

From such an angle, we see that racial difference can provide as important an interpretive context as setting, character types, or cinematography. Specifically, *Ace in the Hole* emerges as one of Hollywood's compelling "racialized dramas of interiority," in which, as Lott explains, "the troping of white darkness . . . has a racial source that is all the more insistent for seeming off to the side."[39] White characters in noir are morally "darkened" by their interactions with secondary or background characters of color. Thus, Tatum's exploitative interactions with Native American characters allow his moral corruptness to show. He exploits the myth of the Curse of the Seven Vultures and the Indigenous office worker he manipulates into bringing him lunch and carrying his messages. His bigoted cracks provide examples of his dark soul as a ruthless tabloid journalist who cares nothing for people, only stories that can enhance his success.

Racialized darkness also reflects broader cultural anxieties. Nativism dominated the early 1940s, along with tensions over the place of the returning soldier and changing gender roles.[40] We see such context reflected within *Ace in the Hole* during a scene in which Leo Minosa's femme fatale wife, Lorraine, expresses her disdain for her husband to Tatum. The camera lingers on her bleached hair, which emphasizes a heightened, artificial racial white-

34 Hirsch, *Dark Side*, 83.

35 Smith, *In Lonely Places*, 177. Smith specifically reads the western imagery of lonely, open spaces in *Ace in the Hole* as a demonstration of "how American culture is weakened by the addiction to myth and spectacle."

36 Eric Lott, "The Whiteness of Film Noir," *American Literary History* 9, no. 3 (Autumn 1997): 542–566 and 544, https://www.jstor.org/stable/490180.

37 Lott, 545.

38 Lott, 545.

39 Lott, 545.

40 See Sheri Chinen Biesen, *Blackout: World War II and the Origins of Film Noir* (Baltimore: Johns Hopkins University Press, 2005).

ness. Her desire to connect emotionally to Tatum manifests in her description of her changed perspective on Leo. When they first met, Lorraine saw Leo as a "good-looking kid in his uniform . . . along with eight million other guys." While she does not say "other white guys," racial implication appears when we consider Lorraine's life selling Indian curios alongside Leo's dark-skinned Mexican mother in Escudero. She has become symbolically darkened by her proximity to racial otherness that was not visible to her when she first met Leo as a soldier.

Leo's most obvious connection to Native Americans is his pursuit of loot within the cave that traps him. Unlike the original story of Floyd Collins from which *Ace in the Hole* is partially derived (and openly referenced in dialogue), Leo is not a caver, not a boy who grew up exploring every hole and shaft of the local caves, but a treasure hunter who cares nothing for the sacredness of the site he plunders. Once he is trapped, Leo does worry that the ancient Native American curse has doomed him, but he does not connect this curse to his own racial complexity, which is never explicitly addressed in the film. Minosa is a predominantly Italian surname, and Richard Benedict, who plays Leo Minosa, was himself Italian American.[41] Within the film, however, Leo's mother is marked as Mexican, with her dark skin suggesting at least some Indigenous heritage. She does not speak English onscreen; instead, she murmurs Catholic prayers in Spanish. Her sole function in the film is to pray for her son's rescue. She thus comprises yet another Indigenous background character. Mama Minosa does receive a film credit, however, unlike the other Native American characters in the film; she was portrayed by Mexican actress Frances Dominguez. This credit superficially separates her from the absent presence of the other Native American characters in the film, although several others have Anglophone dialogue while she does not. Her greatest significance, then, for the film's narrative and racialized economy of noir anxiety, is that she is not white. Her racial otherness exists to haunt Leo's dark eyes, thick stubble, and hairy chest (see Figure 1).

By 1951, Italian Americans had largely assimilated into mainstream US culture, along with Irish, Jewish, and other white ethnic immigrants who came to the United States between the 1880s and the 1920s. As scholars have shown, Americans' common cause during World War II had some positive impact on earlier ethnic prejudice, in that it "greatly expanded many people's sense of who should be included in the category of whiteness."[42] Hispanic and Latinx immigrants, however, faced less stability in their racial and ethnic designation and treatment in the United States. While they were classified as white by the US armed forces, they faced more discrimination in daily life. As Flory argues, "People identified as Hispanic or Latino have long suffered from a cultural confusion over whether they are members of a race or an ethnicity; they have an ambiguous status with respect to whiteness that has only been partly resolved even in the present day."[43] More crucially, Indigenous heritage has been largely erased, for the terms *Hispanic* and *Latino/a/x* were

41 See "Minosa," namespedia.com, https://www.namespedia.com/details/Minosa.

42 Flory, "Ethnicity and Race," 392.

43 Flory, 394.

Figure 1. Richard Benedict as Leo Minosa in a publicity photo for *Ace in the Hole* (Paramount Pictures, 1951) that highlights a Native American clay pot as well as the actor's dark features.

coined to identify Spanish-speaking people from Mexico, Central America, and South America. As Santy Quinde Baidal argues, however, many Latinx people come from Indigenous or mixed-Indigenous heritage.[44] Furthermore, as Simon Romero reports in the *New York Times*, a significant number of Hispanic families have long known of their ancestry but seek to differentiate themselves from Native American peoples as well as from Mexican or other

44 Santy Quinde Baidal, "Don't Be Fooled: Latino = Indigenous," *Indian Country Today*, April 5, 2014, https://indiancountrytoday.com/archive/dont-be-fooled-latino-indigenous.

Latin American immigrants. Recent genetic testing in New Mexico, for example, has revealed that people identifying as Hispanic are 30 percent to 40 percent Native American.[45] If we return to Dominguez's portrayal of Mama Minosa with this context in mind, we see that dark skin, apparent inability to speak English, and stock character typing reflect both the vagueness and complexity of Latinx identity and its film representation.

The presentation of Leo Minosa's father is also central to reading Leo's racial identity in the film. Papa Minosa is played by Irish American actor John Berkes (born John Patrick Feehan). Berkes is a slight, pale individual who portrays Leo's father with a slight Southwestern regional drawl. He does not speak Spanish or any language other than English in the film, but he is able to translate for the Indigenous family we meet briefly at the cave entrance. Significantly, *Ace in the Hole* never shows the elder Minosas together; their interracial relationship is thus not allowed to illustrate the complexity of interracial relations in postwar New Mexico. Furthermore, visually separating the couple downplays the bicultural heritage of their son. In this way, *Ace in the Hole* is less racially progressive than other dark dramas of its day.[46]

Leo Minosa's mixed parentage suggests that he is not a white man corrupted by proximity to racial others, as in Lott's formulation of racialized darkness; rather, he exemplifies the fluid boundaries of race and nation that operate beneath the surface of the film's plot. Leo is a complex, condensed figure, for he is of mixed racial heritage yet plunders from Indigenous people to whom he is broadly connected by birth, if not upbringing. Despite his efforts at scavenging, moreover, the film portrays Leo as the hapless, innocent victim of Tatum's brutal quest for tabloid success that will help him escape New Mexico and return to New York, two states whose names announce suggestive links to nationality and race (the nation of Mexico and England's city of York, respectively).

Tatum is the central focus of *Ace in the Hole*, to be sure. He begins the film corrupt and dies from a stab wound inflicted by Leo's morally darkened wife after he attempts to strangle her in frustration over the fact that she refuses to play the role of devoted wife for the public. Critics and reviewers unsurprisingly label the film thoroughly cynical; most blame its box office failure on its critique of a media-duped public rather than on its harsh treatment of Tatum.[47] As Ed Sikov describes, the film reveals "American culture as the shithole Wilder saw it to be."[48] Particularly scorned in the film is the

45 Simon Romero, "Indian Slavery Once Thrived in New Mexico. Latinos Are Finding Family Ties to It," *New York Times*, January 28, 2018, https://www.nytimes.com/2018/01/28/us/indian-slaves-genizaros.html.

46 Noir films such as *Ride the Pink Horse* (Robert Montgomery, 1947), *Border Incident* (Anthony Mann, 1949), and *The Lawless* (Joseph Losey, 1950)—as well as the later *Touch of Evil* (Orson Welles, 1958)—feature Mexican settings and characters and foreground questions of racism and racial discrimination.

47 For example, see Roger Ebert, "Dirty Rotten Scoundrel," RogerEbert.com, August 12, 2007, https://www.rogerebert.com/reviews/great-movie-ace-in-the-hole-1951; and Graham Daseler, "Evil Under the Sun: *Ace in the Hole*," *Offscreen* 17, no. 2 (February 2013), https://offscreen.com/view/ace_in_the_hole. Ebert's 2007 review of the film begins, "There's not a soft or sentimental passage in Billy Wilder's 'Ace in the Hole,'" whereas Daseler opens his review by asking, "Was there ever a filmmaker more cynical than Billy Wilder?"

48 Sikov, *On Sunset Boulevard*, 311.

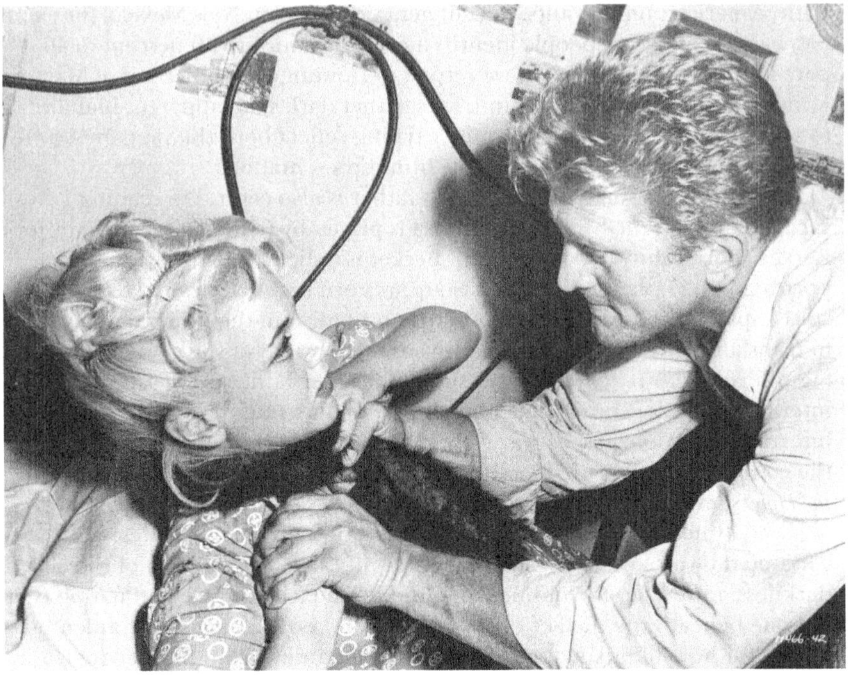

Figure 2. Unfaithful wife and femme fatale Lorraine Minosa (Jan Sterling) faces the darkness of Chuck Tatum's (Kirk Douglas) corrupt soul in *Ace in the Hole* (Paramount, 1951).

Federber family, a white suburbanite couple with young sons, who are first to park their mobile home in the lot beside the cave. The husband refers to their stop as part of a family vacation, identifying their privileged class and racial status while casually linking their pleasure with Leo Minosa's suffering. The film pointedly critiques the Federbers in shots that reveal their sons wearing culturally appropriative headdresses. Neither this offensive display nor the harsh portrayal of Tatum raised concerns for the Production Code Administration, however, because Tatum was ultimately punished for his despicable actions (see Figure 2).

Beyond meeting the demands of the Production Code, narrative closure in classical Hollywood cinema resolved audience anxiety by fulfilling moral expectations. Such gratification allowed viewers to leave the theater clear on the difference between right and wrong and confident justice would triumph. For *Ace in the Hole*, such closure would have meant that Leo Minosa, despite his trespasses, would survive his ordeal, while Chuck Tatum would be punished for his exploitation. That neither positive eventuality occurs suggests that audiences might leave the theater unsatisfied or with their anxieties reinforced. This may explain another facet of American viewers' dislike of the film upon its release. Film noir, however, does not depend on a satisfying resolution. Heightening viewer tensions and ensuring they are unrelieved by socially normative, optimistic formulas are key to the noir mood of *Ace in the Hole*.

COVERT JEWISHNESS

For Chuck Tatum, one of many alter egos in Wilder's films, the director chose actor Kirk Douglas, for what Sikov identifies as his "dynamic on-screen physicality (not to mention his notorious offscreen ballsiness)."[49] Wilder kept this casting determination even when forced to work around Douglas's Warner Bros. contract, which involved a series of threatening letters between Warner's and Douglas's lawyers.[50] Born a decade and thousands of miles apart, Wilder and Douglas nevertheless shared the status of sought-after Hollywood commodities during the immediate postwar era for their talent and self-determination. Both were also Jewish, showing clear awareness of antisemitism as it impacted—in different ways and to different degrees—their professional lives. Such connections offer a suggestive starting point for exploring the presence and impact of Jewishness on ambiguities of race in *Ace in the Hole.*

After fleeing Nazi-controlled Austria, Wilder basked in the freedom for Jews in New York and then Hollywood, where Jews were thriving. As Sikov describes, "It was just like Berlin, except that here nobody had to run for their lives."[51] While he had to learn English rapidly if he wished to write for Hollywood, at least his name was easy enough to change to fit his new nation's tongue. The German pronunciation of his surname (the opening consonant like the English "V," followed by a short "i" vowel) was Americanized (shifted to the English "W" sound with a long "i" vowel), and he simply formalized his already-American nickname, Billie (changing the "ie" to "y" to suit American spelling). He then adopted what he identified as the first lesson of Hollywood: "Don't offend the Catholics, the Jews, the dentists" or any other group.[52] Although he was a European Jew in exile, Wilder had been raised in an assimilated family, so his Jewishness in America reflected cultural difference more than religious practice or faith. For instance, Wilder took issue with Hollywood self-censorship as enforced by Jewish studio executives, which limited depictions of Jews onscreen and "impeded the effort to articulate the urgency to fight Hitler."[53]

By contrast, Kirk Douglas was born Issur Danielovitch in upstate Amsterdam, New York, to an impoverished Jewish family in 1916. As a teen, he rejected a post–bar mitzvah offer by the Sons of Israel Synagogue to underwrite his rabbinical studies; instead, he attended Saint Lawrence University on a wrestling scholarship and grew determined to become an actor. Like most Jewish Americans bound for Hollywood, Douglas was encouraged by the studios and the nation's antisemitism to obscure his background. Douglas, in fact, did so even before he moved from New York.[54] As his success rose,

49 Sikov, 314, 315. For discussion of Wilder's alter ego characters, see Steffen-Fluhr, "Palimpsest."

50 Sikov, *On Sunset Boulevard*, 315.

51 Sikov, 102.

52 Phillips, *Some Like It Wilder*, 269.

53 Gemünden, *Foreign Affair*, 26.

54 Todd Tugend, "Kirk Douglas, an Iconic Star Who Reconnected to Judaism after Near-Fatal Crash," *Times of Israel*, February 6, 2020, https://www.timesofisrael.com/kirk-douglas-an-iconic-star-who-reconnected-to-judaism-after-near-fatal-crash/.

Douglas remained a practicing Jew—if only on the High Holidays. "I always fasted on Yom Kippur," the actor stated. "I still worked on the movie set[s], but I fasted."[55] Only after a much later near-fatal air collision did Douglas fully embrace his faith, including a second bar mitzvah at age eighty-three, although he showed Zionist fervor throughout most of his adult life.[56]

Beginning his Hollywood career in the 1940s, Douglas became known for rough masculinity and antiheroic performances. Such roles, notes George Elkind, were "not often associated with Jewish actors." Blue-eyed and blond-haired, Douglas "had the privilege and ability to pass, integrating into a Hollywood mainstream that would likely have proved hostile to a clearer embrace of his identity or childhood faith."[57] Unlike Douglas, Wilder's foreign accent always marked him as an outsider. Rather than "pass" as did Douglas, Wilder became a man of "innate, bristling independence," posits Gerd Gemünden, never feeling "one of the natives."[58] Wilder shifted in others' perceptions throughout his life: in his youth, he was a "German-speaking Jew in a Polish peasant country; . . . [f]or the Viennese, he was a Polak from the province; for the Berliners of the Weimar Republic, he was an Austrian; for the Nazis, he was a Jew; for the Parisians, he was a *métèque*; and in Hollywood, he was a Central European refugee from a faraway continent."[59] Perhaps both Wilder and Douglas are best described in the words of Jewish American director Steven Spielberg, when presenting Douglas with the Honorary Award at the Academy Awards in 1996: "Most stars of his stature are shaped out of mythic clay," singular in their "drive to be inimitable."[60] This may be what allows Sikov to assert that Douglas's Tatum is not only a Wilder "surrogate" but a "muscular heartthrob—a Jewish one at that."[61]

Of course, a reading of Douglas's Tatum as an alter ego for Wilder need

55 Tugend.

56 Tony Shaw and Giora Goodman, "Star Power: Kirk Douglas, Celebrity Activism and the Hollywood-Israel Connection," *Historical Research* 93, no. 259 (2020): 153.

57 George Elkind, "Kirk Douglas Grappled with Jewish Identity as a Film Star," *Detroit Jewish News*, February 7, 2020, https://thejewishnews.com/2020/02/07/kirk-douglas-grappled-with-jewish-identity-as-a-film-star/.

58 Gemünden, *Foreign Affair*, 3. Here, the term *native* means American born, with its own fraught history as a white supremacist concept that erases the existence of Indigenous Americans.

59 Gemünden, 3.

60 JTA and Tom Tugend, "How Kirk Douglas Came to Grips 'With What It Means to Be Jewish,'" *Haaretz*, February 6, 2020, https://www.haaretz.com/us-news/how-kirk-douglas-came-to-grips-with-what-it-means-to-be-jewish-1.8503042. Worth noting here is the Jewishness in Spielberg's apparent allusion to the Golem in his description of Douglas and stars of his ilk as shaped from "mythic clay." If Douglas's Tatum is like the Golem of Jewish folklore, who was brought to life by Rabbi Loew to protect the Jews of medieval Prague, then the allusion is clearly ironic, for this larger-than-life reporter, created at least in part by a greedy media culture machine, harms or destroys Leo Minosa, his family, and everyone else he encounters in the film.

61 Sikov, *On Sunset Boulevard*, 314. In the fifteen years following *Ace in the Hole*, Douglas would go on to portray several openly Jewish roles, including a Holocaust survivor in *The Juggler* (Edward Dmytryk, 1953) and a heroic World War II veteran in *Cast a Giant Shadow* (Melville Shavelson, 1966). Both films are set in Israel (in 1949 and 1948, respectively), and they represent the binary of Hollywood Jewish male characters of the postwar era: the passive victim or the heroic fighter. For more on this distinction, see Boaz Hagin, "'The Catskill Mountains with Arabs': Pluralizing the Meanings of Melville Shavelson's *Cast a Giant Shadow*," *Jewish Film and New Media* 6, no. 1 (Spring 2018): 1–27.

not (solely) rely on the pair's shared but differently experienced Jewish origins. Gemünden persuasively posits that Jewishness and the Holocaust (which I will discuss presently) are central to Wilder's films, "but they enter in circuitous and contradictory fashion. While there are few characters in Wilder's films clearly marked as Jewish, there are many who possess attributes often associated specifically with Jewishness," including the bungling schlemiels played by Jack Lemmon in several Wilder pictures and others who reflect Wilder's own "restlessness and power of gab."[62] Character typing is always a complex matter, of course. We can emphasize "visual and linguistic performance codes" and work to avoid essentialist tendencies to link performers' origins with their characters, but we may ultimately find that a trait such as Jewishness is created primarily in "the performer-spectator interaction."[63] Thus, to engage with Jewishness in Wilder's films, we must attend to a combination of studio-era preferences and prohibitions and Wilder's writing style alongside his personal history. While remaining cautious of issues of stereotyping and other forms of oversimplification, I do share Gemünden's contention that Wilder's films reflect "his particular brand of Jewishness"—one shaped by outsider experiences and the impulse to assimilate—and the opinion that this renders his films, including *Ace in the Hole*, "much more complex than often claimed—especially by [Wilder] himself."[64]

Chuck Tatum is ruthless, displaced, and, as I read him, Jewish. He is not only an urban man in a small town but also a New Yorker in New Mexico. The character shows his big city bravado when he arrives in Albuquerque in his towed convertible coupe. By the time he gives his own eulogy as he dies from a stab wound in the final scene of the film, he has described during the course of the narrative only two things that matter to him beyond achieving journalistic success: chopped liver and garlic pickles. These items are widely recognized signifiers for New York Jewish culture.

Beyond such cultural markers, *Ace in the Hole* links Tatum to Judaism through the film's overt and covert religious allusions. To begin with one of the subtler examples, we see that while covering the Minosa story, Tatum stays in Mama and Papa Minosa's room at the back of the trading post. In one scene, he stands before Mama's altar to the Virgin Mary and undoes his suspenders. Though the altar suggests Mama Minosa's Catholic faith, the suspenders "hang from under his shirt like the fringe on a *tallis katan* [prayer shawl]," argues Steffen-Fluhr, and Tatum also wears a deputy's star—six-pointed like the Star of David.[65] Tatum's Jewishness is more overtly implied during his announcement of Leo's death to the massive crowd outside the cave, where he is framed like Moses on the mountaintop.[66] He is shot first from behind, grabbing and yelling into a microphone on the high ground from which he has previously convinced workers to drill down to save Leo rather than taking the expedient route of drilling at Leo's level into the

62 Gemünden, *Foreign Affair*, 26.

63 Henry Bial, *Acting Jewish: Negotiating Ethnicity on the American Stage and Screen* (Ann Arbor: University of Michigan Press, 2005), 1–2.

64 Gemünden, *Foreign Affair*, 25.

65 Steffen-Fluhr, "Palimpsest," 190.

66 See Steffen-Fluhr, 191.

cave. There are then a series of quick cuts, beginning with a high angle shot behind the crowds, showing the rows of cars, then a carnival ride in action as upbeat music plays loudly. Tatum loudly commands the music be silenced and attention paid to him behind views of multiple audience clusters, now turning their eyes upward, including a longer shot of Papa Minosa, who stops filling a car with gas and runs toward the gathering mass at the base of the mountain. The file then cuts back to Tatum, this time in close-up, telling those gathered that Leo is dead. I read the moment biblically, with Tatum the tabloid sensationalist figured, satirically, as God's messenger, delivering the Word to an eager, if cynical, audience. He brings forth the Law as they worship the idol he has helped them make of Leo. The irony is powerful because Leo is dead, even as the carnival atmosphere continues to flourish.

Of course, Tatum himself has already broken multiple commandments, which is why he was banished from New York. Of particular relevance are Tatum's specific words to the unruly mob that has taken the media-hyped story of Leo Minosa as an object of obsession, a kind of metaphoric golden calf: "Listen! Listen to me!" he commands. "Listen" (or "Hear") is the first word of the most important Hebrew prayer, to be recited twice daily as fulfillment of a commandment to worship the one God of Judaism: the Shema, or "Shema Yisroel." The opening words, in English, are "Hear, O Israel: the Lord is thy God, the Lord is One," a declaration of avowed monotheism. Continuing the film's ironic tone, we may note that the Shema has been recited as the last words of many Jewish martyrs.[67] Tatum is anything but a martyr, though his death is imminent. The only truth he declares is that of Leo's mortality. For the crowds amassed beneath him, moreover, this is the end of belief, not its declaration.

In addition to Tatum's implied Jewish heritage, there are additional Judaic allusions in *Ace in the Hole.* Bernard F. Dick's volume on Wilder, for example, points to the film's references to the Book of Genesis. "We are back in the archetypal Garden," Dick writes, where "an innocent Adam lies transfixed in a cave for six days [as] his Eve sinks her teeth into an apple."[68] The author refers to a literal scene in which femme fatale Lorraine bites into an apple. There is also a literal serpent in the film to complete Dick's scenario, the menacing snake that the sheriff (Ray Teal) carries around in a cardboard box.[69] Escudero and the Cave of the Seven Vultures are hardly innocent, let alone a paradise, and Dick seems to miss the cynicism in the imagery that I find so evident. More vividly, the film repeatedly links Tatum to rattlesnakes, for example. He first uncovers the Minosa story while en route to cover a rattlesnake hunt. He ponders what would happen if fifty were let loose in the city with all but one discovered. The story could run for days, especially if he hid the last snake, revealing it only after the paper had milked the situation for all it was worth. In this imagined scenario, Tatum controls the story and the last rattler, foreshadowing his control of Leo's entrapment and associating himself with the treacherous serpent in the dusty "garden" of Escudero.

67 See Dorothy A. Richman, "Hear and Act," *My Jewish Learning*, https://www.myjewishlearning.com/article/hear-amp-act/.

68 Bernard F. Dick, *Billy Wilder* (Boston: Twayne, 1980), 60.

69 Dick, *Billy Wilder*, 60.

In this barren town, of course, Lorraine-as-Eve is already corrupt, and the innocence of Leo-as-Adam is tainted by his multiracial heritage and plundering of Indigenous artifacts from a cursed cave.[70]

HOLOCAUST SURVIVOR GUILT

Wilder's Jewishness, and the way it impacts *Ace in the Hole,* is inseparable from the historical context in which he experienced his religious heritage, particularly his forced immigration. After working in tabloid journalism in Vienna and subsequently achieving success in the early Weimar film industry, Wilder fled Europe in 1933 upon the rise of Adolf Hitler, the day after the Reichstag fire, rightly assessing that neither Germany nor his homeland of Austria would long remain a safe place for Jews. His mother, stepfather, and grandmother, however, stayed behind and eventually died at the hands of the Nazis. "To the end of his life, he felt 'fury, tears, and reproaches' over the loss of his family to the Holocaust," writes Gene D. Phillips.[71] Wilder did not talk in depth on the subject, but his few words tend to speak volumes, such as "I learned many things about human nature [during the World War II era], none of them favorable."[72] What he learned involved the realities of ghettos and the concentration and death camps, including firsthand observation as the reluctant editor of the darkly graphic *Death Mills* (Billy Wilder and Hanuš Burger, 1945), a propaganda film produced by the United States Department of War intended to educate postwar audiences about Nazi atrocities.[73]

According to biographer Tom Wood, Wilder's experiences left him a "heartless cynic" with an "excessive contempt for humanity."[74] Wilder, however, nuanced this description, reflecting the direction and limits of his contempt. Soon after the release of the first negative reviews of *Ace in the Hole,* Wilder happened to witness a car accident, to which an exploitative newspaper photographer ran over to take pictures of the injured. Wilder called to him, "You'd better call an ambulance." The photographer dismissed the suggestion, saying, "I've got to get [this photo] to the *Los Angeles Times*!" Of this experience, Wilder concluded, "You put that in a movie, and the critics think you're exaggerating."[75] In a 1960 interview for *Playboy,* Wilder recalled being directly asked how he felt when he learned his mother had died at the hands of the Nazis. He was disgusted and pointedly concluded that such a question "makes you wonder just how cynical *Ace in the Hole* really was."[76] Such exam-

70 Notably, the biblical Moses is a descendant of the revered Jewish patriarch Jacob, which happens to be the given name of Tatum's Albuquerque newspaper editor, Jacob Q. Boot. Like his namesake, this Jacob has strong faith, albeit in facts rather than God; this is illustrated by the framed needlepoint outside his door that reads "Tell the Truth." False prophet Tatum scorns the adage, but we find it validated by the film's conclusion, in which Tatum dies, banished from his holy land, New York City.

71 Phillips, *Some Like It Wilder*, 21.

72 Phillips, 21.

73 For details about the creation and editing of this film, see David Bathrick, "Billy Wilder's Cold War Berlin," *New German Critique* 37, no. 2 (Summer 2010), 31–47. *Death Mills* was the English-language version of *Die Todesmühlen* (with Hanuš Burger, 1945).

74 Wood, *Bright Side*, 103.

75 Phillips, *Some Like It Wilder*, 139.

76 Phillips, 139.

ples illustrate Wilder's perspective on the callousness of journalists, including queries about his relationship to the Holocaust. Others also felt his wrath in relation to the Nazi genocide, including an assistant editor on his earlier film *A Foreign Affair* (1948), set in postwar Berlin. The man lamented that Allied bombings had destroyed the once magnificent city. Wilder scoffed at the implications, stating that the Nazis were solely responsible. "To hell with those bastards!" he shouted. "They burned most of my family in their damned ovens!"[77] Moreover, in a 1999 interview with Cameron Crowe, he reversed earlier statements that he'd have come to the United States with or without the rise of Nazism when he flatly stated that he immigrated "because I did not want to be in an oven."[78] Here, we see anger, determination, and survivor's guilt, a trio of emotions we also see in the images of his films.[79]

Beyond such comments, Wilder seldom talked about the Holocaust, and critics have rarely referenced Wilder's response to the murder of his family in readings of his films, including *Ace in the Hole*, where it is far less visible than in *A Foreign Affair*, for example. Haskell draws a link that others do not, declaring that the character of Tatum "bear[s] the brunt of Wilder's angst—not just corruption, anxiety, but the survivor's guilt of a man whose family died in Auschwitz."[80] One method for coping with such inconceivable loss is to maintain control over all aspects of life going forward, a trait Wilder had and gave to Tatum. The stakes and pressure were high for this first excursion into both writing and directing for Wilder, and we can see his determination to control his project in the note stapled to the first page of the original draft of the screenplay: "Do not give out under any circumstances to anyone!"[81] More generally, as Steffen-Fluhr argues, "Wilder's status as a non-victim is contingent upon the stick remaining in his hand. He can never let go."[82] Tatum, a product of Wilder's cynicism and commanding personality, is a character who can never let go of control. Both creator and creation suffer

77 Phillips, 102.

78 Cameron Crowe, *Conversations with Wilder* (New York: Alfred A. Knopf, 1999), 19.

79 My emphasis on the relationship of Wilder's personal experiences of the Holocaust to his filmmaking shares some of its strategy with Milan Hain's focus on trauma and survivor guilt in the films of émigré Czech Jewish actor and director Hugo Haas. Like Wilder, Haas lost multiple family members to Nazi concentration camps, sought success in Hollywood, and kept his strong accent and feelings of outsider status throughout his life. There were many differences between the two men, including Haas's stardom and popularity in Czechoslovakia before the rise of fascism and his more obvious inclusion of personal trauma in his independent US films (such as giving a character the same name and occupation as his murdered brother and then playing that role). Yet Haas—and, I posit, Wilder—also inscribed his trauma implicitly into his films, sometimes unconsciously or despite overt intention. And, like Wilder, Haas was able at times to vent his incredible anger at what the Nazi genocide had done to him. In a letter for a former colleague in 1946, he explained, "my life has taught me to hate in a very uncompromising way." Milan Hain, "Hollywood Film as Therapy: Hugo Haas, Trauma, and Survivor Guilt," *Jewish Film and New Media* 7, no. 1 (Spring 2019): 7.

80 Haskell, "*Ace in the Hole*." Haskell (like many Wilder critics and biographers before her) seems literal in her reference to Auschwitz as the deathplace of Wilder's relatives, but she is incorrect. Andreas Hutter and Heinz Peters reported in 2011 that Wilder's mother actually died at Płaszów, his stepfather at Belzec, and his grandmother in the ghetto in Nowy Targ. Andreas Hutter and Heinz Peters, "Gitla stand nicht auf Schindlers Liste," *Neue Zuercher Zeitung*, October 6, 2011.

81 Phillips, *Some Like It Wilder*, 131.

82 Steffen-Fluhr, "Palimpsest," 179.

a complex combination of self-aggrandizement and self-doubt, with the key difference being Wilder's ability to turn his anger and guilt into successful art, in part by projecting bravado and self-loathing onto characters such as Tatum. Wilder's survivor guilt thus offers an intriguing extratextual explanation for how and why the director created what Leland Poague describes as a "parable of the irresponsible artist," featuring a protagonist more perpetrator than victim.[83]

If Holocaust survivor guilt provides a persuasive contextual tool for understanding *Ace in the Hole*, precious little guilt of any kind is expressed in the film. Tatum may loathe himself, but he covers his doubts with boldness and bullying. Papa Minosa regrets letting Tatum take over the rescue operation but does not openly blame himself for its failure, while Mama Minosa immerses herself in prayer. Meanwhile, Lorraine uses Leo's peril to make money and then her getaway, without any apparent sense of remorse or responsibility. If the sheriff has regret over Leo's death, it is primarily that he will now not be reelected. Ultimately, instead of passionate displays of guilt among its characters, *Ace in the Hole* provokes guilt in its spectator. Viewers are encouraged to loathe the corruption they see in Tatum, Lorraine, and those who want to profit from Leo's suffering; however, they are also invited to identify with the crowds who flock to witness the cave rescue as a carnivalesque spectator event. Moviegoers have purchased a ticket (and today's viewers, a DVD) to find themselves critiqued as they watch the tragedy unfold.

The crowd at the cave, eating popcorn and riding the Ferris wheel, stands in for the figure of the Holocaust bystander, who does wrong by doing nothing. In the words of Elie Wiesel, "[W]e must take sides. Neutrality helps the oppressor, never the victim. Silence encourages the tormentor, never the tormented."[84] Those in the film who help turn Leo Minosa's suffering into a circus neither actively aid the victim nor even pay much attention to him. A few make money while the masses enjoy a strange holiday that betrays their apathy to the suffering of others. What, then, does it mean to silently, neutrally watch a motion picture centered on this disturbing spectacle? Such questions, read within the early postwar, post-Holocaust era of the picture's release, may help explain why American audiences disliked *Ace in the Hole* so vehemently.

Many Americans in 1951 knew little about the Holocaust—either its perpetrators or its victims.[85] As Catherine Portuges argues, "In some cases there

83 Leland A. Poague, *The Hollywood Professionals*, vol. 7, *Wilder and McCarey* (San Diego: A. S. Barnes, 1980), 145. Only Humphrey Bogart, working on *Sabrina* in 1954, would in anger actually link Wilder with the architects of the Holocaust. Bogart mocked his accent, attacked him for being overly authoritative, and is even reported to have called him a "kraut bastard Nazi son-of-a-bitch." Phillips, *Some Like It Wilder*, 159.

84 Elie Wiesel, "Nobel Prize Speech," The Elie Wiesel Foundation for Humanity, December 10, 1986, http://eliewieselfoundation.org/elie-wiesel/nobelprizespeech/.

85 Among scholars, there is a general consensus that public awareness of the Holocaust was low in 1945 to 1960, especially in nations that were not invaded or attacked by Nazi Germany. See Neil Levi and Michael Rothberg, "General Introduction: Theory and the Holocaust," in *The Holocaust: Theoretical Readings* (New Brunswick, NJ: Rutgers University Press, 2003), 6.

was hostility and even rejection of the traumatic circumstances that had brought the [Jewish] émigrés to Hollywood," from refusal of membership in professional unions to official designation as "enemy aliens" by the US government. Hollywood culture, moreover, could be a radical shock to this group of escapees and survivors, for whom Americans could seem "provincial, lacking in curiosity about 'foreigners,' even oblivious to the tragedy of Hitler's Europe."[86]

Stretching the film's Holocaust symbolism further, Haskell reads Leo Minosa as akin to Wilder's murdered mother and grandmother, for he was "snuffed in a cave that bears a metaphoric resemblance to a concentration camp."[87] Dachau survivor Herbert G. Luft, in an excoriating critique of Wilder published in 1952, shifts the metaphor, reading Papa Minosa's desolation at knowing his son is doomed as akin to concentration camp survivors watching what Luft considers emotional "indifference" at the heart of Wilder's war-era and postwar films. He argues that, in *Ace in the Hole* and elsewhere, Wilder treats his characters "with an obscene, obnoxious witticism," and he then reaches further, arguing that *A Foreign Affair* "helped to increase animosity against America among those who have lived under the yoke of the Nazis." He also misidentifies Wilder as a German (and not a Jew) and compares him to "the philosophers of the Third Reich."[88] Such misstatements and biases make it difficult to credit Luft's reading, which the editors of the *Quarterly of Film, Radio, and Television* published within a section titled "Two Views of a Director—Billy Wilder," pairing it with a direct rebuttal by Wilder's former writing partner, Charles Brackett. Brackett begins by likening Luft's analysis to an essay about Vincent van Gogh by someone who is not only colorblind but also "made actively ill by the painter's favorite color." He goes on to accuse Luft of a "limitation of nature" brought on by his experience as a concentration camp prisoner: a lack of any sense of humor (or irony). Of *Ace in the Hole,* Brackett identifies Tatum as a "ruthless heel" within a story about "certain cynical qualities in the press and certain appalling habits of behavior in crowds." He places the film within the major media and literary vein of "American self-criticism."[89]

Steffen-Fluhr reads *Ace in the Hole* as "the most metaphorical of all [of Wilder's] films, and the most emotional." Within the context of exile and "living death," she sees Leo as "a synecdoche for all the Jews of Europe who did not get out in time." Reading (Wilder) symptomatically, she argues that Tatum "mirrors the psychic status" of Leo.[90] Rather than a literal reading of a ruthless reporter who intentionally endangers a man's life for the demands

86 Catherine Portuges, "Jewish Immigrant Directors and Their Impact on Hollywood," in *Hollywood's Chosen People: The Jewish Experience in American Cinema*, ed. Daniel Bernardi, Murray Pomerance, and Hava Tirosh-Samuelson (Detroit: Wayne State University Press, 2012), 40–41.

87 Haskell, "*Ace in the Hole.*" I confess to finding this comparison excessive in multiple ways, from issues of choice to public response.

88 Herbert G. Luft, "A Matter of Decadence," *Quarterly of Film, Radio, and Television* 7, no. 1 (1952): 61, 65, https://doi.org/10.2307/1209758.

89 Charles Brackett, "A Matter of Humor," *Quarterly of Film, Radio, and Television* 7, no. 1 (1952): 66, 69, https://doi.org/10.2307/1209759.

90 Steffen-Fluhr, "Palimpsest," 189.

of his career, Tatum is instead a liminal figure, homeless and no more alive than Leo languishing in the cave. The film serves in this analysis to suggest the depth of a survivor's guilt in which Wilder renders himself both perpetrator *and* victim, then invites an audience in to watch him pay for his sins.

Ultimately, as Brackett's response to Luft makes plain, *Ace in the Hole* is perhaps best interpreted as satire, and there is productive purpose in critiquing the media and decrying the passivity of the masses. Audiences could leave the theater determined not to be bystanders. So can we today when we watch the film on DVD or stream it. Indeed, audiences today might even reconsider its message in light of contemporary antisemitism, anti-immigrant politics, anti-Black police violence (and the uprisings against it), and the ongoing mistreatment of Native Americans by the US government.

CONCLUSION

The failure of *Ace in the Hole* did not deter Wilder from expressing his concerns about the ills of humanity, particularly those related to the Holocaust. The next film he directed was *Stalag 17* (1953). Based on Donald Bevan and Edmund Trzcinski's Broadway play of the same name, the film depicts American airmen in a squalid Nazi prisoner of war camp in Austria. Like *Ace in the Hole*, the setting is bleak and the tone despairing, but *Stalag 17* offers "raucous barracks humor" alongside the successful exposure of a Nazi informer.[91] Moreover, the film's relationship to the Holocaust appears in the casting of fellow Austrian émigré director Otto Preminger as the commandant. Like Wilder, Preminger was a Jewish refugee who fled Austria upon the invasion by Nazi Germany. To the satisfaction of Paramount executives and Wilder's own relief, this film was a hit. The Jewish émigré thus, in my reading, showed he could continue to process his cynicism and his survivor's guilt through directing profitable motion pictures.

There are certainly limits to reading race and heritage primarily through symbolism and metaphor. Whiteness and racism are central to the imagery and concerns of *Ace in the Hole*, no matter how one approaches the film. If we reduce the film to a manifestation of survivor's guilt, we pathologize Wilder and deny the reality of the relatively collaborative environment in which the film was conceived and written.[92] And if we read the film's mobilization of racial otherness as an indirect commentary on white emotional and ethical failure, the actors and characters of color are reduced to mere vehicles through which to see whiteness. Put another way, the symbolism of white darkness is intrinsically racist, for it links characters of color and exoticized or denigrated locales to psychological darkness and cultural ills. Therefore, as Lott reminds us, by "relying on race to convey that pathology, [noir films] in effect erected a *cordon sanitaire* around the circle of corruption it sought to

91 Phillips, *Some Like It Wilder*, 142.

92 Wilder selected twenty-year-old radio writer Walter Newman to assist him with *Ace in the Hole*, and Lesser Samuels also contributed to the script. While neither of these younger men controlled the writing or the process, Newman brought the idea and original film treatment to Wilder for consideration, and both Newman and Samuels actively wrote parts of the screenplay.

penetrate," no matter how merciless their exposure of white corruption.[93]

Nonetheless, exploring racialized darkness within *Ace in the Hole* through its literal and metaphoric invocations of Native Americans and Jewishness reveals a film that speaks in a complex manner about the racism, antisemitism, and Holocaust survivor trauma of its day. By reading within and beyond its acknowledged condemnation of tabloid journalism, gullible mass audiences, and consumerism in America at midcentury, we find underlying pathologies that operate below surface realism and offer subtle and complex commentary on difference, injustice, and death. Ultimately, we see how Wilder—as Jewish émigré, Holocaust survivor, and successful Hollywood filmmaker—channeled his experience and his vision during an era of cultural transition into a film with greater poignancy and social resonance than has yet been adequately acknowledged.

I am grateful for Matthew Zumwalt's contribution to this study as my graduate research assistant at Middle Tennessee State University in 2017. I also thank the anonymous readers and journal editors who helped to make this manuscript far stronger than it would have been without their input.

Elyce Rae Helford is a professor of English at Middle Tennessee State University, author of *What Price Hollywood? Gender and Sex in the Films of George Cukor* (University Press of Kentucky, 2020), and co-editor of a forthcoming collection on international liminal noir (Edinburgh University Press, forthcoming).

93 Lott, "Whiteness of Film Noir," 545–546.

Patrick Keating

Light and Time in the Narrative Fiction Film

ABSTRACT
This article turns to the ideas of Paul Ricœur to develop an account of film lighting grounded in the theory of narrative as temporal experience. Narrative films structure lighting as an unfolding configuration, pointing forward and back in time. When we interpret a film's lighting as part of such a configuration, experiences of memory and expectation enrich our attention to the image before us. The narrative power of lighting rests in its ability to create this experience of a threefold present. Examples draw from a range of films, including *Umberto D.* (Vittorio De Sica, 1952), *Apocalypse Now Redux* (Francis Ford Coppola, 2001), and *Mudbound* (Dee Rees, 2017).

In the neorealist classic *Umberto D.* (Vittorio De Sica, 1952), the title character, played by Carlo Battisti, goes outside one evening to sell some books to raise money for overdue rent. When he returns, night has fallen, and the hallway of the apartment is dim. Patterns of light move back and forth across the walls, suggesting the presence of trams passing by on the streets below. I have long found this moment to be one of the most beautiful instances of lighting in all of cinema. The lights from the trams appear, hop from one wall to another, and then disappear, creating ephemeral layers of lines and shapes on top of the already intricate wallpaper. Although the film includes scenes photographed on location, this shot was captured on a studio-built set, and cinematographer G. R. Aldo's lighting is designed intentionally to look accidental. By planting the idea of trams in our minds, the effect builds toward two long-term narrative payoffs, preparing us for the moments when the despairing protagonist will contemplate jumping out of his window onto the tracks below and when he boards the tram to depart the neighborhood, possibly forever. But the shot's beauty remains rooted in the sensory present,

Patrick Keating, "Light and Time in the Narrative Fiction Film," *JCMS* 61, no. 3 (Spring 2022): 59–81.

not in the yet unknown future. The lights flash by, this way and that, and then they are gone. To appreciate the light, we must pay attention to what we see right now.

This account explains the scene's lighting in both narrative and descriptive terms. As a narrative tool, the lighting measures the passage of time while Umberto attempts to raise money before the end of the night. As a descriptive tool, the lighting reveals the shape of the window, the size of the entryway, and the speed of the tram. As Seymour Chatman explains, these frameworks—narrative and description—are distinct but interlocking, handling time and space in different ways. Considering the distinction in written texts before turning his attention to cinema, Chatman initially draws a sharp line between narrative and description, on the grounds that only the former follows a double temporal logic: "Narrative entails movement through time not only 'externally' (the duration of the presentation of the novel, film, play) but also 'internally' (the duration of the sequence of events that constitute the plot)."[1] By contrast, a description takes time to read, view, or hear, but its internal structure may be atemporal, as when a description merely renders "the properties of things—typically, though not necessarily, objects visible to or imaginable by the senses."[2] By describing the physical appearance of a house, a novel might freeze story time for several pages before shifting to narrative mode and recounting the events that happen inside that house. This distinction seems absolute, but Chatman recognizes that it raises certain theoretical problems—especially when it comes to film, with its special capacity to render visible properties in motion. An establishing shot of a house may serve a descriptive purpose, but if the shot depicts movement—say, the movement of a cloud casting a shadow over the roof—then it also represents a change unfolding over time, which is a prototypical narrative activity. Rather than insist that any given shot must be one or the other, Chatman suggests that description might serve narrative, or vice versa.[3] According to Chatman, the cinema "cannot help describing, though usually it does so only tacitly. Its evocation of details is incessantly rich."[4] On this account, the images in a narrative film are typically narrative and descriptive at the same time, advancing the story even as they depict a wealth of attributes with a particularity that a literary text would strain to match.

If we accept Chatman's idea that a prototypical description renders sensory attributes, then it would seem that the craft of film lighting is

1 Seymour Chatman, *Coming to Terms: The Rhetoric of Narrative in Fiction and Film* (Ithaca, NY: Cornell University Press, 1990), 9.

2 Chatman, 9. See also Marie-Laure Ryan's argument that a descriptive text requires the recipient to construct a "static text world" as opposed to a storyworld, which is a "dynamic model of evolving situations." Marie-Laure Ryan, "Story/Worlds/Media: Tuning the Instruments of a Media-Conscious Narratology," in *Storyworlds across Media: Toward a Media-Conscious Narratology*, ed. Marie-Laure Ryan and Jan-Noël Thon (Lincoln: University of Nebraska Press, 2014), 33.

3 Some might use the term *depiction* here, preferring to reserve *description* for texts. For a consideration of this terminology, see Werner Wolf, "Description as a Transmedial Mode of Representation: General Features and Possibilities of Realization in Painting, Fiction and Music," in *Description in Literature and Other Media*, ed. Werner Wolf and Walter Bernhart (Amsterdam: Rodopi, 2007), 3n1.

4 Chatman, *Coming to Terms*, 40.

eminently well suited to the tasks of description. Lighting is a spatial art, shaping the surface of everything it touches. But is the stylistic tool of film lighting equally well suited to the tasks of narrative? The answer will depend on the definition of narrative that we choose to adopt. Many theorists define narrative as the representation of change over time. For instance, in *Film Narratology*, Peter Verstraten writes, "Narrative is the representation of a (perceptible) temporal development."[5] Under this definition, the hallway shot from *Umberto D.* is a mini narrative, even before Umberto walks into the room. The trams audibly roll by, and shadows crawl across the walls. This is a story: a situation changing over time. Other definitions propose additional requirements: that a narrative show a series of events (rather than just one), for instance, or that those events be linked.[6] David Bordwell, Kristin Thompson, and Jeff Smith "consider narrative to be a chain of events linked by cause and effect and occurring in time and space."[7] Even with the addition of causality as a requirement, the moment from *Umberto D.* passes the test, both because the trams are causing the movement of the shadows and because the trams function as what Thompson would call a "dangling cause," preparing us for consequences that will become more salient later in the film.[8] Other narrative theorists adopt a gradable approach to the problem of defining what a narrative is—not a matter of *yes* or *no*, but a matter of *more* or *less*. The transmedia narrative theorist Marie-Laure Ryan writes, "I suggest regarding the set of all narratives as fuzzy, and narrativity (or 'storiness') as a scalar property rather than as a rigidly binary feature that divides mental representations into stories and nonstories."[9] She proceeds to offer eight conditions for narrativity, while granting that some readers and viewers might put more weight on some conditions than on others. The image of a light flickering across a wall meets some conditions ("the world must be situated in time and undergo significant transformations") but not others ("some of the events must be purposeful actions").[10] The shadow play in *Umberto D.* has some narrativity, but it is not a purposeful action; the narrativity increases only when Umberto barges in and asks the maid, Maria (Maria-Pia Casilio), to take the money to the landlord (Lina Gennari).

All of these definitions are valuable; each one brings distinct aspects of narrative to the fore. In this article, I propose to explore the narrative (and descriptive) functions of film lighting in relation to Paul Ricœur's theory of time and narrative. Admittedly, Ricœur's three-volume *Time and Narra-*

5 Peter Verstraten, *Film Narratology*, trans. Stefan van der Lecq (Toronto: University of Toronto Press, 2009), 9.

6 Emma Kafalenos defines narrative as "a sequential representation of sequential events" in *Narrative Causalities* (Columbus: Ohio State University Press, 2006), 15. Brian Richardson defines narrative as "the representation of a causally related series of events" in *Unlikely Stories: Causality and the Nature of Modern Narrative* (Newark: University of Delaware Press, 1997), 106.

7 David Bordwell, Kristin Thompson, and Jeff Smith, *Film Art: An Introduction*, 12th ed. (New York: McGraw Hill, 2020), 73.

8 For more on the "dangling cause," which is particularly common in Hollywood films, see Kristin Thompson, *Storytelling in the New Hollywood: Understanding Classical Narrative Technique* (Cambridge, MA: Harvard University Press, 1999), 12.

9 Marie-Laure Ryan, *Avatars of Story* (Minneapolis: University of Minnesota Press, 2006), 7.

10 Ryan, 8.

tive series from the 1980s seems like a counterintuitive choice for a study of cinematic lighting because Ricœur's books, working at the intersection of literary theory and philosophy, have little to say about film.[11] But Ricœur's sustained examination of time in narrative is ideally suited to the problem I have sketched above—the problem of understanding how film lighting, so good at the spatial tasks of description, may contribute to the temporal unfolding that is characteristic of narrative. Drawing on Ricœur's theory, I show how narrative films structure lighting as part of an unfolding configuration, pointing forward and back while molding each space with descriptive precision. When we interpret a film's lighting as part of such a configuration, experiences of memory and expectation enrich our attention to the image before us. The narrative power of lighting thus rests in its ability to create this experience of a threefold present.[12]

LIGHT UNFOLDING IN TIME

Ricœur opens *Time and Narrative* with the assertion that "the world unfolded by every narrative work is always a temporal world."[13] This brief statement, referring both to a world and to its unfolding, alludes to two distinct levels of temporality: the story's world is temporal, but so is the work itself, which discloses the changing aspects of that world gradually or quickly. After two preparatory chapters on Augustine's theory of temporal experience and Aristotle's theory of emplotment, Ricœur spells out his own proposal in chapter 3 of volume 1, defining plot as "a synthesis of the heterogeneous."[14] An artwork may unfold a succession of scenes, but the respondent makes sense of this succession as a configuration—as a "grasping together" that "draws from this manifold of events the unity of one temporal whole."[15] The result is a dialectic between discordance and concordance, whereby seemingly disconnected features make sense as contributions to a larger pattern.

What is it that turns a succession of events into a narrative configuration? Many narrative theorists have considered this question over the years. For instance, Brian Richardson offers the following thought experiment: "Cut two or three sentences of reported action from a newspaper, paste them together, and they will not, even if presented in chronological sequence, necessarily constitute a narrative. More is needed." For Richardson, the "more" is "some kind of causal connection, however oblique or indirect."[16] By

11 For some of Paul Ricœur's thoughts on cinema, see his preface to André Gaudreault, *From Plato to Lumière: Narration and Monstration in Literature and Cinema*, trans. Timothy Barnard (Toronto: University of Toronto Press, 2009), xi–xv. Alberto Baracco has applied Ricœur's theory of understanding and explanation to film studies in *Hermeneutics of the Film World: A Ricœurian Method for Film Interpretation* (London: Palgrave Macmillan, 2017).

12 Almost all of my examples come from narrative fiction films. How Ricœur's model might apply to other modes is a topic for other research, but I see no reason why his theory would not produce insights for the study of narrative documentary. When focusing on written texts, Ricœur explicitly considers both fiction and history.

13 Paul Ricœur, *Time and Narrative*, vol. 1, trans. Kathleen McLaughlin and David Pellauer (Chicago: University of Chicago Press, 1984), 3.

14 Ricœur, 1:66.

15 Ricœur, 1:66.

16 Richardson, *Unlikely Stories*, 93–94. Richardson defines causality broadly, including chance as a way of understanding events in relation to a causal logic.

contrast, Robert Belknap proposes five different organizational principles: "Authors can relate one incident to another only chronologically, spatially, causally, associatively, or narratively."[17] Plots must hold events together somehow, but they may do so in many ways.

Ricœur's discussion of Aristotle places special emphasis on the logic of action: "In the final analysis, narratives have acting and suffering as their theme."[18] Here, "suffering" may refer to physical or emotional pain, but it also may refer to the sense of being acted upon. At first glance, it would appear that Ricœur is proposing a clear principle of coherence: the object of a narrative representation is an action or set of actions. However, Ricœur's proposal is actually more fluid, shifting attention away from the object or theme toward the reader's temporal experience. When we grasp a story as it unfolds in time, we say that we *follow* it. This process involves searching for some kind of concordance, even as the work presents us with a series of discordances: "To follow a story is to move forward in the midst of contingencies and peripeteia under the guidance of an expectation that finds its fulfillment in the 'conclusion' of the story. This conclusion is not logically implied by some previous premises. It gives the story an 'end point,' which, in turn, furnishes the point of view from which the story can be perceived as forming a whole."[19] This account is thoroughly temporal: one moves forward toward the ending, which reshapes one's understanding of the past. With its reference to peripeteia (or reversal of fortune), the passage's debt to Aristotle is clear. But the debt to Augustine is equally important. As Ricœur explains, Augustine pondered how we experience time as a "threefold present," considered as "a relation between expectation, memory, and attention."[20] This notion of the threefold present gives Ricœur's account of *following the story* much of its richness. When a reader follows a story, memories of what has happened previously work alongside expectations about what might happen next to shape the reader's attention to each unfolding event. The process is dynamic, shifting as the work unfolds. As Ricœur explains in a later volume, "throughout the reading process there is a continual interplay between modified expectations and transformed memories."[21] The reader is constantly grasping for a pattern, but the shape of that pattern is ever-changing.

In a recent analysis of Ricœur's theory, Jonas Grethlein argues that Ricœur's discussion of the temporal character of human experience retains great value for the study of narrative—as long as we remember to apply these insights to the *dual* chronology that characterizes the mode. He writes, "In narrative there is a double tension between expectations and experiences. It can first be found at the level of the action. . . . Characters have expectations that are disappointed or fulfilled or remain open in the plot of narratives." This timeline interacts with another: "Second, the recipients of narrative

17 Robert L. Belknap, *Plots* (New York: Columbia University Press, 2016), 19. In this context, *narratively* refers to plots in which one character tells a story to another.

18 Ricœur, *Time and Narrative*, 1:56.

19 Ricœur, 1:66–67.

20 Ricœur, 1:9.

21 Paul Ricœur, *Time and Narrative*, vol. 3, trans. Kathleen Blamey and David Pellauer (Chicago: University of Chicago Press, 1988), 168. In this passage, Ricœur is offering a favorable account of Wolfgang Iser's theory of the implied reader.

have expectations as to the development of the plot and have experiences depending on whether these expectations are fulfilled or disappointed."[22] Both of these features of Ricœur's theory—his Aristotelian emphasis on the characters' actions and his Augustinian concern for the reader's threefold temporal experience—suggest that his theory is fully applicable to drama and cinema, as well as literature.[23]

A brief example from *Mata Hari* (George Fitzmaurice, 1931) illustrates how this model might explain the narrative powers of film lighting while hinting at a significant limitation I must address. When Greta Garbo's title character seduces Rosanoff, the naïve Russian officer played by Ramon Novarro, she asks him to blow out the candle illuminating a religious icon above the bed. Secretly, she knows that extinguishing the light will serve as a signal for another spy to enter the room and steal the information she needs. The plot hinges on a change in lighting located firmly within the storyworld. For the characters, the act of blowing out the candle is intensely meaningful, shaped by both memory (Rosanoff's memory that he always keeps the candle lit) and expectation (Mata Hari's expectation that the action will help her accomplish her goal). The candle scene is consequential for spectators, as well, temporarily dashing any hopes that Mata Hari's emerging feelings for Rosanoff might triumph over her obligation to betray him. One cannot tell this part of the story without mentioning the candle. In lighting this scene, cinematographer William H. Daniels's immediate goal was inevitably somewhat descriptive—that is, to render the appearance of candlelight clearly and accurately—but his descriptive achievement served a narrative purpose, telling a story wherein candlelight would have causal consequences.

But now we come to a crucial point: while this account addresses two key aspects of Ricœur's model—action and temporal experience—the analysis of light's role in narrative cannot rest on examples like this. They are simply too rare, confined to scenarios where a lamp or a candle has the power to affect the course of events. More commonly, when a character hits a switch, the lamp turns on, but there are no repercussions further down the causal chain. A viewer could summarize the story perfectly well without mentioning the lighting. Even more, there are plenty of scenes in which light is just there, emerging from no source in particular. The characters enter the room, and the room seems to be bright, but we don't see a specific lamp motivating this backlight or that sidelight. In such cases, the lighting is often clearly descrip-

22 Jonas Grethlein, "The Narrative Reconfiguration of Time beyond Ricœur," *Poetics Today* 31, no. 2 (Summer 2010): 316, https://doi.org/10.1215/03335372-2009-022. Grethlein's reading of Ricœur draws on Meir Sternberg's theory of narrative, which has influenced my own thinking for years. See, in particular, the account of narrativity "as the play of suspense/curiosity/surprise between represented and communicative time" in Meir Sternberg, "Telling in Time (II): Chronology, Teleology, Narrativity," *Poetics Today* 13, no. 3 (Autumn 1992): 529, https://doi.org/10.2307/1772872.

23 Ricœur specifically notes that the "distinction between the diegetic mode and the dramatic mode moves into the background." See Paul Ricœur, *Time and Narrative*, vol. 2, trans. Kathleen McLaughlin and David Pellauer (Chicago: University of Chicago Press, 1985), 153. For a detailed discussion of how Plato and Aristotle used these terms differently, see Gaudreault, *From Plato to Lumière*, 38–51.

tive, rendering the shape of the actors' features, but the narrative effect of such lighting may remain unclear. The light is not an action or a cause; it might not even change onscreen. So how does it contribute to the narrative?

Ricœur offers a solution to this problem, precisely because he supplements the action-oriented definition of narrative with the appeal to the reader's experience of the threefold present. Even when we cannot answer the action-oriented question, "How does lighting advance a character's goals?" we may ask, "How does lighting contribute to (or benefit from) the dynamics of temporal experience, with its play of attention, expectation, and memory?" This question allows us to consider how we might experience a moving image as a description, as a narrative, or (most often) as both. When we experience a scene as a description, we attend to the image presently before us, appreciating how the lighting renders the nuances of this particular subject in time and space. When we experience a scene as a narrative, we still attend to the present image (for we could hardly do otherwise), but our experience of the present comes charged with expectation and memory, based on the scene's place within a larger configuration. The two experiences may co-exist and even reinforce each other, but they remain conceptually distinct, offering interlocking appeals to the spectator. The remainder of this article considers how filmmakers balance those appeals—the narrative and the descriptive—in different ways.

The lighting need not be as consequential as the lighting in *Mata Hari* to produce such temporal effects. For instance, mood lighting often shapes the temporal experience of the viewer even when it seems utterly routine to the characters. At the end of *Laura* (Otto Preminger, 1944), Gene Tierney's title character turns off three lamps and walks into a back room. The camera whip-pans to the doorway, where Waldo (Clifton Webb) sneaks in and grabs a gun hidden in a nearby clock. Within the storyworld, Laura has turned off the lamps because she is going to sleep for the night. It is a very minor action: the causal chain would be largely unchanged if she decided to keep the lamps on. Instead, Laura's action provides motivation for the film's shift in mood: the shift from moderately high-key lighting to decisively low-key lighting creates the expectation of a crime scene, arousing fears that the newly silhouetted Waldo will succeed in his second attempt to murder Laura. For the present moment, the film depicts an innocuous image: Laura turns off a lamp. But that innocuous image comes charged with emotions—emotions grounded in expectations about the future (Laura may be killed) and in recollections of the past (as the first half of the film misleadingly implied that Laura was dead). Note that light itself is not the target of these emotions. The filmmakers do not ask us to fear the darkened room itself. The darkened room functions as a conventional signifier of the crime scene, asking us to fear for Laura's fate.

In contrast to *Mata Hari*, *Laura* shifts the weight of the explanation from the object of the narrative (the characters' actions) toward the viewer's temporal experience. Indeed, it opens up the possibility that we might experience a scene as narrative even when it depicts very little action at all. Consider a scene of a character sitting in a room and doing nothing. If we have reason to believe that this character is a murderer (let us suppose that the character is lit ominously), then this scene may generate feelings of dread as we fear what the character is about to do. My reading of Ricœur urges a definition of narrative that is expansive enough to include seemingly uneventful scenes such as this, on the grounds that they produce an emotionally charged experience of the threefold present, playing on expectations, attention, and memories even when their causal contributions are minimal.[24] Indeed, we could reduce the scene's causal consequences to zero. Perhaps we later learn that we have been misled; this character is not a murderer at all. The scene will have engaged our expectations, attention, and memory nonetheless. We follow a story even when the emplotment leads us down false paths.

For Ricœur, emplotment "draws a configuration out of a simple succession."[25] Making sense of a plot requires an ongoing process of interpretation, looking at the succession of details and seeing them as parts of a temporal configuration—that is, as potential beginnings or middles or ends and not as mere moments in an undifferentiated series. In the narrative fiction film, cinematographers create patterns of light that shift over the course of the story, encouraging viewers to find meaningful progression. *The Shape of Water* (Guillermo del Toro, 2017) contains several scenes set in the bathroom where the protagonist, Elisa (Sally Hawkins), hides the Amphibian Man (Doug Jones). Cinematographer Dan Laustsen explains that director Guillermo del Toro established a strict color palette for these scenes.[26] As Elisa and the Amphibian Man fall in love, the lighting in the bathroom grows noticeably warmer. The color palette for this space abruptly reverts to blue-green near the end of the film, however, when the villain (Michael Shannon) enters the bathroom and realizes that the Amphibian Man is no longer there. These color shifts do not merely illustrate a succession of moments; rather, they form a configuration—a pattern with a beginning (moderately cool before the romance blossoms), middle (increasingly warm as Elisa initiates a relationship with the creature), and end (harshly blue-green as the villain arrives to defeat them).

The preceding examples from *Laura* and *The Shape of Water* are suspenseful, in part, because they open up multiple possibilities: Laura might survive, or she might not; Elisa's romance might succeed, or it might not. This openness is a crucial feature of Ricœur's temporal approach to narrative. In the previously quoted passage, Ricœur insisted that a story's conclusion is "not logically implied by some previous premises."[27] He expands upon this claim in the second section of volume 1. The immediate context is an exegesis on historiography. This subject admittedly seems rather remote from the narrative fiction film, but Ricœur's comments about predictability will prove directly relevant to my discussion of light and time. Ricœur writes, "A story that includes no surprises or coincidences or encounters or recognition scenes would not hold our attention. This is why we have to follow a story to

24 Some might be less willing to go this far. As we have seen, many theorists define narrative as the representation of an event or a sequence of events. See, for instance, H. Porter Abbott's survey of the field in *The Cambridge Introduction to Narrative*, 2nd ed. (Cambridge: Cambridge University Press, 2008), 13.

25 Ricœur, *Time and Narrative*, 1:65.

26 See Dan Laustsen, "Love on the Run," interview by Jean Oppenheimer, *American Cinematographer* 99, no. 1 (January 2018): 40.

27 Ricœur, *Time and Narrative*, 1:66.

its conclusion, which is something completely different than following an argument whose conclusion is compelled to be what it is."[28] Excessive predictability poses a challenge for storytelling. A story worth following presents a chain of events that cannot be determined in advance, at least not perfectly. Whether history or fiction, narratives hold more interest in this account when they contain contingencies: events that happened even though they could have happened some other way. To be sure, causes play an important role in the construction of most narratives, but the understanding of a story may involve both nomic and teleological explanations—that is, explanations in terms of natural laws and explanations in terms of purposes (means and ends), including purposes that do not go as planned.[29]

Light fits uneasily into this model because light's progress seems more inevitable than a character's actions. In the real world, the flow of electricity and the movement of the sun are nomic processes, governed by natural laws that are entirely predictable. Without additional emplotment, such processes seem ill suited to the sorts of open-ended stories that Ricœur has in mind. One could make a film about the movement of the sunlight, slowly inching its way across the room, but the experience of watching such an inexorable film would be unlike that of following a story about a person pursuing a goal or stumbling on an accident, where what happens gains in significance because it might have happened otherwise.[30] Andy Warhol's *Empire* (1964) is, among other things, a record of the changing sky. Over the course of eight hours, a very spare story of light unfolds, with a beginning, middle, and end: the evening sky grows dim, the illuminated Empire State Building stands against the darkness for several hours, and then suddenly the floodlights turn off. The movie's minimal emplotment generates an unusual structure of expectations, founded on the near-certainty that the building will appear more or less unchanged for several hours. This expectation of sameness allows the film to generate occasional surprises, as when the floodlights finally turn off or when a window reflection reveals the presence of the filmmakers.[31] Such surprises are narrative effects, but it seems strange to describe *Empire* as a narrative work, at least in Ricœur's sense of the term. Concluding the third volume of *Time and Narrative*, Ricœur compares narrated time to a bridge spanning the gap "between phenomenological time and cosmological time."[32] *Empire* leaves this gap exposed, offering a record of cosmological time but refusing to represent it in human terms. The movie's appeals lie elsewhere: in its foregrounding of the film stock's texture, in its philosophical interrogation of the nature of cinema, or perhaps in its sheer audacity.

28 Ricœur, 1:150.

29 Ricœur, 1:142.

30 Peter Hühn draws a distinction between "proper narratives," which typically include at least one unexpected event, and "process narration," which is more descriptive and informative. See Peter Hühn, "Functions and Forms of Eventfulness in Narrative Fiction," in *Theorizing Narrativity*, ed. John Pier and José Ángel García Landa (Berlin: Walter de Gruyter, 2008), 145n30.

31 For a more detailed account of the film's progression, see J. J. Murphy, *The Black Hole of the Camera: The Films of Andy Warhol* (Berkeley: University of California Press, 2012), 29–35.

32 Ricœur, *Time and Narrative*, 3:244.

Movies that are more committed to narrative engagement consistently shape and reshape the horizon of expectation. For Ricœur, "the term 'expectation' is broad enough to include hope and fear, what is wished for and what is chosen, rational calculations, curiosity—in short, every private or public manifestation aimed at the future."[33] To grasp the stories of *Mata Hari*, *Laura*, or *The Shape of Water*, the viewer must situate the events within a much larger field of possibilities, considering events that almost happened but did not, events that did happen even though they were unlikely, events that characters willed to happen but came to regret, and events that happened totally by chance. Each film's chain of causes and effects is a part of this shifting pattern, but only a part.

Like Ricœur, several scholars have stressed the importance of possibility to the theory of narrative. For instance, Marie-Laure Ryan has analyzed "virtual events": events that exist in the minds of characters, who hope, expect, plan, imagine, or worry that a particular event may occur.[34] Some of these events come to be realized, and some do not; either way, we experience the events that do happen differently because we understand them in the context of a vast cluster of virtual events. Similarly, Gary Saul Morson associates "narrativeness" with the openness of time: "For a present moment to matter, to have real weight, more than one thing must be possible at the next moment. . . . For a determinist, one and only one thing can happen at any given moment; what did not happen could not have happened. In open time, at least one thing that did not happen could have."[35] Morson illustrates his point by imagining a child telling a mind-numbingly repetitive story about an ant moving a grain of sand, followed by another ant moving another grain of sand, followed by another, and so on. This story may display some narrative features, such as a chain of linked events, but it is hard to imagine someone listening to the story and saying, "Wow! What happens next?"[36] When a story grabs attention, it opens up the possibility of surprise and suspense. Even in a well-lit narrative film, it is usually not lighting itself that generates the engagement associated with open time. We rarely say, "I hope that lamp goes dim soon!" Instead, the lighting forms a pattern that amplifies the viewer's expectations and memories vis-à-vis the characters and their world. In *The Shape of Water*, the pattern of warm and cool lighting mimics the progression of Elisa's story, intensifying her arc's ups, downs, and uncertainties.

What about films for which we know the ending in advance? Watching *Julie & Julia* (Nora Ephron, 2009), we know that Julia Child (Meryl Streep) will succeed in her goal of publishing a cookbook—not just because Child is a well-known historical figure but also because the film employs an alternating timeline, using the modern-day story of Julie Powell (Amy Adams) to establish in the first few minutes of the film that Child's decades-old story

33 Ricœur, 3:208.

34 Marie-Laure Ryan, "Virtuality and Tellability," in *Possible Worlds, Artificial Intelligence, and Narrative Theory* (Bloomington: Indiana University Press, 1991), 156.

35 Gary Saul Morson, "Narrativeness," *New Literary History* 34, no. 1 (Winter 2003): 62, http://www.jstor.org/stable/20057765. I discuss the theories of Ryan and Morson in Patrick Keating, *Harry Potter and the Prisoner of Azkaban* (Austin: University of Texas Press, 2021), 29, 39–42.

36 Morson, "Narrativeness," 68.

will end in lasting fame and accomplishment. In the film's final scene, a dissolve transitions from the Julia Child exhibit at the Smithsonian to the Childs' Cambridge home; the dim artificial lighting of the museum gives way to warm sunlight beaming through an implied window as Julia opens the package containing her newly published book. The bright sunlight is another instance of mood lighting, but the mood in question is a foregone conclusion. A skeptic might wonder why this conclusion is emotionally engaging at all, given that it has been known all along. Ricœur's theory can help us understand why. He writes that one of the functions of history "is to lead us back to those moments in the past where the future was not yet decided, where the past was itself a space of experience open to a horizon of expectation."[37] The movie allows us to experience the life of Julia Child in two ways: as a past that has already been decided (in Julie's timeline) and as a present with a still-open future (in Julia's timeline). Whenever the film cuts back to Julia's timeline, Child's success reemerges as a contingent event. The fact that we know it did happen does not contradict the fact that it might have happened otherwise. Indeed, Nora Ephron's film takes pains to remind us that Julia worked hard for many years to bring her goal to fruition. The possibility of failure was ever present. Throughout the film, lighting aids this process of leading us back into a past when its future was still open by making these temporal shifts more tangible. The film represents Julia not just in Paris but in the Paris of the postwar years, and even more particularly on days that are sunny or cloudy and at hours that are early or late, with a corresponding sense that Julia is living in an unfolding present.

This insistence on temporal experience offers a new way of understanding the many ways that lighting contributes to a narrative film. In a previous work, *Hollywood Lighting from the Silent Era to Film Noir,* I explained how studio-era cinematographers justified their craft in functional terms—that is, in terms of glamour, realism, or storytelling.[38] These functions contained various subfunctions, and *storytelling* brought together at least four distinct subfunctions: characterization, mood, the denotation of time and place, and the control of the spectator's attention. While I still find this list useful, I have come to realize that these four subfunctions cannot be counted as storytelling functions until we conceive of them in temporal terms. Lighting might perform any one of these tasks—characterization, denotation, attention, and mood—in a purely descriptive work such as a nonnarrative painting. In a portrait of an old woman, lighting may enhance characterization by emphasizing the subject's eyes and wrinkles, expressing her underlying disposition. In a painting of an empty room, lighting may indicate that the time is sunset; the skillful rendering of a single moment in time may be the point of the painting. In a still life painting of a bowl of vegetables, lighting may draw attention to a perfectly goalless onion resting on the edge of the bowl. In a landscape painting of a mountain, lighting may convey a somber mood without suggesting anything about the mood of the mountain the day before or after. In a

37 Ricœur, *Time and Narrative*, 3:227.

38 Patrick Keating, *Hollywood Lighting from the Silent Era to Film Noir* (New York: Columbia University Press, 2010), 6.

narrative film, lighting may do all of these tasks—but with a difference that I failed to spell out before. The difference is the appeal to temporal experience: a threefold present shaped by shifting interpretations of the film's shifting configurations. Careful figure lighting may represent a character as old or young or tired or lively, but these traits carry different meanings if we see them as the beginning of an unfolding configuration or as the end of an unfolded configuration. Careful effect lighting may represent a given space or time as poor or wealthy or ancient or modern, but again we see these traits differently when we read them as irrevocable qualities or as open features susceptible to change over the course of the story.

This time-oriented theory of the narrative functions of film lighting recognizes the important role of description in the craft of cinematography—both as tacit support for narrative unfolding and as an independent interest. Many cinematographers take great pride in crafting precisely rendered pictures of their subjects. It is a matter of getting the details just right: adjusting the key light so the shadows capture the shape of the actor's cheekbones or setting the lamp outside the window so it mimics the appearance of early morning sunlight peeking through the blinds. Think of Miyagawa Kazuo's rendering of rooms illuminated by a single candle, as in *Chikamatsu monogatari* (*A Story from Chikamatsu*, Mizoguchi Kenji, 1954); working with artificial lamps, Miyagawa exercised great care to create a convincing impression that there is only one shadow on the back wall and that the shadow comes from that particular candle.[39] Or think of Gordon Willis's precise depiction of the difference between a dim interior and a bright exterior in the opening sequence of *The Godfather* (Francis Ford Coppola, 1972), with shadows and highlights placed just within the limits of the film stock. For such cinematographers, description is far from tacit.

My question is not whether lighting should be narrative or descriptive, but how a filmmaker might balance the two goals, which may be mutually supportive or in tension with each other. Consider again the hallway shot from *Umberto D.*, discussed in the introduction. Even as the film continues to tell its story about a character pursuing a consequential goal, the images represent the much more predictable process of evening turning to night. Prior to the hallway shot, Umberto leaves his bedroom, and a window brightens in a distant apartment to suggest the arrival of evening. When Umberto goes outside, the sky is almost black, and the primary illumination appears to come from a lamp at the bookseller's stand. The shot showing Umberto's return functions as the culmination of a trajectory, signifying that the transition to night is complete. The configuration we see in the film's depiction of nightfall (an inexorable process that happens in roughly the same way every night) remains distinct from the configuration of Umberto's story (an open narrative wherein he may or may not get kicked out of the apartment).

Alternatively, a filmmaker might situate a film's changing patterns of light very tightly within the teleological framework of goals and counter-

39 For a definitive analysis of Miyagawa's handling of light and shadow, see Daisuke Miyao, "The Cinematography of Miyagawa Kazuo," in *The Aesthetics of Shadow: Lighting and Japanese Cinema* (Durham, NC: Duke University Press, 2013), 255–282.

goals, as in *Strangers on a Train* (Alfred Hitchcock, 1951).[40] In one celebrated sequence, Guy (Farley Granger) tries to reach the fairground before nightfall to prevent Bruno (Robert Walker) from planting incriminating evidence on the island where the murder occurred. As do the director and cinematographer of *Umberto D.*, director Alfred Hitchcock and cinematographer Robert Burks take special care to represent the passage of time. A series of effect-laden shots depict the position of the sun and represent the changing illumination on the characters' faces. When Bruno sits on a bench and looks at the sun, his face appears dim, suggesting that the sunlight is fading, and a sidelight blinks on and off, evoking the presence of the carousel nearby. Later, as Bruno stands in line to buy a ticket, the sky behind him looks black, and his face looks much darker than before as two backlights separate him from the background. Hitchcock and Burks clearly care about lighting's descriptive powers; their attention to detail shows that they want to get the scene right. But the overriding function of the lighting progression is to increase suspense. Bruno cannot plant the evidence until it is dark. Knowing this, Guy hopes to arrive at the park while there is still daylight in the sky. The rendering of nightfall feeds into the larger dynamic of hope and fear, calibrating our expectations about whether Guy or Bruno will succeed in accomplishing their competing goals.

A similar function is at work in *Umberto D.*, as Umberto tries to finish his task before the night ends, but the link between Umberto's goal and the sky's darkening is much weaker. Whereas Guy and Bruno repeatedly look at the sun, Umberto barely notices the sky because an hour here or there makes little difference. This looser linkage between the changing light and Umberto's changing prospects creates more room for the viewer to experience and appreciate the sequence's descriptive achievement as an apt rendering of time passing over the course of a night in Rome. The filmmakers detail the transition from evening to night because the transition is inherently interesting. The lighting's sensory appeal encourages us to savor each present moment in all its ephemerality.

THE INTERACTION OF NARRATIVE AND DESCRIPTION

With neorealism and its successors in mind, the French lighting theorist Fabrice Revault d'Allonnes proposes a useful distinction between classical lighting and modern lighting.[41] Whether in a studio-era film or a contemporary blockbuster, classical lighting dramatizes; it shifts to suit the changing demands of the story. Modern lighting refuses such gestures. The light may change over time, depending on the hour, setting, or weather, but it does not change to alter the mood or even to pick out a plot point. Instead, the film respects the fact that light usually lacks significance in the real world. As Revault puts it, "In reality, you can die, and the sky will not darken; you can

40 I have compared these sequences from *Umberto D.* and *Strangers on a Train* in a video essay. See Patrick Keating, "From Evening to Night: A New Look at Neorealist Lighting," *Movie: A Journal of Film Criticism* 8 (2019), https://warwick.ac.uk/fac/arts/film/movie/8_audio_visuals.pdf and https://vimeo.com/275646845.

41 Fabrice Revault d'Allonnes, *La Lumière au cinéma* (Paris: Cahiers du cinéma, 1991), 7–8.

be hero or saint, you will not glow."[42] In contrast to classical lighting, modern lighting disconnects the representation of time from the line of meaningful actions.

Beau travail (Claire Denis, 1999) demonstrates the power of the modern approach. Much of the film takes place under natural sunlight, and cinematographer Agnès Godard records the many different forms that sunlight might take. Godard's craft involves selecting the right time of day to shoot each scene, positioning the camera with careful attention to the sun's place in the sky, and selecting the right exposure to ensure that photographic detail remains in the highlights and shadows, given the constraints of the film stock. The resulting film is descriptively rich, not just because it captures the nuances of light itself (for instance, the bright overhead sunlight of Djibouti contrasts with the less severe, often overcast light of Marseille), but also because the play of light and shade renders the shape of the actors' faces and bodies.[43] As Judith Mayne explains, "the bodies that receive the most attention in Denis's films are the bodies of men, and these bodies are presented as 'strange'—not necessarily in a pejorative sense. Although plenty of female bodies inhabit Denis's works, the male body is more consistently an object of curiosity and fascination."[44] Many of the film's sequences show members of the Foreign Legion conducting highly choreographed exercises. In one scene, Galoup (Denis Lavant) and Sentain (Grégoire Colin) circle around each other while all the other legionnaires look on. The director Denis and the cinematographer Godard have selected a time of day when the sun is placed above and to the side of the actors' heads. The resulting light emphasizes the texture of each man's skin, allowing us to notice how the roughness of Galoup's skin contrasts with the smoothness of Sentain's. Here are two different bodies standing under the same sun (see Figure 1). Figure 1 gives some idea of the effect, but it is more evocative in cinematic form because the shadows constantly change as the actors move through space. The skillful rendering of these contrasting textures conveys a narrative point, hinting at Galoup's simmering awareness that he lacks Sentain's physical beauty. In this sense, we may read the scene as part of a configuration—that is, as the continuation of an ongoing arc in a tale of jealousy and desire. And yet this experience of the story does not preclude us from experiencing the same scene as a *succession* of moments, as we notice what Galoup's face looks like under the sunlight at this moment and now at the next, never quite identical to the way it looked a split second ago.

Beau travail is a challenging film, with a complex structure that evokes the high modernist exemplars that Ricœur favored, such as Virginia Woolf's *Mrs. Dalloway* (1925). Whereas more conventional narratives make it relatively easy for readers to find a configuration within the text's succession of events,

42 Revault, 13 (my translation). Thanks to Colin Burnett, who has collaborated with me in translating another portion of Revault's text.

43 Some psychologists refer to this effect as *shape from shading*, whereby a pattern of shadows allows viewers to see a depicted object as concave or convex. See Vilayanur S. Ramachandran, "Perceiving Shape from Shading," *Scientific American* 259, no. 2 (August 1988): 76–83.

44 Judith Mayne, *Claire Denis* (Urbana: University of Illinois Press, 2005), 80–81.

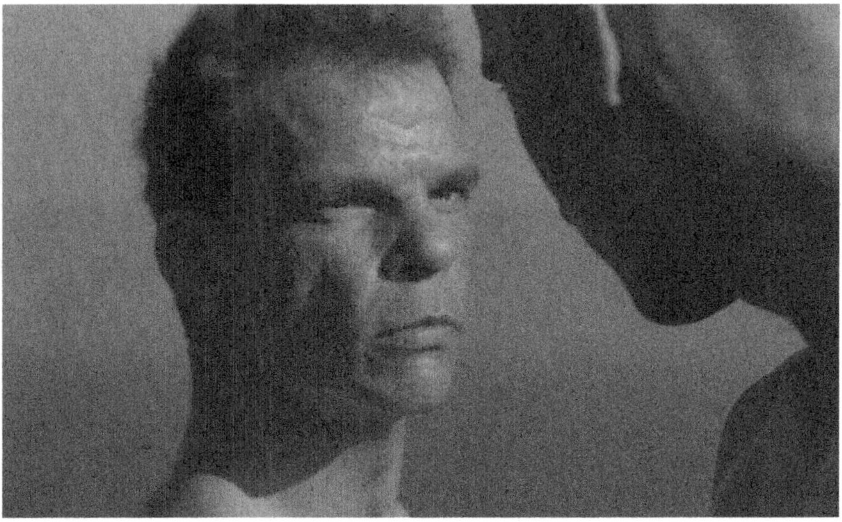

Figure 1. In *Beau travail* (1999; The Criterion Collection, 2020), shadows emphasize the rough texture of Galoup's (Denis Lavant) face; the texture changes moment by moment as he circles around.

these books create an effect of *discordant concordance,* making us aware of divergent elements as we struggle to find appropriate connections.[45] *Beau travail* is a loose adaptation of a famous narrative template (Herman Melville's novella *Billy Budd, Sailor,* posthumously published in 1924), but the movie spends long passages showing men doing activities without accomplishing any actions. With an analeptic structure that skips over key scenes, a tendency to favor repetitive exercises over narrative turning points, and an ambiguous ending that is impossible to place within the storyworld's timeline, the movie blocks viewers' attempts to construct a coherent configuration that will make sense of the whole. In so doing, it brings sensory pleasures to the fore—including the sensory pleasures of watching light as its shapes the bodies onscreen moment by moment.

Other modernist films combine this attention to sensory details with other configurations, such as the symbolic configurations crafted by cinematographer Vittorio Storaro. Francis Ford Coppola's Vietnam War epic *Apocalypse Now Redux* (2001) contains an extraordinary sequence that was cut from the 1979 theatrically released version of the film. Willard (Martin Sheen) visits an old French plantation, where he attends a dinner as the sun sets. The orange sunlight shines directly into Willard's face. The widow Roxanne (Aurore Clément) sits across from him; the sunlight creates a halo around her red hair (see Figure 2). Hubert (Christian Marquand) sits at the end of the table, outside the range of the direct sunlight; his lighting is less warm and slightly dimmer. For most of the scene, Hubert angrily explains why he has no intention of leaving the country. When his temper subsides,

45 Ricœur, *Time and Narrative*, 2:101.

Figure 2. The lighting changes over the course of the scene to suggest a sunset in *Apocalypse Now Redux* (2001; Lionsgate, 2019).

he tells Willard, "Go on with your war." At that moment, the light changes, getting darker, softer, and bluer. Without showing the sun itself, Storaro has rendered the sunset—the precise shift from golden hour to magic hour.[46]

The fact that Coppola cut this scene from the original release suggests that it makes a negligible contribution to the ongoing assassination plot. While there is plenty of story here, from the conflict between Hubert and Willard to the romance between Willard and Roxanne, much of the appeal is sensory. Storaro later wrote a three-volume book theorizing the symbolic significance of every conceivable form of light: daylight, moonlight, soft light, hard light, red light, green light, and more. He insisted that each type of illumination carries layers of hidden meanings; hard light, for instance, with its crisp separation between light and shade, might imply "the division between two worlds: Good and Evil, Male and Female, Conscious and Unconscious."[47] In this scene from *Apocalypse Now Redux,* Storaro represents time passing to evoke the larger theme of the fate of empires: the fall of the French empire seems as inevitable as the setting of the sun. In the face of such inevitability, the plantation owner's insistence on holding onto the land seems absurd. The overwhelming mood of nostalgia softens this critique, as the beauty of the sunset enhances the beauty of the verdant plantation setting. This opposition between nostalgia and critique develops along gendered lines: Roxanne looks beautiful, her orange hair ablaze in the orange backlight; Hubert looks worn out, only dimly visible, cut off from the sunlight shining into the room.

46 Coppola recently released *Apocalypse Now: Final Cut* (2019). This version changes the timing of the sunset. The line "Go on with your war" has been eliminated, and the sunset now coincides with Hubert's previous line, "You are fighting for the biggest nothing in history."

47 Vittorio Storaro, *Writing with Light*, vol. 1, *The Light* (New York: Aperture, 2003), 52. I discuss Storaro's theories in more detail in "What Does It Mean to Say That Cinematography Is Like Painting with Light?," in *Transnational Cinematography Studies*, ed. Lindsay Coleman, Daisuke Miyao, and Roberto Schaefer (Lanham, MD: Lexington Books, 2016), 106–110.

Willard's position evokes both knowledge and ignorance: he can see Roxanne and Hubert, and yet the blinding sunlight forces him to shield his eyes. For much of the scene, the brightness of Willard contrasts with the dimness of Hubert, just as the power of the American empire contrasts with the weakness of the French. But then the sun goes down at the precise moment when Hubert refers to "your war." Willard, too, darkens. The opposition between the French and the Americans becomes an analogy. Both will fall into darkness. Meanwhile, the Vietnamese servants seem completely excluded from this battle of empires: they stand on the edges of the scene, out of focus, barely visible. Coppola's film consistently fails to consider Vietnamese subjectivity, and Storaro's imagery, which is characteristically structured along binary lines, has magnified that failure by keeping the white protagonists in the center and relegating the Vietnamese characters to the periphery.

As we have seen, many classical films use description more tacitly, in the service of narrative. However, even studio-era Hollywood movies linger on passages of descriptive richness, especially in close-ups of female stars. Laura Mulvey has long pondered this paradox: classical Hollywood favored propulsive storytelling, but Hollywood close-ups also provide "a mechanism of delay, slowing cinema down into contemplation of the human face."[48] An example from *Chained* (Clarence Brown, 1934) shows this interaction at work, developing the story while offering a striking moment of pure stasis. Diane (Joan Crawford) is in love with her boss, Richard (Otto Kruger). Richard asks his wife, Louise (Marjorie Gateson), for a divorce; when Louise declines the request and stands to confront him, the film cuts to a close-up of Diane. Formally, the close-up seems indistinguishable from a studio portrait. Crawford holds her gaze upward, catching a point of light in each eye. The darkened setting foregrounds the abstract play of curves and triangles in her coat, echoing the curve of her cap, all outlined in backlight. Most remarkably of all, Crawford does not move an inch over the course of the shot—not a blink, not a shift, not a twitch. On the story level, Diane's stillness simultaneously evokes powerlessness and strength—powerlessness, because Diane knows that there is nothing she can do to change Louise's mind, and strength, because Diane remains stoic while her heart breaks. Beyond the story, the evocation of still photography may shift the viewer's attention from Diane to the actor who plays her.

The type of relationship introduced here—between Diane as a character and Joan Crawford as actor and star—is specific to this historical film industry and cannot be found in the literary examples that Ricœur discusses. However, Ricœur's theory of temporal experience remains relevant because Crawford's changing star persona creates another narrative for viewers to follow, another configuration moving from a beginning toward a (possible) end point. While telling the story of Diane, each close-up adds to the ongoing story of Crawford's career, developed by the studio and the star over the course of many years and spread across many sorts of representations, from films to publicity photos to magazine articles. Crawford's calm, mature image

48 Laura Mulvey, *Death 24x a Second: Stillness and the Moving Image* (London: Reaktion Books, 2006), 163–164.

Figure 3. Joan Crawford remains perfectly still during a dramatic close-up in *Chained* (1934; Warner Home Video, 2009).

in 1934 contrasts with the more exuberant star image she projected during the silent era. With this context in mind, the spectator may experience each close-up as a densely detailed and largely stationary description of a woman's face, as a piece of the unfolding configuration of Crawford's career, as a piece of the unfolding configuration of Diane's story—or as all three.

Crawford's image remains elegant throughout *Chained*, but some films sacrificed glamour for characterization in crucial scenes, even at glamour-conscious Metro-Goldwyn-Mayer. In the Norma Shearer vehicle *Marie Antoinette* (W. S. Van Dyke, 1938), the lighting follows a progression, growing more glamorous as the title character indulges in the pleasures of being a queen, then shifting briefly but powerfully away from glamour when she is imprisoned. In the prison cell, a hard key light illuminates one side of Shearer's face, and a dimmer fill light illuminates the other. Because the two lamps are positioned on opposite sides, they create triangular shadows underneath each eye (see Figure 4). Cinematographer William H. Daniels could have eliminated both eye shadows by moving the lamps closer to the camera and softening them with diffusion; instead, the harsh lighting scheme works in concert with Shearer's makeup to emphasize how tired the protagonist is, especially when one compares this close-up with the more flattering images of Tyrone Power. Shearer boldly plays into the lighting scheme, raising her hand to cover her face partially, thereby drawing more attention to the shadows around her eyes. The conspicuous lack of glamour enhances characterization by heightening her arc. The younger Marie Antoinette seemed friv-

Figure 4. A shift away from glamorous lighting marks a turning point for the protagonist in *Marie Antoinette* (1938; Warner Home Video, 2013).

olous, obsessed with meaningless beauty. Now, her glamour has been taken away, and she is preparing to face her fate with courage. There is a double change in fortune here: the privileged royal has fallen in status, but she has risen in moral worth.

Temporal unfolding allows filmic characterization to work via an onscreen progression; the lighting changes to mark Marie Antoinette's changing character. A progression differs from a simple binary opposition in that it includes a temporal direction; a film that progresses from light to darkness feels different from a film that progresses from darkness to light. As Ricœur argues, such patterns make an "implicit recourse to phenomenology."[49] Before seeing *Marie Antoinette*, each spectator has a culturally specific experiential understanding of what it is like to look one's best and what it is like to look one's worst. This preexisting phenomenology shapes the temporal experience of the film's visual progressions.

More radically, a film might subject the very idea of a *progression* to scrutiny, as in *Mudbound* (Dee Rees, 2017), photographed by Rachel Morrison, who became the first woman nominated for Best Cinematography in the ninety-year-long history of the Academy Awards. The story is about two families—the Black Jacksons and the white McAllans—living on the same difficult land in the 1930s and 1940s. Given the genre of the historical drama, we might expect *Mudbound* to adopt visual strategies evoking

49 Ricœur, *Time and Narrative*, 2:59.

the idea of gradual progress, suggesting that race relations have improved over time. This is a common strategy for Hollywood period films with Black protagonists. In *Hidden Figures* (Theodore Melfi, 2016), for instance, cinematographer Mandy Walker gradually changed the camera's height over the course of the film, to suggest how the three protagonists were initially treated intentionally as inferiors by the white characters and reflect that they had achieved greater equality by the end of the film.[50] *Mudbound* refuses to adopt this arc of gradual progress. It may end on a tentative note of hope, but it spends the bulk of its running time showing that racist oppression continued in full force, even after the end of a war (World War II) in which many Black soldiers fought for a Double Victory that would defeat fascism abroad and white supremacy at home. Several characters grow and change over the course of the film, but these shifts occur in the context of stalled progress against racism.

Structurally, *Mudbound* juxtaposes two distinct kinds of story time. A lot happens in Rees's film (e.g., romance, friendship, torture, and murder); it is also a film where nothing happens (e.g., society fails to change). The slower first half of the film is occasionally reminiscent of a Terrence Malick film, with passages of voice-over narration dipping into the thoughts of multiple characters. The second half is more intensely dramatic, building up to a white supremacist attack on Ronsel Jackson (Jason Mitchell), a soldier who returned from WWII with hopes for a better future. Fittingly for a film that combines heightened drama with lyricism, Morrison's cinematography synthesizes classical and modernist approaches. In some scenes, the lighting and photography exaggerate the dramatic arc of the story. As Morrison told interviewer Emily Buder, "I call it subjective naturalism because you can kind of exaggerate within the stakes of the story—when the stakes are high, often I'll use higher contrasts than I would if it were just a [regular] scene. But it should still feel believable."[51] Such exaggeration is a variation on the strategy of modulation that Hollywood cinematographers practiced throughout the classical period, as in *Mata Hari*, *Laura*, and *Strangers on a Train*, all three of which shift to stronger contrasts and deeper shadows for turning point scenes. In an equally classical vein, Morrison created *before* and *after* arcs to heighten thematically significant causal transitions. At the beginning of the film, the white McAllan family lives in relative comfort. Then Henry McAllan (Jason Clarke) gets swindled, and the family must move to a muddy shack much closer to the home of their Black tenants, the Jacksons. Morrison explained, "We definitely had a bit of a different plan for before they go to the farm and after they go to the farm [in the movie's plot]. Before

50 Agatha French, "*Hidden Figures*: An Interview with Cinematographer Mandy Walker," *Cinema Thread*, accessed April 15, 2017. I discuss Walker's work on this film in "The Art of Cinematography," in *The Palgrave Handbook of the Philosophy of Film and Motion Pictures*, ed. Noël Carroll, Laura T. Di Summa-Knoop, and Shawn Loht (Cham, Switzerland: Palgrave Macmillan, 2019), 90.

51 Rachel Morrison, quoted in Emily Buder, "How 'Mudbound' DP Rachel Morrison Created 'Natural Light' by Lighting Heavily," *No Film School*, December 1, 2017, https://nofilmschool.com/2017/11/mudbound-rachel-morrison-cinematographer-dp-interview. Buder's in-depth interview also provides much of the technical information I discuss below.

they get to the farm, the colors are much more poppy and saturated. . . . But after they get to the farm, [I used a grittier] color palette."[52] The visual shift amplifies the sense that the new house represents a narrative turning point for the McAllans, some of whom will react with deep hostility to the prospect of living under conditions that they associate with Blackness.

Morrison has also explained her approach in descriptive terms reminiscent of documentary photography, as an art of rendering spatial and temporal details with nuance and precision. With Rees's encouragement, Morrison turned to the photographs of Dorothea Lange and Gordon Parks for inspiration.[53] Both the Jacksons and the McAllans live in wood houses with small windows. Arriving on set, Morrison hoped to photograph interior scenes without losing the view through the windows, but she found a huge (eight- or ten-stop) difference between interior and exterior illumination levels.[54] In order to capture detail inside without losing detail outside, she asked the production designer to add a few hidden openings to the set, and then she blasted powerful lights (up to eighteen thousand watts) through the openings and windows. The crew also placed light-reducing neutral density filters over selected windows. According to Morrison, "I used a lot of lighting to make it look like it wasn't lit."[55] For instance, one image shows a backlit Hap Jackson (Rob Morgan) sitting near a doorway in the Jackson family home (see Figure 5). The background exterior registers at the upper limit of the image's tonal range: it is very bright, with just a hint of detail in the landscape beyond. The foreground interior registers closer to the other end of the tonal range: it is much darker, but there is still sufficient detail to capture the worried expression on Hap's face, the pattern of his shirt and suspenders, and the texture of the newspaper lining the walls behind him. The lighting situates the location in time, on a day when the sun is bright and in a decade when electricity has not yet come to the rural South.

This strategy for representing the farmhouses remains relatively consistent over the course of the film, even though the timeline spans several years. The resulting pattern of repetition supports the film's political critique of a society that failed to change. Many of the film's visual contrasts are spatial rather than temporal. One contrast involves the opposition between the two houses. The Jackson house is rendered in moderately warm tones, suggesting that the Jacksons have succeeded in building a genuine home in a hostile environment; the less loving McAllan household is rendered in a more desaturated palette.[56] Another contrast involves the opposition between the United States and Europe. During the war, Ronsel enjoys a relationship with Resl (Samantha Hoefer), a German woman. When the war ends, we see

52 Morrison, quoted in Buder, "DP Rachel Morrison." Bracketed text in the original.

53 Mark Dillon, "Delta Blues," *American Cinematographer* 98, no. 12 (December 2017): 79.

54 Each stop represents a doubling of the light level. If the exterior is ten stops brighter than the interior, then it has over a thousand times the amount of light. This extreme difference can be difficult to capture.

55 Morrison, quoted in Buder, "DP Rachel Morrison."

56 Rees discusses this contrast in Tommy Cook, "'Mudbound' Director Dee Rees on Her Adaptation Process & Changing the Ending," *Collider*, November 16, 2017, https://collider.com/dee-rees-interview-mudbound/.

Figure 5. The lighting creates a strong contrast between the interior and exterior, without losing detail, in *Mudbound* (Netflix, 2017).

Ronsel and Resl standing next to a window, recalling previous scenes at the Jackson home. Morrison lights this sequence more evenly, without the stark contrasts between interior and exterior lighting that characterizes the home scenes. The visual shift heightens the thematic contrast between Ronsel's experiences in Europe and his experiences in the United States, especially when he returns home and the imagery remains much the same as before.

For all the horror of the film's climactic lynch mob scene, *Mudbound* ends on a stubborn note of determination.[57] The Jacksons hide Ronsel in a carriage and leave town for good. A lyrical final sequence shows the Jacksons living in a new home and Ronsel reunited with Resl and his son in Europe. In voice-over, Ronsel introduces the finale by asking, "Should my story end there, silenced and defeated?" He reopens time by imagining and then enacting the continuation of his story. When we see the Jacksons at their new home, the lighting has changed decisively to mark this hard-won turning point. Gone are the harsh contrasts between interior and exterior; instead, we see the Jacksons on or in front of a broad open porch, where the lighting on each character blends seamlessly with the light of the sun.

CONCLUSION

Ricœur's theory combines an Aristotelian interest in narrative as action with an Augustinian interest in the reader's threefold experience of time. Throughout this article, I have argued that it rarely makes sense to ask how light advances the action in film. Even when the lighting regularly changes in the storyworld, it does so in ways that characters barely notice, perhaps because the shifts in illumination seem utterly ordinary to them or because those shifts are simply irrelevant to the characters' goals. But the lighting may contribute powerfully to the narrative nonetheless, and Ricœur's discus-

57 The film's co-writer, Virgil Williams, explains the decision to end this bleak film on a hopeful note in Andrew Karpan, "Why Virgil Williams Changed the Ending to 'Mudbound,'" *Film School Rejects*, November 27, 2017, https://filmschoolrejects.com/virgil-williams-changed-ending-mudbound/. See also Rees's comments on the ending in Cook, "'Mudbound' Director Dee Rees."

sion of time helps us understand how. It is because lighting is such an effective means of detailed description that it can show us characters acting in a present moment, a present shaped by past experiences and open to a horizon of expectations. When we experience the film as a narrative, we draw a configuration out of this succession of moments. In this way, we too experience a threefold present, looking ahead and looking back, without losing sight of what is in front of our eyes.

The author would like to thank Lisa Jasinski, Meraj Dhir, the two anonymous readers, and the editors of *JCMS* for their helpful comments about the ideas in this article.

Patrick Keating is a professor in the Department of Communication at Trinity University, where he teaches courses in film studies and video production. He is the author of *The Dynamic Frame: Camera Movement in Classical Hollywood* (Columbia University Press, 2019).

Ido Lewit

The Coroner and the Real: Death, Media, and "Deep Truth" in Werner Herzog's *The Enigma of Kaspar Hauser* and *Grizzly Man*

ABSTRACT

This article looks at media technologies as inflecting the concept of truth in films by Werner Herzog. The first section characterizes Herzog's approach to the image as informed by an investment in poesis and a dialectics of real and artifice. The second section examines two sequences, one from a fiction film (*Jeder für sich und Gott gegen alle*; *The Enigma of Kaspar Hauser*, 1974) and one from a documentary (*Grizzly Man*, 2005), through the theme of autopsy. Applying Friedrich Kittler's media theory to this analysis highlights *truth* as a concept contingent on the technological media that these films incorporate.

Soon after Kaspar Hauser, the protagonist of *Jeder für sich und Gott gegen alle* (*The Enigma of Kaspar Hauser*, Werner Herzog, 1974), appears in the town of Nuremberg, he is taken to a stable where the town's officials examine him. During the examination, the officials find several objects in Kaspar's possession previously accorded to him by his captor: a letter of introduction, two prayer books, a rosary with a metal cross, and a paper containing gold leaf. In his director's commentary on the scene, Werner Herzog stresses that it is based on real descriptions of the historical Kaspar Hauser and that the objects were those actually found in Hauser's possession. Pondering over the

Ido Lewit, "The Coroner and the Real: Death, Media, and 'Deep Truth' in Werner Herzog's *The Enigma of Kaspar Hauser* and *Grizzly Man*," *JCMS* 61, no. 3 (Spring 2022): 82–106.

meaning of some of these objects—"Gold leaves, why? Totally mysterious"—Herzog suggests not only a distinct link between the film and the historical real but also the notion that the film carries no clear univocal signification.[1] Conversely, in her analysis of the film, Kaja Silverman emphasizes the Oedipal signification and cultural value of the items featured in the scene: the sacramental objects are "emblems of guilt and faith," the gold signifies "monetary exchange," and the letter "assures the officials . . . that [Kaspar] wants to serve his king faithfully." Kaspar's captor, furthermore, is rendered "the symbolic father."[2] Through their comments, Herzog and Silverman promote two distinct approaches toward the cinematic image: while Silverman's textual analysis is rooted in a structuralist tradition according to which every element in a given text is decodable within an adequate key (in this case, Lacanian psychoanalysis), Herzog promotes an attitude we might term nonreferential, according to which the elements do not primarily signify but rather primarily *are* (that is, exist) and as such carry some enigmatic quality. Herzog often expresses such an attitude. In interviews and DVD commentaries, he repeatedly expresses the desire to achieve moments of deep truth (or "ecstatic truth") in the form of new, unknown, and mysterious images and stresses the primacy of the look and quality of the image over narrative content and syntactic value as the means to reach this truth.[3]

This nonreferential investment in the image has been noted or alluded to in several studies of Herzog. Matthew Gandy, for instance, claims that Herzog's cinematic imagery achieves "a kind of aesthetic transcendence that instills thoughts and sensations that are not easily conveyed through conventional narrative structures."[4] In a separate study, Lutz Koepnick asserts that "[p]owerful images, in Herzog's work, often seem to suspend questions about narrative coherence and plausibility."[5] Finally, Brad Prager argues that "Herzog is uninterested in depicting the world as it generally appears to us, [rather] he is striving for the aesthetic heights akin to that attainable by poetry," a theory that accounts for the motivation behind Herzog's nonreferential tendency.[6] This article expands on these comments by investigating the relationship between Herzog's nonreferential tendency and his concept of cinematic deep truth with regard to his dual investment in fiction and

1 Werner Herzog, "DVD Commentary," *Jeder für sich und Gott gegen alle* (1974; Munich, West Germany: BFI [The Werner Herzog Collection], 2014), DVD.

2 Kaja Silverman, "Kaspar Hauser's 'Terrible Fall' into Narrative," *New German Critique*, no. 24/25 (Autumn 1981–Winter 1982): 76, https://doi.org/10.2307/488044.

3 Werner Herzog, *Herzog on Herzog*, ed. Paul Cronin (London: Faber and Faber, 2002), 301, 66–67. See also Les Blank, *Werner Herzog Eats His Shoe* (1980; Berkeley, CA: BFI [The Werner Herzog Collection], 2014), DVD, in which Herzog attacks the popular images of television and commercials: "It kills us with talk-shows, we have to declare holy war on what we see on television. Real war against TV. We lack adequate images; our civilization doesn't have adequate images. . . . [I]t is not understood yet that a problem of the same magnitude [such as environmental issues, energy crisis, and world hunger] is that we do not have adequate images, and that's what I'm working on. A new grammar of images."

4 Matthew Gandy, "The Melancholy Observer: Landscape, Neo-Romanticism, and the Politics of Documentary Filmmaking," in *A Companion to Werner Herzog*, ed. Brad Prager (Oxford: Wiley-Blackwell, 2012), 529.

5 Lutz Koepnick, *Fitzcarraldo* (Rochester, NY: Camden House, 2019), 21.

6 Brad Prager, *The Cinema of Werner Herzog: Aesthetic Ecstasy and Truth* (New York: Wallflower Press, 2007), 5.

documentary filmmaking. Utilizing Friedrich Kittler's media theory for the task, the ultimate aim of this study is to present German media theory as a theoretical grid with particular applicability to the study of Herzog's idea of cinematic truth.

Herzog's approach to the cinematic image—his prioritization of film as visual experience rather than a decodable text—echoes German media theorists' post-semiotic tendencies, specifically Kittler's insistence that cultural interpretation is always-already mediated and shaped by technology. By looking at technological media and material substrates as forming the conditions for the generation of "discourse-networks," German media theory relocates the center of attention from the analysis of content to the study of the technological-material conditions of the production and constitution of knowledge and meaning.[7] In Kittler's words, "technologically possible manipulations determine what in fact can become a discourse."[8] While German media theory arose in the 1980s out of an intellectual discontent with hermeneutics, my own intervention in this tradition, which I describe as post-semiotic hermeneutics, does not dismiss interpretation but rather proposes hermeneutics that is based on technological-material aspects of media, aspects that commonly remain invisible, or at least irrelevant, in most textual analyses. When applied to the interpretation of films, my approach not only reveals the symbolic signification of objects and media but also scrutinizes the value of these media and objects, homing in on their technical operations and how these operations' specific applications determine discourse and meaning in the films that feature them. This approach is particularly relevant with regard to the enigmatic, the ineffable, the elusive, and the unsayable in movies, which generally resist traditional hermeneutics. Thus, German media theory further contributes to film theory by helping scholars better understand the way these filmic phenomena function, rather than what they signify.

In the next section, I characterize Herzog's approach to the cinematic image—his quest for "deep truth"—as informed by an investment in poesis rather than referentiality and by a dialectics of real and artifice, two aspects that are echoed in his distinctive work in fiction and documentary.[9] The second section moves on to closely look at two sequences, one from a fiction film (*Jeder für sich und Gott gegen alle*) and one from a documentary (*Grizzly Man*, 2005), that together epitomize the two aspects of Herzog's "deep

7 Friedrich A. Kittler, *Discourse Networks 1800/1900*, trans. Michael Metteer with Chris Cullens (Stanford, CA: Stanford University Press, 1990), 369. Kittler defines "discourse-network" as "the network of technologies and institutions that allow a given culture to select, store, and process relevant data." He introduces the issue of print as an example of a discourse's reliance on technology: "Technologies like that of book printing and the institutions coupled to it, such as literature and the university, thus constituted a historically very powerful formation, which in the Europe of the age of Goethe became the condition of possibility for literary criticism." Bernhard Siegert, *Cultural Techniques: Grids, Filters, Doors, and Other Articulations of the Real*, trans. Geoffrey Winthrop-Young (New York: Fordham University Press, 2015), 2.

8 Kittler, *Discourse Networks*, 232.

9 Throughout this article I use the term *real* to designate prediscursive aspects of the world and existence that cannot be captured through traditional representational means.

truth" through the theme of autopsy. Applying Kittler's media theory to this analysis shows how the concept of *truth* in these films, specifically in the films' manifestation of the tension between the unfathomability of death and the attempt to embed it into discourse, is generated and negotiated not only through cinematic style but also significantly by means of the technological and material media that the films incorporate.

FROM REFERENTIALITY TO POESIS

Inspecting several instances from Herzog's oeuvre aids in pointing out his tendency to diminish the image's referential function. In *Grizzly Man*, a moment that Herzog's voice-over describes as fulfilling the "inexplicable magic of cinema"—something that a filmmaker "couldn't expect, never even dream of"—is provided by two foxes that unexpectedly cross the frame. The value of the scene does not stem from any symbolic, narrative, or structural signification but rather from the contingency and authenticity of the filmed event.

Herzog invests his films with a potentiality for chance and authenticity in two distinct ways. In the first, he works with unexpected and ungovernable contents including natural forces—such as an active volcano, the Peruvian jungle, or the extreme conditions of Antarctica and Siberia—and idiosyncratic actors Klaus Kinski and Bruno Schleinstein. The second involves directorial decisions such as leaving the camera rolling several seconds after the scripted content is concluded (as he often does in *Grizzly Man*) or hypnotizing the cast throughout the shooting, as he did in *Herz aus Glas* (*Heart of Glass*, 1976). *Herz aus Glas* is also a useful example of what landscape means for Herzog; according to Gandy, it is "not a straightforward dimension to cinematic realism, in the sense of neo-realist or cinéma vérité approaches, but rather an exploratory terrain in itself that is capable of revealing insights beyond surface appearances."[10] The long landscape scenes in *Herz aus Glas* evoke transcendence and sublimity in the tradition of German Romantic painting and are for Herzog a part of a search for "ecstatic truth."[11] These shots introduce, according to Timothy Corrigan, "a world whose meaning lies not in any significance attained from the human order but in their own self-conspicuous vitality."[12] Indeed, Herzog searches for his ecstatic truth in generally nonnarrative moments, whose signification is in their atmospheric value.[13] Truth, it thus seems for Herzog, is opposed to conventional human meaning.

This opposition between truth and meaning is furthermore echoed in Herzog's mistrust in language in its capacity as referential signification, or, as Brigitte Peucker puts it, "the recurrent Herzog theme of the insufficiency

10 Gandy, "Melancholy Observer," 528.

11 Werner Herzog, "DVD Commentary," *Herz aus Glas* (1979; Munich, West Germany: BFI [The Werner Herzog Collection], 2014), DVD. On the affinity of Herzog's rendition of landscapes to German Romanticism, see Gandy, "Melancholy Observer."

12 Timothy Corrigan, "The Original Tradition: Hypnotic Space in Herzog's *The Mystery of Kaspar Hauser*," in *New German Film: The Displaced Image*, rev. ed. (Austin: University of Texas Press, 1994), 132.

13 Some of the attributes Herzog gives the landscape scenes in *Herz aus Glas* are "ecstatic" and "very very mysterious."

of language."[14] For Herzog, much like for the German Romantics who have doubtlessly influenced him, the sublime is antithetical to language.[15] As Prager claims, Herzog's search for truth exceeds language's expressive capacity: "Language, to speak at least of prose rather than of poetry, is unlikely to evoke the sublime insofar as language is always already part of our everyday world; it is always profane, and only an earthly tool by which we name earthly things."[16]

Herzog's prioritization of the visual impact of the image over its referential meaning is also evident in his essay-films *Fata Morgana* (1971) and *Lektionen in Finsternis* (*Lessons of Darkness*, 1992). Phantasma and actual mirages dominate *Fata Morgana*, while *Lektionen in Finsternis* features the combination of slow-moving aerial shots of an uncanny blazing landscape, romantic tropes, and Richard Wagner's music, a combination that according to Gandy achieves a "cinematic sublime."[17] Both films thus fulfill "a quest for images you have not really seen."[18] In that regard, the two films crystalize an important additional aspect of Herzog's elusive conception of the image. The image is not only a striving for authenticity and contingency; it is also a pursuit of mystery and uncanniness. In other words, these films epitomize Herzog's investment in the filmed event, presenting it not as it is commonly observed and experienced, but as it is mediated through the aestheticizing filters of cinema. In this way, the films betray Herzog's prioritization of the poetic over the referential. Prager concisely encapsulates this prioritization, stating that if Herzog's films document anything, it is "the constant search for a standpoint beyond conventional means of experiencing the world—an aesthetic standpoint."[19]

At the heart of Herzog's approach to the image, then, is an ambition to experience reality as an event that somehow both precedes its cultural signification and is subsequent to its aesthetic rendition. In terms of subject matter, this ambition is most clearly articulated in *Jeder für sich und Gott gegen alle* and *Land des Schweigens und der Dunkelheit* (*Land of Silence and Darkness*, 1971). Although the first is fiction and the second a documentary, both films deal with humans who remain outside the symbolic order due to their special life circumstances. Kaspar Hauser was locked in a dark room and had no interaction with other beings until his adolescence, while the subjects in *Land des Schweigens und der Dunkelheit* are severely sight- and hearing-impaired individuals whose sensorium is significantly atypical.[20]

14 Brigitte Peucker, "Herzog and Auteurism: Performing Authenticity," in Prager, *Companion to Werner Herzog*, 37.

15 On Herzog and Romanticism, see Brigitte Peucker, "Werner Herzog: In Quest of the Sublime," in *New German Filmmakers: From Oberhausen through the 1970s*, ed. Klaus Phillips (New York: Ungar, 1984), 168–194. See also Gandy, "Melancholy Observer"; and Laurie Johnson, "Werner Herzog's Romantic Spaces," in Prager, *Companion to Werner Herzog*, 510–527.

16 Prager, *Cinema of Werner Herzog*, 5.

17 Gandy, "Melancholy Observer," 531.

18 Werner Herzog, "DVD Commentary," *Fata Morgana* (1979; Munich, West Germany: BFI [The Werner Herzog Collection], 2014), DVD.

19 Prager, *Cinema of Werner Herzog*, 198.

20 In *Land des Schweigens und der Dunkelheit*, viewers meet Vladimir Kokol, a deaf and blind twenty-two-year-old who had never left his home or learned to speak, an eerie example of a modern-day Kaspar Hauser.

The interaction with the world for these people constitutes both Kaspar Hauser and the subjects of *Land des Schweigens und der Dunkelheit* as embodiments of the epistemological search in Herzog's cinema, a search whose aim is not just to show that culture and language keep us from truth—what Silverman aptly refers to as "the censorship of signification"[21]—but also, and primarily, to render this unrepresentable truth in the form of aestheticized images.

In both films, the images that delineate the consciousness of these outsiders of symbolic order feature aestheticized renderings of documentary actualities: in *Land des Schweigens und der Dunkelheit,* the documentary subject's vision that opens the film—described by Gertrud Koch as "the gloomy, flickering, out of focus view of a field path above which clouds are drifting"—is a stylized manipulation of landscape footage (see Figure 1).[22] Similarly, in *Jeder für sich und Gott gegen alle,* the protagonist's dream-visions are all incorporations—in most cases by means of substantial processing—of existing documentary footage shot on Super 8mm (see Figure 2).[23] Corrigan points out that these dream-visions employ a different, rougher film stock from that which is used for the rest of the film and notes that while this correlates to Kaspar's primal imagination, equally important for the effect of the scenes are "the realistic roots of these dreams": namely, that they "all originate in actual stories or daily events."[24] Again, Herzog's cinematic vision is the product of a dialectics of documentary actual and filmic manipulation. The interpretation of pre-signified inner worlds in *Land des Schweigens und der Dunkelheit* and *Jeder für sich und Gott gegen alle* reveals Herzog, the "experimenter in new sights," as someone whose interest lies in a heightened aestheticized mediation of the profilmic real.[25]

BETWEEN REAL AND ARTIFICE

Both *Jeder für sich und Gott gegen alle* and *Land des Schweigens und der Dunkelheit* deal with authenticity. This aspect, as I illustrated earlier, is central to Herzog's vision of the true image. Yet, as I've shown, in these films, authenticity is inseparable from artificiality. In her essay on performance and authenticity in Herzog, Peucker investigates this disconcerting duality and points to how central the physical act of filmmaking is to Herzog's idea of authenticity. She writes, "It is the extraordinary human effort required to perform this act, when registered by the camera, that renders the image authentic." At the same time, however, she observes that Herzog's films also welcome "all manner of artifice" provided they lend the image poetic qualities that promote

21 Silverman, "Kaspar Hauser's 'Terrible Fall,'" 91.

22 Gertrud Koch, "Blindness as Insight: Visions of the Unseen in *Land of Silence and Darkness*," in *The Films of Werner Herzog: Between Mirage and History*, ed. Timothy Corrigan (New York: Methuen, 1986), 78.

23 Herzog, *Herzog on Herzog*, 108. The imagery of Kaspar's dream on the Caucasus, for example, was produced by filming in 35mm and, in different speed, the backward projection of an 8mm shot made by Lucki Stipetić (Herzog's half-brother) in Burma some years earlier.

24 Corrigan, "Original Tradition," 141.

25 Corrigan, 130.

ecstatic truth.[26] In what seems like a contradiction in terms, Peucker argues that "the 'authenticity' of the Herzog film is equally predicated on the belief in a relation to the real conferred upon the image by physical investment *and* by the repeated recourse to artifice."[27] This blurring of the boundaries between the authentic and the fabricated, between the real and artifice, plays a central role in Herzog's vision of cinematic truth and in his dual investment in documentary and fiction filmmaking.

Herzog's search for truth by way of images naturally directs him to documentary film practice. Indeed, according to Eric Ames, "documentary cinema appeals to Herzog . . . for its privileged relationship to knowledge."[28] And yet, this privileged relationship to knowledge is not that which one usually associates with documentary, nor even with realism in fiction film. Herzog's documentaries, Ames writes, "are scripted, staged, arranged, and fabricated," but at the same time, he continues, "they are also unscripted, improvised, contingent, and exploratory."[29] This contradiction is most succinctly epitomized in a remark by Ed Lachman, one of Herzog's cinematographers, who once said that "Herzog will lie to get to the truth."[30] Lachman thus affirms that Herzog's aim is not simply a Bazinian realism of contingency and authenticity, nor is it pure observational documentation. Cinematic deep truth, for Herzog, is distinct from such straightforward notions of realism and documentary, which begs the question: What is cinematic truth for Herzog? In the DVD commentary on the scene from *Jeder für sich und Gott gegen alle* with which I opened this article, Herzog is asked whether he is after a documentary feel in depicting the story of Kaspar Hauser. He replies:

> It's not documentary, it's not realism, it's something I've always been after, and I see it more clearly in recent years. I've always tried to find a deeper strata [*sic*] of truth that are inherent in cinema. . . . You know there is some deep truth within it and you don't have to analyze, you don't have to ask, you don't have to read books to extract what is the truth, you just know it. . . . A deep truth. This is possible also in cinema, and it is not the accountant's truth of cinéma vérité, it is something else, it is an ecstatic truth, and I'm after an ecstatic truth. I see it very very clearly and I have actually written it down in a very short manifesto, the so-called "Minnesota Declaration" and you can find it on my website printed out.[31]

Herzog presented his twelve-point "Minnesota Declaration" as a protest against certain types of documentary filmmaking.[32] Essentially, the declara-

26 Peucker, "Herzog and Auteurism," 36–37; and Prager, *Cinema of Werner Herzog*, 2. Prager suggests that in Herzog's films "the body is integrated into the work, as it would be in the act of sculpting or painting."

27 Peucker, "Herzog and Auteurism," 37 (italics in the original).

28 Eric Ames, *Ferocious Reality: Documentary According to Werner Herzog* (Minneapolis: University of Minnesota Press, 2012), 10.

29 Ames, 6.

30 Quoted in Prager, *Cinema of Werner Herzog*, 8.

31 Herzog, "DVD Commentary," *Jeder für sich und Gott gegen alle*.

32 "Werner Herzog Reads His Minnesota Declaration: Truth and Fact in Documentary

tion insists on a dichotomy between facts and truth, or between "accountant's truth," which creates norms, and deep "ecstatic truth," which creates illumination.[33] According to the fifth point of the declaration, the deeper strata of truth in cinema are "mysterious and elusive" and "can be reached only through fabrication and imagination and stylization."[34] This is, of course, a provocative claim, not only for devotees of direct cinema but also for the documentary project as such.

Prager rightly notes that "the capacity to transfigure reality, in Herzog's view, is what separates the poets from the accountants."[35] But what is the meaning of this transfiguration when it comes to Herzog's understanding of truth? I argue that Herzog's insistence on fabrication, imagination, and stylization promotes a dialectics of the real and artifice as a means for achieving truth in cinema.[36] This dialectics affords a poetic treatment of the actual and authentic; as such, it achieves an expression of aspects of existence that cannot be captured in a straightforward positivistic discourse. That, in a nutshell, is the link between a dialectics of the real and artifice and Herzog's conception of deep or ecstatic truth. While this dialectics is more provocative as a practice for documentary filmmaking, it pervades Herzog's fiction films as well. Herzog's investment in both documentary and fiction and his stated lack of discrimination between the two modes beget a corpus that gravitates toward a synergy of real and artifice.[37] *The Wild Blue Yonder* (2005), which produces a science fiction narrative by recontextualizing documentary footage, embodies this synergy, but many other films in Herzog's oeuvre—one thinks, for example, of *Fitzcarraldo* (1982), *Wo die grünen Ameisen träumen* (*Where the Green Ants Dream*, 1984), *Tod für fünf Stimmen* (*Gesualdo: Death for Five Voices*, 1995), and *Flucht aus Laos* (*Little Dieter Needs to Fly*, 1997)—demonstrate the same inclination, where the general rule is that the documentaries strive to accentuate and augment their artificiality while the fictions labor to ground their commitment to the real.

The dialectical operations of fiction and documentary in search for truth should be most illuminating in cases where the two cinematic modes deal with the same subject matter. Herzog's oeuvre makes it possible to detect such intrinsic links and affinities across decades and genres.[38] When

---

Cinema," *Crosscuts*, April 30, 1999, https://walkerart.org/magazine/minnesota-declaration-truth-documentary-cinema-1999. The declaration is meant to address the problem that "there's something ultimately and deeply wrong about the concept of what constitutes fact and what constitutes truth in documentaries in particular." On Herzog's misuse of the term *cinéma vérité* and his assault on the French documentary movement of the 1950s, see Ames, *Ferocious Reality*, 9–10.

33 Herzog, *Herzog on Herzog*, 301.

34 Herzog, 301.

35 Prager, *Cinema of Werner Herzog*, 5.

36 While *fabrication*, *imagination*, and *stylization* designate different operations, all three concepts stand in opposition to notions of factuality and can be grouped as various approaches to artifice.

37 Herzog, *Herzog on Herzog*, 95. Herzog stated that he "never made a distinction between [his] feature films and [his] 'documentaries.' For [him], they are all just films." Prager, *Cinema of Werner Herzog*, 8. Prager, nevertheless, makes the observation that the features and documentaries are distinct in that features are mostly shot in 35mm and documentaries mostly in 16mm, Super 16, or high-definition video.

38 *Flucht aus Laos* and *Rescue Dawn* (2006) make an obvious pair, but one can think

Figures 1 and 2. Visions of the protagonists in *Jeder für sich und Gott gegen alle* (Werner Herzog Filmproduktion, 1974) and *Land des Schweigens und der Dunkelheit* (Werner Herzog Filmproduktion, 1971).

inspected synchronically, as in what follows, these links and affinities testify to the director's doctrine.

THE CORONER AND THE REAL

Given that film is already an artifact, it makes sense to study a dialectics of artifice and the real in film by looking at films with a subject matter as intensively related to the real as possible. In this conviction, I follow a suggestion by Ivone Margulies in her study of cinematic realism: "How can one recall an event's concrete peculiarity or reproduce its original urgency through a medium that so clearly defers? One way to invite such hard questions is to represent those events that most stubbornly resist the notion of duplication because of their close association with the carnality of the body and decay."[39] Herzog's work repeatedly engages with what Margulies calls "visceral signifier[s] for the real."[40] His films deal with issues of corporeality such as disability, the body in pain or physical danger, and, of course, death. As Seung-hoon Jeong and Dudley Andrew pertinently note, "Herzog's cinema of risk aims to embalm not life but death. A fetishist, he gets as close as possible to the real thing, embellishing everything that has to do with death."[41]

Death is often treated as the archetypal locus of the real; it earns this status partly by being the inevitable end of all of us and partly by being directly and intensively linked to the physicality of the body. Death presents a challenge for representation and mediation partly because it is the great unknown of human existence and partly, as Philippe Ariès argues, because of its disappearance from the public sphere in Western modernity and its increasing conceptualization as "a transgression which tears man from his daily life, from rational society."[42] Mostly, however, it is the incongruity between death as a locus of the real, on the one hand, and representation as always necessarily removed from the real, on the other, that constitutes the greatest challenge in the mediation of death. This incongruity is evident in symbolic representations, such as language. But when death is represented not by the symbolic grid of language but in ways that are "authenticated by the object itself" (e.g., in phonographic and cinematographic media) and as such escape all symbolic grids, the mediation of death becomes an even more complex issue.[43]

---

of less straightforward "twins": *Aguirre, der Zorn Gottes* (*Aguirre, the Wrath of God*, 1972) and *Die große Ekstase des Bildschnitzers Steiner* (*The Great Ecstasy of Woodcarver Steiner*, 1974); *Fata Morgana* and *The Wild Blue Yonder*; *Beobachtungen zu einer neuen Sprache* (*How Much Wood Would a Woodchuck Chuck*, 1976) and *Stroszek* (1977); and *Land des Schweigens und der Dunkelheit* and *Jeder für sich und Gott gegen alle*.

39 Ivone Margulies, "Bodies Too Much," in *Rites of Realism: Essays on Corporeal Cinema*, ed. Ivone Margulies (Durham, NC: Duke University Press, 2003), 1.

40 Margulies, 3.

41 Seung-hoon Jeong and Dudley Andrew, "Grizzly Ghost: Herzog, Bazin and the Cinematic Animal," *Screen* 49, no. 1 (Spring 2008): 2, https://doi.org/10.1093/screen/hjn001.

42 Philippe Ariès, *Western Attitudes toward Death: From the Middle Ages to the Present*, trans. Patricia M. Ranum (Baltimore: Johns Hopkins University Press, 1974), 57–58.

43 Kittler, *Discourse Networks*, 12. On this complexity, see Jennifer Malkowski, introduction to *Dying in Full Detail: Mortality and Digital Documentary* (Durham, NC: Duke University Press, 2017), 1–22.

Film's indexical relation to the real has often been treated as the reason why filming death is an obscenity. For André Bazin, sex and death "must be experienced and cannot be represented."[44] Violating this prohibition is obscene; in the case of sex, it is a moral obscenity and, in the case of death, a metaphysical one, since "we do not die twice."[45] Vivian Sobchack adds that since death is a taboo subject in Western society, it is rendered unnamable in both social relations and the representations that indexically point to those social relations. The result is that "the event of death as it is perceived in our culture points to and interrogates the very limits of representation in all its present forms."[46] Death, in other words, constitutes a succinct case of the pre-signified real, a truth beyond the censorship of signification.

Herzog has long been attracted to Bazin's two cinematic taboos. Explaining the background for his "Minnesota Declaration," Herzog recalls watching television one night and being confronted "by a very stupid, uninspiring documentary" followed by "something equally bad, the same kind of crap you find on television wherever you go."[47] At four o'clock in the morning, however, Herzog recalls, "I found some hard-core porno, and I sat up and said to myself, 'My God, finally something straightforward, something real, even if it is purely physical.' For me the porno had real naked truth."[48] Herzog's attraction to the pornographic film, Peucker notes, lies in its "zero-degree realism," its value of the "real beyond signification."[49] At the same time, she adds, "the privileging of the pornographic image points to Herzog's assertions concerning the physicality of filmmaking, as well as to a mystical belief that its corporeality will somehow be taken up into the image to reside there as 'truth' or 'authenticity.'"[50] Similarly, it is the corporeality and the value of the "real beyond signification" that privilege death for Herzog. Serge Daney's comment (on Bazin's filmic realism), according to which "filming as risk and of risk" is what "justifies the making of the film" and what "confers on it a certain surplus value," might also explain Herzog's repeated experimentation with death, such as his attraction to genuinely dangerous filming locations.[51] As Peucker succinctly puts it, Herzog is someone for whom "landscapes produce essential images because death lurks in the natural world."[52] Herzog would probably nod at Daney's explication of Bazin's "fetishism" for realist cinema: "You have to go to the point of dying for your images."[53]

If death presents an "'undomesticated' and 'irrational' behavior of the body," then the dead body under the scrutiny of autopsy presents a quintes-

44 André Bazin, "Death Every Afternoon," in Margulies, *Rites of Realism*, 30.

45 Bazin, 30.

46 Vivian Sobchack, "Inscribing Ethical Space: Ten Propositions on Death, Representation, and Documentary," *Quarterly Review of Film Studies* 9, no. 4 (1984): 286, https://doi.org/10.1080/10509208409361220.

47 Herzog, *Herzog on Herzog*, 239.

48 Herzog, 239.

49 Peucker, "Herzog and Auteurism," 36.

50 Peucker, 36.

51 Serge Daney, "The Screen of Fantasy (Bazin and Animals)," trans. Mark A. Cohen, in Margulies, *Rites of Realism*, 37.

52 Peucker, "Herzog and Auteurism," 35.

53 Daney, "Screen of Fantasy," 37.

sential example of modern Western culture's tendency to confine the real into empirical positivistic discourse and to discipline aberrations of irrationality and unrepresentability.[54] In other words, the autopsy itself testifies to a dialectics of reality and discourse. As such, it provides an optimal case to study Herzog's dialectics of reality and artifice. Whereas the literal translation of the ancient Greek word *autopsíā*, as Stan Brakhage reminds us with the title of his 1971 film, *The Act of Seeing with One's Own Eyes*, is "seeing with one's own eyes," the very conflation of film with this procedure implies its subversion. But this subversion, which is nevertheless not a cancellation but a modification of the act of seeing with one's own eyes, is exactly what Herzog is after. Indeed, in *Jeder für sich und Gott gegen alle* and *Grizzly Man*, the negotiation of death and discourse revolves around sequences that are centered on an autopsy. These sequences are the focus of the following discussions.

JEDER FÜR SICH UND GOTT GEGEN ALLE

Jeder für sich und Gott gegen alle tells the story of Kaspar Hauser, a person who has been kept in complete isolation throughout the first years of his life. As a young adult, Hauser is taken out of confinement and is left in the center of a town. Taken under supervision by various parties, the film traces society's reaction to the outsider and Kaspar's process of socialization. According to Herzog, Kaspar Hauser's is a story about "what civilization does to us all, how it deforms and destroys us by bringing us into societal line."[55] This perspective on the film—essentially a Foucauldian critique of socialization through normalization—has been elaborated in the works of various commentators.[56] Silverman, for example, interprets Kaspar's process of civilization in the film as a violent fall from an "oceanic" plentitude into difference—language, subjectivity, narrative, and meaning.[57] Corrigan, conversely, presents the conflict between Kaspar and society primarily as a struggle for "an original vision," which finds its most prominent articulation through the film's three dream-visions.[58] I take Silverman's and Corrigan's accounts to be complementary. In Lacanian terms, it may be said that while Silverman points at the repressive function of the symbolic, Corrigan calls attention to the reparatory function of the imaginary.

I will expand on these scholars' readings by focusing on the significance of technologies, tools, and media for the particular form that Kaspar's process of confinement into discourse takes in the film. If this process is understood as essentially Foucauldian, then my approach may be defined as Kittlerian to the extent that it seeks to reveal the material factors that regulate the storage and recording of information as governing the formation of discourse.[59] My analysis focuses on the film's final sequence, composed of

54 Sobchack, "Inscribing Ethical Space," 284.

55 Herzog, *Herzog on Herzog*, 111.

56 See Michel Foucault, *Discipline and Punish: The Birth of the Prison*, trans. Alan Sheridan (New York: Vintage Books, 1995). First published in French in 1975.

57 Silverman, "Kaspar Hauser's 'Terrible Fall,'" 74–75, 79.

58 Corrigan, "Original Tradition," 132.

59 "In *The Order of Things*, Foucault presents a discontinuous sequence of epistemes without explaining why new discursive orders appear. Kittler, in turn, refers these shifts to medial changes." Geoffrey Winthrop-Young and Nicholas Gane, "Friedrich Kittler: An Introduction," *Theory, Culture & Society* 23, no. 7–8 (December 2006): 10.

three scenes: Kaspar's deathbed, whereupon he relates his third and final dream-vision; the autopsy of his body; and a final short scene of the town's scribe, endowed with the autopsy results, exiting the operating room and on his way to write the autopsy report. I will show that in tracing a trajectory that leads from a portrayal of Kaspar's unique nature in the form of a filmic vision to an explanation of his unique nature in the form of a written report, the sequence manifests the role of technological and procedural instruments in the formation of discourse. The sequence moreover illuminates the effect of the intermedial encounter between technologies utilized in the film and the medium of film itself.

On his deathbed, Kaspar relates a story of which he knows its beginning. Like his dream about the Caucasus and his vision of death earlier in the film, the story, about a caravan led by a blind man lost in the Sahara Desert, forms a separate visual segment. The grainy, flickering, slow-motioned image is aesthetically distinct from the rest of the film. Certainly, Kaspar's original vision coincides with Herzog's own quest for deep truth: "there is a much more profound level of truth than that of everyday reality, for example in the dreams that Kaspar talks of," says Herzog, continuing, "it is my job to seek them out."[60]

In Silverman's reading of the scene, the old blind caravan leader provides an alternative image of Kaspar's symbolic father. Moreover, the story's open-ended narrative denies traditional boundaries such as narrative closure.[61] In other words, Kaspar's story points to an alternative social order and an alternative process of socialization that take the form of an aesthetic vision in which "the film's visual diegesis fractures, giving way to an alternative landscape."[62] If, as Peucker claims, "Kaspar's image-oriented dreams are akin to the art of the cinema," then the visual alternative provided in Kaspar's dream-vision constitutes Herzog's "ecstatic" and essentially cinematic way of portraying Kaspar as an original and vital being.[63]

But the attainment of this cinematic truth soon makes way for a competing account of *what* (rather than *who*) Kaspar is. After he finishes telling his story, the film cuts to Kaspar's feet, now tagged in a clinic, his body under examination by three coroners. They give special attention to a study of his brain, which is also shown in the film at length and close-up; that organ that produced the original vision we just witnessed is now literally opened up, lending itself to observation and scrutiny. Unlike the extraordinary visions produced by the living organ, however, the dissected brain and body produce a different sort of knowledge: the autopsy reveals that the left lobe of Hauser's liver "is greatly enlarged" and the brain's shape is "rather unusual."

In *The Birth of the Clinic* (1963), Michel Foucault traces a break in the history of Western medicine around the turn of the nineteenth century during which the autopsy made death into "an object and source of knowledge" to the extent that "the corpse became the brightest moment in the figures of

60 Herzog, *Herzog on Herzog*, 113.

61 Silverman, "Kaspar Hauser's 'Terrible Fall,'" 91.

62 Silverman, 89.

63 Brigitte Peucker, "Literature and Writing in the Films of Werner Herzog," in Corrigan, *Films of Werner Herzog*, 111.

Figure 3. Kaspar's caravan story constitutes Herzog's essentially cinematic way of portraying Kaspar as an original and vital being in *Jeder für sich und Gott gegen alle* (Werner Herzog Filmproduktion, 1974).

truth."[64] If for the Renaissance and the eighteenth century "the knowledge of life was based on the essence of the living," then for the medical perception of the nineteenth century (during which the story of Kaspar Hauser takes place), along with its development of pathological anatomy and its rigorous analysis of corpses, "knowledge of life finds its origin in the destruction of life and in its extreme opposite; it is at death that disease and life speak their truth: a specific, irreducible truth."[65]

The break in the history of Western medicine traced by Foucault in *The Birth of the Clinic* corresponds to the epistemic shift between the Classical and Modern eras revealed in his study in *The Order of Things* (1966). Curiously, Foucault describes the epistemic shift from Classical to Modern in terms of topography and visibility, where the "great, universal expanse" of Classical Western knowledge is rearranged in the nineteenth century according to "a verticality" that provides "the foundation for perceptible arrangements," which displaces "all the great horizontal deployments of the *taxinomia*."[66] Descending into the body in order to explain its visible surface phenomena, the autopsy appears to be the archetypical emblem of the Modern ordering and acquisition of knowledge. Accordingly, the medical eye of the nineteenth century, Foucault insists in *The Birth of the Clinic*, penetrates the body in order to find in its depths explanations in the form of deformations, accidents, and displaced, destroyed, or modified elements.[67]

64 Michel Foucault, "Open Up a Few Corpses," in *The Birth of the Clinic: An Archaeology of Medical Perception*, trans. A. M. Sheridan (London: Routledge, 2003), 125. First published in French in 1963.

65 Foucault, 145.

66 Michel Foucault, *The Order of Things: An Archaeology of the Human Sciences*, trans. Alan Sheridan (New York: Routledge, 2002), 273–274 (italics in the original).

67 Foucault, "Open Up," 136.

Consonant with the explanatory weight that Foucault links with the study of corpses in the Modern clinical perspective, the deformations and abnormalities revealed in Kaspar's autopsy give great satisfaction to the coroners, who exclaim, "That explains a great deal! This should be recorded." Intriguingly, the coroners' exclamation juxtaposes knowledge ("That explains a great deal!") and documentation ("This should be recorded"). For the coroners, the explanatory value of the autopsy is coupled with a desire to archive knowledge and make it available for future reference. Indeed, the discovery specifically brings great joy to the town's scribe (*Schreiber*)—a recording and archiving apparatus in the form of a human bureaucrat. As he leaves the operating room in the film's final scene, the scribe says to himself with satisfaction, "What a wonderful, what a precise report this will make! Deformities discovered in Kaspar Hauser's brain and liver! Finally, we have got an explanation for this strange man." The scribe's fetishization of the report attests to a culture's compulsion to transform things (and people) into writing, thereby converting them into decodable, storable, translatable, and processable data.[68] And so, reified, arrested, and reduced to his corporeal materiality, Kaspar can finally be dissected, studied, classified, assessed, recorded, and filed. The enigma of a human being whose special life circumstances have rendered them an outsider of society is finally confined and accounted for through their circumscription into modern clinical discourse. As this scene of the autopsy makes abundantly evident, the enigma of Kaspar Hauser is explained via media. The process of explicating Kaspar Hauser includes studying his body with medical instruments, articulating any findings in language, recording those words in writing on paper (and, one assumes, storing these papers in an archive). These cultural techniques, instruments, and procedures (medical devices, language, alphabetization, ink, paper, filing, and so on) facilitate and promote a material-empirical conception of knowledge that is imposed on Kaspar's undomesticated ways of thinking and being. Clearly, this kind of knowledge fails in precisely the place where the visual medium of film triumphs, that is, in conveying the vitality and uniqueness of the figure of Kaspar Hauser, his original vision.

Prager points out that in contrast to Kaspar's unfinished story about the caravan, "the Scribe maintains the pretense—the illusion—that a satisfactory explanation, and thereby closure, can be found."[69] True, yet the main dichotomy between Kaspar's story and the scribe's explanation does not pivot the degree of phenomena's explicability; it rather involves the different types of knowledge that different technological operations and procedures—writing/dissecting (the scribe's report), on the one hand, and filmmaking (the visual rendition of Kaspar's caravan story), on the other—accommodate.

Kaspar's final confinement into discourse is the achievement of the scalpel and the pen, of the joined operation of the explanatory value of the autopsy in the Modern episteme and the capacity of writing to record. Peucker notes that the word *Schreiben* (writing) is the first word that Kaspar

68 In the original German, the word for *report* (*Protokoll*) is repeated three times in the town recorder's monologue: "Ein schönes Protokoll, ein genaues Protokoll. Ich werde zu Protokoll geben, daß man an Hauser Deformationen entdeckt hat."

69 Prager, *Cinema of Werner Herzog*, 70.

hears in the film and that "with this word difference or otherness is introduced into his previously hermetic existence."[70] Peucker moreover shows that in *Kaspar Hauser* the written word functions as a source of social alienation.[71] Furthermore, in pointing out that prior to conjuring up his vision of the Sahara, Kaspar has been *told* about it, Peucker asserts that in his dream-vision, Kaspar "converts and subverts verbal representation . . . into visual images."[72] Eventually, however, it is the counter-conversion that has the upper hand: the process that begins with *Schreiben* concludes with the *Schreiber* (the scribe), and what began with teaching Kaspar the word *writing* ends with the conversion of Kaspar *into* writing.

The notion that writing is not only a central emblem of Kaspar's socialization but also a kind of death for him is alluded to by Silverman and explicitly pointed out by Prager.[73] But it is Corrigan who implies an association between the functions of writing and dissecting; he remarks that writing as manifested by the scribe "becomes an absurdly repetitive exercise generated by its own self-serving momentum" and that, at its worst, this writing "*dissects* in a search for simple explanations where there are none."[74] Indeed, the tools of writing and dissecting are isomorphic to the extent that both trace lines in a surface (or a medium) in order to produce difference and meaning. As such, both the scalpel and the pen—unlike the camera—are tools used in the service of the selection, excavation, analysis, storage, and communication of "great *hidden* forces," namely, in the service of the production and accumulation of knowledge that Foucault associates with the Modern episteme, Kittler with the Discourse Network 1800, and Herzog with accountants.[75]

The dichotomy between camera and pen/scalpel that the film advances corresponds to a break that Kittler detects between the nineteenth and twentieth centuries. In *Discourse Networks 1800/1900* (1985), Kittler shows that the widespread phonetic method of language teaching in Germany around 1800, coupled with the expanding role of mothers as educators of children, resulted, in the words of Gill Partington, in "a new set of relationships between subjectivity and language: language is not 'imposed' on the human mind, but is seen as having something like an organic link with it."[76] Language becomes oral, letters become sounds, and the inner-voice of the self coincides with the "mother's mouth." Consequently, in the Discourse Network 1800, "[t]he 'system of equivalents' Woman=Nature=Mother . . . gives language an 'absolute origin': all arbitrariness disappears and language becomes instead an ideal of nature."[77] This naturalized status of language gives rise to transcendental entities such as souls and subjects. As it affords

70 Peucker, "Literature and Writing," 108. On the relation between writing and acculturalization to the dominant tradition in *Jeder für sich und Gott gegen alle*, see also Silverman, "Kaspar Hauser's 'Terrible Fall,'" 75, 78–79.

71 Peucker, "Literature and Writing," 109.

72 Peucker, 111.

73 Prager, *Cinema of Werner Herzog*, 65.

74 Corrigan, "Original Tradition," 135 (italics added).

75 Foucault, *Order of Things*, 274 (italics added).

76 Gill Partington, "Friedrich Kittler's *Aufschreibsystem*," *Science Fiction Studies* 33, no. 1 (March 2006): 58.

77 Partington, 59.

the "smooth, effortless transition of graphemes into acoustic and visual signs, and vice versa,"[78] the Discourse Network 1800 blurs the boundaries between speaking, listening, reading, and writing. As such, language becomes "a homogenous alpha-medium, able to weave together nature and culture in a continuum of meaning."[79]

Emanating from analog recording and storage technologies, the Discourse Network 1900 destroys the continuity of language as a communication system. The ability of photographic and phonographic media to record and store optical and acoustic excerpts of the real without recourse to symbolic mediation results in a "*technological differentiation of data streams.*"[80] Gramophone, film, and typewriter execute this differentiation and dissolve the status that language enjoys in the Discourse Network 1800: speaking, listening, reading, and writing become separate functions that are related to and associated with different media. As a result, the Mother-Woman-Nature configuration is eradicated and along with it "the guarantee of meaningfulness."[81] I will next show that the abolition of language's guarantee of meaningfulness through a differentiation of data streams—film being one of them—makes possible the emergence of an aesthetic effect in *Jeder für sich und Gott gegen alle* that coincides with Herzog's notion of a deep truth. In her analysis of *Jeder für sich und Gott gegen alle*, Peucker shows how Herzog "assert[s] his preference for the visual over the literary."[82] The animosity that Peucker detects between the visual and the literary in Herzog's work may be placed in the context of the break that Kittler detects between the Discourse Network 1800 and the Discourse Network 1900 and their respective media. Herzog's utilization of film's distinctness from the technologies of 1800, which serve the scribe and the coroners, protest Kaspar's "terrible fall" into the discourse-network of 1800.

Thus, Herzog takes a number of steps to try to reduce the gap between sign and reference in his cinematic portrayal of the imposition of discourse over Kaspar's body. The text spoken by the coroners is taken from the actual autopsy report of the coroner who studied the body of the historical Kaspar Hauser; the brain used and dissected in the scene is a real human brain; and the three men who study Kaspar are in fact real coroners, not professional actors.[83] Herzog thus introduces surrogates for the real by including metonyms for death.[84] At the same time, and in line with what I detect as Herzog's dialectics of the real and artifice, the scene also foregrounds artificiality. This emerges primarily through intermedial and intertextual references to canonical works of Western art. The mise-en-scène and subject of the

78 Geoffrey Winthrop-Young, *Kittler and the Media* (Cambridge: Polity, 2011), 62.

79 Winthrop-Young, 62.

80 Winthrop-Young, 62 (italics in the original).

81 Winthrop-Young, 71.

82 Peucker, "Literature and Writing," 112.

83 Herzog, "DVD Commentary," *The Enigma of Kaspar Hauser.*

84 The fact that these elements cannot be recognized as referring to the real without Herzog's extra-textual explication matters little. For Herzog such gestures make their imprint on the film whether the viewer consciously notices them or not. This is why Herzog insisted on using real human labor to drag a real steamboat over a mountain in *Fitzcarraldo*, as the documentary *Burden of Dreams* (Les Blank, 1982) shows.

autopsy recall the painting *De anatomische les van Dr. Nicolaes Tulp* (*The Anatomy Lesson of Dr. Nicolaes Tulp*, Rembrandt van Rijn, 1632); the final shot of the film, in which the scribe walks off into the distance, alludes to the iconic endings of Charlie Chaplin films such as *The Tramp* (1915), *The Circus* (1928), and *Modern Times* (1936); and the accompanying score is an old hissing vinyl recording of an aria from Mozart's *Die Zauberflöte* (*The Magic Flute*, 1791). These intermedial and intertextual references foreground various media-inflected discourses. The rendition of death and autopsy emerges in the medium of painting (in Rembrandt); the construction of the concept ending in the medium of film (in Chaplin); and the expression of the concept love in the medium of opera (in Mozart).

The passage from *The Magic Flute* used in the scene is the aria Tamino sings when he is falling in love with Pamina's image through a portrait (act 1, scene 4). In bestowing magical-aesthetic qualities to an image, the aria's title (and first line), "This image is enchantingly lovely," echoes Herzog's ideal of the cinematic image as "mysterious and elusive." Furthermore, the fantasmatic moment of falling in love with an image, of reaching ecstatic heights through visual mediation, complies with Herzog's cinematic-epistemological project. Finally, the act of falling in love by looking at a picture without ever *seeing with one's own eyes* the woman painted ("Like no eye has ever beheld!" reads the second line) is the ultimate subversion of *autopsíā* as a means for attaining essential knowledge. The hiss of the phonographic recording appears to play a role too. Old phonograph recordings function similarly to Super 8mm footage in forming a constant reminder to the operation of mediation and its residue of noise (grainy image, hiss). As D. N. Rodowick puts it, "an inescapable quality of all analogical media is that each subsequent copy and every instance of playback introduces noise to the recorded information."[85] The hiss, therefore, attests both to the record's nature as copy and to its ephemerality and fragility. Every instance of playback becomes unique and advances the record's own eventual expiration. The "aura" (to use Walter Benjamin's concept) is not destroyed by mechanical reproduction; quite so, it resides in the mechanical reproducibility of analogical media.[86] The old recording of the aria, like Kaspar's vision of the caravan story, adheres to an "enchanting beauty" enabled in the purview of mediation.

Phonograph and film, painting and opera are juxtaposed in the film's closing scenes with the Discourse Network 1800. By foregrounding media that are dominated by non-symbolic representations (painting, film, opera) and juxtaposing them with the epistemic order of the Discourse Network 1800, the scenes expose the mechanisms of discourse production and critique the reduction of truth to facts and the narrowing of image to meaning. Finally, they testify to the potential of film—a medium both indexically

85 D. N. Rodowick, *The Virtual Life of Film* (Cambridge, MA: Harvard University Press, 2007), 113.

86 Walter Benjamin, "The Work of Art in the Age of Its Technological Reproducibility," in *The Work of Art in the Age of Its Technological Reproducibility, and Other Writings on Media*, ed. Michael W. Jennings, Brigid Doherty, and Thomas Y. Levin, trans. Edmund Jephcott et al. (Cambridge, MA: Harvard University Press, 2008), 23–24.

attached to the real and intermedially inclusive—to constitute its own unique concepts and its own deep truth in the form of images and sounds.

The next section, focusing on *Grizzly Man*, explores the ways in which the documentary mode and the incorporation of found footage affect Herzog's dialectics of real and artifice in his quest for deep truth through the cinematic mediation of the autopsy.

GRIZZLY MAN

On October 5, 2003, bear enthusiast Timothy Treadwell and his partner, Amie Huguenard, were mauled and partially consumed by a grizzly bear in Katmai National Park and Preserve in southern Alaska. Herzog's 2005 documentary film *Grizzly Man* brings together video footage taken by Treadwell using a DVCAM camcorder with 16mm film material that was shot by Herzog after Treadwell's death. Herzog describes Treadwell's association with the bears as the crossing of "an invisible borderline." The line metaphor, we may recall, is also used by Herzog to describe *Jeder für sich und Gott gegen alle* as a story about how civilization brings individuals "into societal line." If Kaspar Hauser is brought into societal line, then Treadwell, by conversion, breaches the line that separates civilization from nature, humans from animals. A line, a product of inscribing instruments, is indeed instrumental in the confinement of Kaspar into the Discourse Network 1800. For Treadwell, equipped with a digital camcorder at the turn of the twenty-first century, "the line" he allegedly crossed has already been *crossed out*; as an archetype of inscription, difference, and meaning, the line gives way in *Grizzly Man* to the audiovisual recording. It is therefore the intermedial encounter between Treadwell's footage and Herzog's film (rather than between inscribing instruments and film as in *Jeder für sich und Gott gegen alle*) that negotiates death and discourse in *Grizzly Man*.

While the film does not contain footage of Treadwell's and Huguenard's deaths, it does refer to (but does not include) an audio recording: the audio track of a videotape that was recorded with the lens cap on and presumably captured the sounds of Treadwell's and Huguenard's moments of death. Jeong and Andrew describe *Grizzly Man* as a commercial film that envelops Treadwell's undomesticated footage: "At the centre of the Herzog's professional film lies Treadwell's wild video, and at the core of that video lies the (missing) footage of agony, when a life ends in death."[87] As I shall demonstrate, the facts of the missing footage and of the existing audio are as central to *Grizzly Man* as is the fact of death itself. Although we do not gain direct access to its content, and although it is only the audio track of a recorded event, the audio recording of Treadwell's and Huguenard's horrible deaths functions as the film's structural center and is the driving force behind Herzog's aesthetic choices in it.

Ned Schantz also believes the film to be structured around the fatal bear attack.[88] To appreciate this absent moment, Schantz suggests that "we must

87 Jeong and Andrew, "Grizzly Ghost," 4.

88 Ned Schantz, "Melodramatic Reenactment and the Ghosts of *Grizzly Man*," *Criticism* 55, no. 4 (Fall 2013): 604.

consider an extended sequence that constitutes the very heart of the film: three major scenes of reenactment, back to back to back."[89] The sequence Schantz is referring to begins with a scene of a coroner describing his examination of the remains of Treadwell and Huguenard, followed by a scene in which Herzog is seen listening to the tape that captured the attack, and then fades to unrelated footage, taken by Treadwell, of two grizzly bears wrestling violently. Schantz argues that the nonexistent video haunts Herzog to the extent that "he tries to compensate for it in his own images" and that the three scenes may therefore be approached as a series of reenactments of the missing fatal attack.[90]

I propose taking the sequence that Schantz isolates not as including three reenactments of the attack, but as including three re-mediations of the missing audio recording. Unlike Schantz, who is convinced that Herzog takes the unremoved lens cap to be "Treadwell's ultimate failure as a filmmaker," I see the audiovisual split into an audio track and a (blank) visual track to be an essential motivation behind the entire film project.[91] Recalling his approach to cinematic truth, it seems safe to assume that for Herzog the visceral realness of real death does not leave room for mystery, poesis, and imagination. A representation of the obscene, shocking as it may be, does not amount to anything beyond an "accountants' truth." The motivation behind the sequence should therefore not be understood so much as a compensatory reenactment of the missing moment but as an extraction of the "mysterious and elusive" strata of truth through "fabrication and imagination and stylization."[92] Mediation and re-mediation of the missing event appear to make it, and the project as such, cinematically worthy and epistemologically fascinating for Herzog.

The sequence seems to be tracking two parallel movements. One movement follows the gradual inclusion of the medium of video: if in the coroner's monologue, the recording is merely mentioned in words, then in the next scene, the video camera is visible and the tape of the attack is played (though the audio is restricted to Herzog's ears); in the third scene, a video recording is incorporated into and merges with the cinematic images and sounds. This movement is joined by yet another that traces a gradual renunciation of death: if the coroner delivers his firsthand experience with the remains and with the tape, then the second scene both involves figures whose engagement with the deaths is less direct and reveals less about the content of the tape (even though the tape is playing); the third scene delivers merely an associative metonym of the attack. In short, if the sequence unfolds a quest for the image of death, then the closer we get to the image, the further we withdraw from death, and vice versa. This double movement between the real and its mediations takes form as a dialectics of the real and artifice in the coroner's monologue. A large portion of the coroner's monologue is dedicated to a recounting of the content of the audio recording. Notably, Herzog employs

89 Schantz, 604.
90 Schantz, 605.
91 Schantz, 605.
92 Herzog, *Herzog on Herzog*, 301.

a variety of artificial elements in *Grizzly Man*, a practice that becomes most pronounced in the scene of the coroner's monologue. While the death that he recounts is real, the scene is markedly artificial: the coroner's monologue seems to have been scripted, a surmise suggested by the man's contrived demeanor, exaggerated facial expressions, and use of vernacular language, such as referring to a mortuary box as a "large metal can." In addition, his monologue references issues that exceed common medical expertise, such as his claim, "I know that at the moment of death . . . Amie stayed with her lover." The scene's construction further emphasizes its artificiality. The coroner breaks the fourth wall by directly addressing the camera; the editing cuts abruptly between exterior and interior settings and between varied camera angles and distances in a manner that often creates jump-cuts, and all the while the monologue continues as if uninterrupted.

The coroner scene in *Grizzly Man* is thus opposed to the coroner scene in *Jeder für sich und Gott gegen alle* in various ways. In the latter, the coroner scene is a fictional scene with an actual autopsy report, a real brain, and real coroners, whereas the scene in *Grizzly Man* purports to be documentary yet contains no medical details, no remains from the deceased, and a coroner who appears "professionally dubious"[93] and, in any event, as one who overacts for the camera (see Figure 4). The coroner scene in *Grizzly Man*, like the one in *Jeder für sich und Gott gegen alle*, features a conflation of real and artifice, but as is made clear by the above description, the *Grizzly Man* scene does not emphasize the real as does its equivalent in *Jeder für sich und Gott gegen alle*. Instead, it foregrounds its artificiality. What accounts for this reversal?

The answer is threefold. One reason is video. In *Jeder für sich und Gott gegen alle*, film offers a mediation that diverges from language and print. But in *Grizzly Man*, film's distinction from the medium that it incorporates is not found in its ability to directly record and process visual and acoustic traces of the real (video does that too) but rather in its enhanced molding of these traces in the form of narrative, planned mise-en-scène, editing, professional camera work, musical score, non-diegetic narration, aerial shots, and other markers of a professional cinema that Treadwell's authentic, fragmented, and amateurish footage cannot obtain. In other words, unlike Treadwell's camera, which is "wandering straight into the fearful uncharted zone of the mysterious Real,"[94] Herzog's film cultivates traces of the real, forging them into a meaningful imaginary construction. The second reason for the reversal in the role of film in the dialectics of the real and artifice is the ultimate realization of real death. It is real death—however mediated and at whatever remove—that distinguishes the conflation of the real and artifice in a fiction film like *Jeder für sich und Gott gegen alle* from the same conflation in a documentary like *Grizzly Man*. The third reason for the reversal is the form that the recording of the moments of death takes in *Grizzly Man*, that is, acoustic registration, which for Kittler captures "the waste or residue that neither the mirror of the imaginary nor the grid of the symbolic can catch: the physiological accidents and stochas-

93 Schantz, "Melodramatic Reenactment," 599.
94 Jeong and Andrew, "Grizzly Ghost," 4.

Figure 4. The coroner in *Grizzly Man* (Lionsgate, 2005).

tic disorder of bodies."[95] Video, death, acoustics—*Grizzly Man* mediates and negotiates these three markers of the real.

A central aspect in Kittler's *Gramophone, Film, Typewriter* (1986) is the alignment of gramophone, film, and typewriter with each of Jacques Lacan's three axiomatic registers: the real, the imaginary, and the symbolic. The typewriter's association with the symbolic order is based on its encoding of data into symbols, while film, as has also been established by film scholars, such as Jean-Louis Baudry, Daniel Dayan, and Laura Mulvey during the 1970s, is related to the imaginary order.[96] Finally, sound recording captures the real, because, Kittler argues, "The phonograph does not hear as do ears that have been trained immediately to filter voices, words, and sounds out of noise; it registers acoustic events as such. Articulateness becomes a second order exception in a spectrum of noise."[97]

Of course, digital camcorders do not record sounds by etching grooves like analogical phonographic recordings; they convert visual and acoustic input into an electrical signal that is then recorded onto a medium, a DV cassette in the case of Treadwell's Sony DCR-VX2000 model. As a result, the discrete nature of a digital record fails to fulfill "[t]he continuous undulations recorded by the gramophone and the audiotape," which for Kittler is fundamental for defining analog acoustic recordings as "signatures of the

95 Friedrich A. Kittler, *Gramophone, Film, Typewriter*, trans. Geoffrey Winthrop-Young and Michael Wutz (Stanford, CA: Stanford University Press, 1999), 15–16. First published in German in 1986.

96 See Jean-Louis Baudry, "Ideological Effects of the Basic Cinematographic Apparatus," trans. Alan Williams, *Film Quarterly* 28, no. 2 (1974–1975): 39–47; Daniel Dayan, "The Tutor-Code of Classical Cinema," *Film Quarterly* 28, no. 1 (Autumn 1974): 22–31; and Laura Mulvey, "Visual Pleasure and Narrative Cinema," *Screen* 16, no. 3 (Autumn 1975): 6–18.

97 Kittler, *Gramophone, Film, Typewriter*, 119, 23. Film's relation to the imaginary order is based on it being "scans, excerpts, selections" that are projected in speed to create the illusion of wholeness and continuity.

real, or raw material."[98] Still, I believe that there are reasons to claim that just as Treadwell's digital video footage has little to do with the loss of the index, so his sound recordings—"the horrific sounds that accompanied, indeed constituted, an experience of real death"—are more relevant to the phenomenology of phonography than to that of digital sound recording.[99]

The digitization of any information, be it visual, acoustic, or textual, in what may be cautiously called the Discourse Network 2000, de-differentiates the trilateral Discourse Network 1900. In Kittler's words, "Sound and image, voice and text are reduced to surface effects. . . . Inside the computers themselves everything becomes a number, quantity without image, sound, or voice."[100] But in Treadwell's moment of death, thanks to the camcorder's covered lens, the digital audiovisual track is split into two differentiated data streams and, as such, anachronistically simulates a separation between phonograph and cinematograph. Moreover, the audio track itself appears to exclude symbolic information—from what is told in the film about the content of the tape, it appears that the few words uttered in its beginning ("Stop! Get away! Go away!") are soon replaced by indescribable sounds of agony—and, as such, completes the triadic differentiation characteristic of the Discourse Network 1900. Hence, as it registers Treadwell's and Huguenard's final moments of torment while also obstructing any visual registration that could anchor these sounds in an imaginary construction, Treadwell's lens-covered camcorder fulfills the phonographic conditions of a Kittlerian record of the unseeable and unreadable voices, noises, and utterances that are "produced by the larynx prior to any semiotic order and linguistic meaning."[101]

Although we never hear it, the content of the tape finds its way into Herzog's film in two separate scenes and in two different ways. The first is in the coroner's monologue, which essentially describes the recording's content. In this scene, Treadwell's and Huguenard's deaths—first mediated by the audio recording—are twice more remediated, once by the coroner's verbal description and again by film. In the coroner's verbal description, the symbolic filter of language converts the pre-semiotic noise into a meaningful string of signs, while the cinematic imaginary reconstitution—with obtrusive splicing in the form of prominent editing—increases the effect of imaginary construction. In other words, the phonographic real—Treadwell's "animal scream"—is converted and split into two data streams, symbolic and imaginary, that repress, mediate, distance, and finally make meaningful the raw and obscene sounds of violent death.[102]

And still, something of the obscenity of the sound recording, even if disfigured and transfigured, manages to puncture the symbolic-imaginary shield, invading the words and images of the coroner's scene. Schantz observes that in the later part of his monologue, the coroner "is no longer

98 Kittler, 118.

99 See Schantz, "Melodramatic Reenactment," 593–594; and Jeong and Andrew, "Grizzly Ghost," 5, 12.

100 Kittler, *Gramophone, Film, Typewriter*, 1.

101 Kittler, 16.

102 Jeong and Andrew, "Grizzly Ghost," 11.

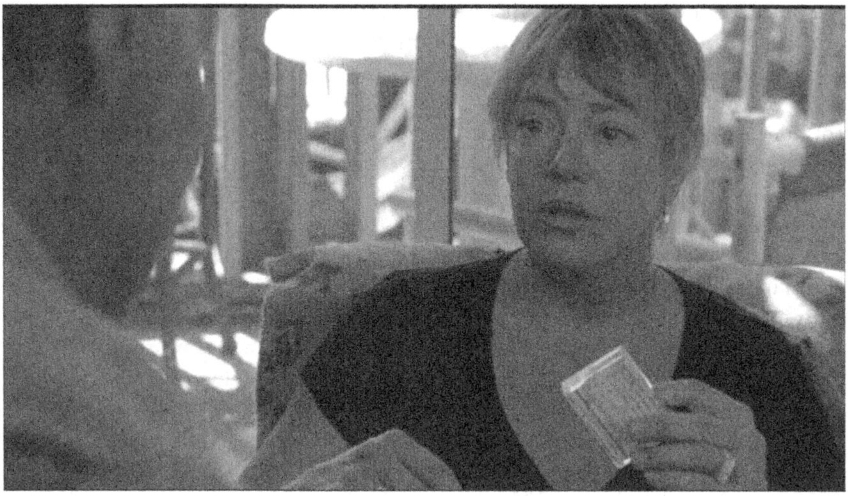

Figure 5. The human face registers the effects of the silenced sounds of real death in *Grizzly Man* (Lionsgate, 2005).

just himself. . . . His voice appropriates both Amie's and Treadwell's words from the tape, while his hand . . . wields Amie's imaginary frying pan to bash an imaginary bear."[103] The coroner becomes himself a medium, a conflation of real and artifice, a cinematic vision in the service of deep truth.

The second moment in which the content of the tape invades the film is in the following scene, which shows Herzog, his back to the camera, as he listens to the tape in the presence of Treadwell's former girlfriend, Jewel Palovak. In a reversal of the conditions of the recording of the attack wherein the image track is obstructed and only sound is recorded, here the audio track is obstructed, and the machine only records the images, thus ensuring that in the mediation of the attack, access to both its sights and sounds is withheld. This exchange between audio and image tracks is echoed in Herzog's own presence in the scene, which momentarily transforms, as Ames notices, a vocal presence into a visual one.[104] Filtering out sounds and sights, the recording of Herzog's camera of the playback of Treadwell's camera of the recording of the attack amounts to a view of Palovak watching Herzog listening. Her face, which the camera gradually frames in a close-up, now registers the effects of the silenced sounds of real death (see Figure 5). As in the previous scene, the human body functions as medium or, more precisely, as a media-component of the cinematic assemblage. But here, it is not the acting and reenacting body that mediates death for us, but the affection-image par excellence: the human face in close-up.[105] This second scene thus achieves

103 Schantz, "Melodramatic Reenactment," 605.

104 Ames, *Ferocious Reality*, 251.

105 Gilles Deleuze, *Cinema 1: The Movement Image*, trans. Hugh Tomlinson and Barbara Habberjam (Minneapolis, MN: University of Minnesota Press, 1986), 87-101. First Published in French in 1983.

what the humor, performativity, and excessiveness of the previous scene precludes: authenticity in the form of emotional discharge.

Commenting on Lillian Gish's performance in a scene from *Way Down East* (D. W. Griffith, 1920), Béla Balázs describes the cinematic rendition of her facial expressions as "something that words are incapable of."[106] For Balázs, the close-up of the face is "film's true terrain," where the medium fulfills its advantage over language, or what we would call symbolic media.[107] It is significant that Balázs is writing in the era of silent film, during which the exclusion of verbal communication crowns "visible man," specifically the human face, as the medium's epitome. Appropriately, Herzog's exclusion of the sounds of the attack from the scene links the close-up on Palovak's face to silent cinema. It is in this moment, in which the attack is most densely filtered and mediated (by Treadwell's capped camera, Herzog's capped ears, Herzog's unseen face, Palovak's reaction to that face, and finally the cinematic close-up), wherein we witness the most authentic—the most real, if you will—response to death in the film. Like Balázs, who finds in the close-up "the poetry of the cinema," Herzog here finds in this face—the last stop on a convoluted path of mediations and remediations—what differentiates poets from accountants.[108]

Ido Lewit teaches at the Steve Tisch School for Film and Television, Tel-Aviv University. His fields of research include German cinema, German media theory, film philosophy, and the discursive impact of technology on film.

106 Béla Balázs, *Béla Balázs: Early Film Theory:* Visible Man *and* The Spirit of Film, ed. Erica Carter, trans. Rodney Livingstone (New York: Berghahn Books, 2010), 35.

107 Balázs, 38.

108 Balázs, 41.

Bo Ruberg

Hungry Holes and Insatiable Balls: Video Games, Queer Mechanics, and the Limits of Design

ABSTRACT

This article presents a queer, comparative reading of the video games *Katamari Damacy* (Namco, 2004) and *Donut County* (Annapurna Interactive, 2018). These games offer contrasting models of consumption. In *Katamari Damacy*, players roll around a ball that gobbles up items. *Donut County* follows a similar premise, with holes that swallow objects. Yet *Donut County* fails to deliver on its queer potential, leaving its holes hungry, whereas the balls of *Katamari Damacy* remain insatiable. Building on the work of Kathryn Bond Stockton, Shira Chess, and Edmond Chang, this article argues that these games, considered together, suggest both the power and the limitations of video game design to reflect queer "appetites."

This article compares two video games, both of which are about gobbling up objects and wreaking havoc on quaint, normative towns: *Katamari Damacy* (Namco, 2004) and *Donut County* (Annapurna Interactive, 2018). In *Katamari Damacy*, players roll around increasingly large, sticky balls that pick up everything from household items to animals to buildings, creating bizarre, colorful masses that are then shot into outer space. Similarly, in *Donut County*, players move around holes in the ground, which widen as they swallow up more items, sucking homes and businesses into a jagged chasm that has formed beneath a sunny, pseudo Los Angeles. Though neither video game includes overt LGBTQ representational content, such as gay characters or

Bo Ruberg, "Hungry Holes and Insatiable Balls: Video Games, Queer Mechanics, and the Limits of Design," *JCMS* 61, no. 3 (Spring 2022): 107–128.

same-sex romances, these games offer examples of what queer game studies scholars and queer game developers have referred to as *queer game mechanics*.[1] *Mechanic* is the term commonly applied to the designed, interactive components of a video game—that is, the things that games allow players to *do* rather than the people or narratives that games present on-screen.[2] Queer game mechanics are those interactive elements of games, either digital or analog, that resonate with non-heteronormative experiences of sexuality or gender. Whether or not they have been implemented intentionally by game designers, these mechanics allow games to engender queer meaning through player experience. Specifically, *Katamari Damacy* and *Donut County* offer two models of what I describe, drawing from Kathryn Bond Stockton and Shira Chess, as mechanics of *queer consumption*: queer forms of eating and the transgressive desire to consume, rendered into video game play.[3]

Despite the many similarities between *Katamari Damacy* and *Donut County*, there are also telling differences between the two games and how they translate queer consumption into queer game mechanics. Whereas the balls of *Katamari Damacy* are insatiable, seemingly capable of eating up an infinite array of haphazardly strewn items, the holes of *Donut County* are merely hungry; they can be sated by a comparatively small number of items carefully placed within levels that have been designed with clear precision. These differences give the games, as "affective systems," notably different feels.[4] Because its gameplay is more loosely structured, *Katamari Damacy* allows for a sense of ecstatic chaos: a queer act of messing up and "messing with" the game world.[5] By contrast, through its careful and overly restrained design, *Donut County* constrains the queer potential of its mechanics and gives play the semblance of tidying up. What ultimately emerges from this juxtaposition of *Katamari Damacy* and *Donut County* is an ambivalent picture of the interplays between game design and queerness. In this way, this article complicates existing scholarship on the queer potential of game design, which has typically celebrated the capacity of video games to engage with queerness "beyond representation" through the interactive elements of games.[6] By contrast, this work demonstrates how queer mechanics themselves, when over-designed, can re-normativize a video game with otherwise queer interactive potential. Placing queer interpretive readings of *Katamari*

1 Edmond Y. Chang, "Queergaming," in *Queer Game Studies*, ed. Bonnie Ruberg and Adrienne Shaw (Minneapolis: University of Minnesota Press, 2017), 15–24; and Naomi Clark, "What *Is* Queerness in Games, Anyway?," in Ruberg and Shaw, *Queer Game Studies*, 3–14.

2 See Chris Swain, "The Mechanic Is the Message: How to Communicate Values in Games through the Mechanics of User Action and System Response," in *Ethics and Game Design: Teaching Values through Play*, ed. Karen Schrier and David Gibson (Hershey, PA: Information Science Reference, 2010), 217–235.

3 Kathryn Bond Stockton, "If Queer Children Were a Video Game," in Ruberg and Shaw, *Queer Game Studies*, 225–238; and Shira Chess, *Ready Player Two: Women Gamers and Designed Identity* (Minneapolis: University of Minnesota Press, 2017).

4 Aubrey Anable, *Playing with Feelings: Video Games and Affect* (Minneapolis: University of Minnesota Press, 2018), xii.

5 Jen Jack Gieseking, "Messing with the Attractiveness Algorithm: A Response to Queering Code/Space," *Gender, Place and Culture* 24, no. 11 (2017): 1660, https://doi.org/10.1080/0966369X.2017.1379955.

6 Bonnie Ruberg, *Video Games Have Always Been Queer* (New York: New York University Press, 2019), 14.

Damacy and *Donut County* side by side draws to the surface both the opportunity for video game mechanics to embody queer experiences as well as the limits of those very mechanics as tools for expressing queerness in video games through design.

Even in the face of such ambivalence, this interpretive critique of *Katamari Damacy* and *Donut County* entails a celebration of the queer body, its place within video games, and the way that play can become synonymous with expressions of queer hungers. For this reason, this work itself playfully revels in the absurdity, humor, and sexual charge of the "holes" and "balls" that become figures of queer corporeality and longing in these two games. In the same sense that queerness can manifest in video games in ways that go beyond literal LGBTQ representation, so, too, can the erotic body, which appears here not in human form but in the shape and movement of the ever-growing balls or the widening holes whose desires ravage placid scenes of the heteronormative world. To describe these figures as "hungry holes" and "insatiable balls" is to deliberately call to mind the terminology of pornography, in particular pornography featuring sex between men. It embraces the meanings suggested by sexual innuendo (a kind of epistemological sideways glance) and plays up the echoes between video games, their mechanics, and lived queer bodies. As hungry holes and insatiable balls, the anus, testicles, and, by extension, the genitals more generally are figured as subjects of longing and sites of agency—places where both pleasure and meaning are made through play.

VIDEO GAMES AND (QUEER) CONSUMPTION

The gameplay of both *Katamari Damacy* and *Donut County* centers on interactive mechanics of consumption. In her book *Ready Player Two* (2017), Shira Chess discusses some of the ways that consumption enters video game design. Chess's broad project is a critique of the development of so-called casual video games, often produced for mobile devices or social platforms, which Chess performs through the lens of gender studies and an attention to the biases faced by women players. Chess addresses how video game mechanics model consumption during her analysis of the immensely popular casual video game *Candy Crush Saga* (King, 2012). One of the most widely played mobile games of the last decade, *Candy Crush Saga* is a match-three game themed around sweets.[7] Typically, in match-three games, players attempt to line up identical symbols to clear them from the board. In *Candy Crush Saga*, once a player makes a match of three identical candy pieces, the pieces disappear in a puff of smoke or a twinkle of stars; making matches also triggers sound effects reminiscent of teeth chomping down on food. Chess refers to the mechanics of match-three–style games as "consuming mechanics." She writes, "the consuming mechanic is one where the player's goal is to perform a series of maneuvers that make an object or series of objects disappear, visually creating a sense that the object has been consumed."[8] In addition, con-

7 Tom McKay, "*Candy Crush* Developer Says 9.2 Million Users Play at Least 3 Hours a Day, but It's Totally Not Addictive," *Gizmodo*, June 26, 2019, https://gizmodo.com/candy-crush-developer-says-9-2-million-users-play-at-le-1835893580.

8 Chess, *Ready Player Two*, 131.

temporary casual games are often characterized by what she terms a "lush" aesthetic: bright colors, shiny objects and interface elements, and rounded edges suggest a kind of visual candy.[9] It is fitting, then, that *Candy Crush Saga* both epitomizes one model of consumption mechanics while also literalizing this emphasis on consumption through its food-related theming and sugary visual style.

Moreover, the cultural implications of consumption mechanics such as those found in match-three–style games are tied to the interrelations between gender and pleasure. Of tasks like clearing items from the board in *Candy Crush Saga*, Chess writes that "there is something *inherently satisfying* within the game mechanic itself. . . . This mechanic is enjoyable . . . because of the disappearing element, which has the effect of neatly clearing the screen."[10] In this sense, in Chess's view, the pleasure of consumption mechanics can be tied to the feminine-coded labor of cleaning. Aubrey Anable, in her book *Playing with Feelings* (2018), also discusses *Candy Crush Saga* and its relationship to gendered play. For Anable, *Candy Crush Saga* is exemplary of the types of games that have frequently been overlooked in serious discussions of video games. To illustrate how games like *Candy Crush Saga* are, in fact, an important part of the culture of the everyday, Anable describes a common scene: a woman plays *Candy Crush Saga* in snippets as she waits for a subway.[11] Through her discussion of this scene, Anable suggests that the pleasures that (women) players take in a casual video game such as *Candy Crush Saga* should be considered equally important as the pleasures that stereotypical straight, cisgender men take in playing so-called hardcore video games. For both Chess and Anable, games such as *Candy Crush Saga* are important objects of analysis because they offer scholars the opportunity to attend to feminine-coded design and women players and thereby challenge dominant notions about what modes of play are meaningful in video games and what types of players consume them.

At the same time, it is important to note the potentially hegemonic overtones of this vision of gendered play, which links women's pleasure to "neatly clearing the screen." Interpreted in this way, the model of consumption mechanics found in match-three games seems to enact what Dimitrios Pavlounis has described as a "straightening up" of the game space.[12] In his analysis of *Gone Home* (Fullbright Company, 2013), a video game well-known for its LGBTQ content, Pavlounis explains that games that appear to have queer meaning can invite players to straighten them, for instance by encouraging them to tidy up objects and archives in order to create linear, homonormative narratives. In this way, such games make players complicit in undoing the mess of queerness: that is, as queer studies scholars have articulated, the ways that queer lives, identities, and communities often look messy to those who hold positions of privilege

9 Chess, 48.

10 Chess, 48 (emphasis in the original).

11 Anable, *Playing with Feelings*, viii.

12 Dimitrios Pavlounis, "Straightening Up the Archive: Queer Historiography, Queer Play, and the Archival Politics of *Gone Home*," *Television and New Media* 17, no. 7 (February 2016): 579–594, https://doi.org/10.1177/1527476416631627.

and power and who therefore set the terms for what constitutes "order."[13] Though games like *Candy Crush Saga* typically forgo substantial attempts at building narratives, we might say that they, too, "straighten things up" in prompting players to create order by matching like objects and whisking them off the cluttered space of the board. Yet through their very emphasis on consumption, *Candy Crush Saga* and similar games themselves seem to resist such one-dimensional readings. Players do not simply clean up but in fact *eat* the candy that appears on-screen. As soon as it is eaten, more candy fills the board instantly and infinitely. In most match-three games, it would be impossible for players to ever actually clear the screen. Consumption becomes an endless task, both Sisyphean and decadent.

This connection between consumption mechanics in video games and the pleasures of indulgence helpfully points toward a broader resonance between consumption, erotics, and queerness. In "The Uses of the Erotic" (1978), Audre Lorde describes the erotic as expressions of "our deepest cravings," which often take the form of a desire to reach out to other people and form affective and intellectual connections across difference.[14] Lorde's use of the term *cravings* to characterize this longing to connect suggests that we might understand desire itself as a kind of hunger—and queer desire, by extension, as a hunger that does not fit with dominant notions of what (and how much) the desiring subject should crave. Indeed, queerness and transgressive consumption are already aligned in the broader cultural imaginary of twenty-first-century America. Both queer bodies and fat bodies are perceived as what Roxane Gay and others have referred to as *unruly bodies*, which are imagined as manifesting a socially unacceptable desire to consume, whether pleasure or food.[15] Relatedly, queerness and fatness are both "scandals of appetite," in the words of Lauren Berlant.[16] In *Carnal Appetites* (2000), Elspeth Probyn describes the similarities between sex and eating. Though Probyn does not present eating as queer per se, her descriptions of the erotics of consumption have clear resonances with queerness. "Practices of preparing and eating food are, of course, highly sensual and sometimes sexual," writes Probyn.[17] "The intricate ways in which food and self intertwine may help to extend our ways of thinking sexuality."[18] Much as eating shares qualities with sex in Probyn's formulation, sex shares qualities with eating. Both acts, argues Probyn, involve "the opening of the body to reveal

13 Martin F. Manalansan IV, "The 'Stuff' of Archives: Mess, Migration, and Queer Lives," *Radical History Review* 2014, no. 120 (2014): 94–107, https://doi.org/10.1215/01636545-2703742.

14 Audre Lorde, "The Uses of the Erotic: The Erotic as Power," in *Sister Outsider*, rev. ed. (Berkeley: Crossing Press, 2007), 57.

15 Constance Grady, "Roxane Gay on Unruly Bodies, the Difficulty of Being Transgressive, and #WhoBitBey," *Vox*, April 3, 2018, https://www.vox.com/culture/2018/4/3/17172642/roxane-gay-interview-unruly-bodies. The term *unruly bodies* has been explored by scholars from a number of areas, notable among them disability studies, long before Gay's popularization of the term. For examples of this work, see Susannah B. Mintz, *Unruly Bodies: Life Writing by Women with Disabilities* (Chapel Hill: University of North Carolina Press, 2007); and Nick Hodge, "Unruly Bodies at Conference," *Disability and Society* 29, no. 4 (March 2014): 655–658.

16 Lauren Berlant, *Cruel Optimism* (Durham, NC: Duke University Press, 2011), 105.

17 Elspeth Probyn, *Carnal Appetites: FoodSexIdentities* (London: Routledge, 2000), 61.

18 Probyn, 64.

a multitude of surfaces that seek out contact with other surfaces."[19] Building from Berlant and Probyn, we might say that the connections between sex and eating color each other with queerness, casting a shadow of the erotic over food and reframing sexual desire in non-heteronormative terms as a hunger for contact between surfaces.

The intersection of these components—video game play, consumption, pleasure, and queerness—is precisely the subject of Stockton's 2017 article, "If Queer Children Were a Video Game." In Stockton's theorization, playing video games itself can be seen as an act of queer consumption. Inspired in part by Georges Bataille, who ties gameplaying to nonreproductive sexual acts, Stockton compares video games to candy.[20] "Clearly, a chocolate bar is not a game. But is it like a game in effect not in fact?" she asks. "The effects of candy are libidinal, captivating, repetitive, time wasting, grandly lateralizing of adults and children, and linked to the pleasures of self-destruction."[21] By "lateralizing," Stockton means that eating candy both literally widens the body and represents a form of "diversion" or sideways movement (rather than forward movement) through which the subject lingers in the pleasures of consumption.[22] Given the context of Stockton's essay, which appears in the volume *Queer Game Studies*, as well as her related writing in *The Queer Child* (2009), it is reasonable to add an additional, inferred adjective to this list of candy's qualities: queer. Stockton observes, "at this point in gaming's history, digital games are becoming more like candy: quickly consumed, 'eaten' in snatches, snacked on in the cracks of our time, especially as they migrate increasingly to smartphones, which are a pantry in our pockets. . . . Games are candy without the calories."[23] As a form of queer candy, video games promote their own sort of libidinal, sideways growth. Building from Stockton's work, Christopher Goetz describes an inherent tension in the notion of "queer growth" within the context of video games.[24] As Goetz explains, those approaching video games from queer perspectives seem simultaneously to call for video games to grow up and become more inclusive and to grow sideways—that is, to resist teleological narratives of upward progress and instead to reach outward for other forms of connection and meaning.

If video game mechanics can model different forms of consumption, and consumption has ties to queerness that intersect in video games, what might it look like for a video game to take on the task of translating queer consumption into interactive gameplay? In what follows, I demonstrate how the designs of *Katamari Damacy* and *Donut County* offer two related yet different models of queer consumption mechanics—both of which are notably distinct

19 Probyn, 63.

20 Georges Bataille, *Visions of Excess: Selected Writings, 1927–1939*, ed. Allan Stoekl, trans. Allan Stoekl, Carl R. Lovitt, and Donald M. Leslie Jr. (Minneapolis: University of Minnesota Press, 1985).

21 Stockton, "If Queer Children," 232.

22 Kathryn Bond Stockton, *The Queer Child, or Growing Sideways in the Twentieth Century* (Durham, NC: Duke University Press, 2009), 25. Although I am focusing on Stockton's essay "If Queer Children Were a Video Game" here, this essay is itself an outgrowth of the writing in her book *The Queer Child*.

23 Stockton, "If Queer Children," 232.

24 Christopher Goetz, "Queer Growth in Video Games," in Ruberg and Shaw, *Queer Game Studies*, 239.

from the models found in casual games that have been discussed in the existing scholarship mentioned above. As I use it here, the term *queer consumption* describes modes of consuming (where *consuming* itself encompasses multiple meanings) that resist heteronormative notions of what constitutes an acceptable appetite or object of hunger. Queer consumption operates around alternative logics of longing—whether for food or flesh. If to consume is to eat, in one form or another, then to consume queerly is to eat in ways that do not fit the dominant dictates of society: to eat *what* one is not supposed to, to eat *for reasons* that one is not supposed to, and, by extension, to inhabit a body that bears the markers of stigmatized forms of eating. Queer consumption is about what (and whom) we desire, what (and whom) we take into our bodies, and why we do so. To think about consumption in a conceptual sense is always also to be thinking about the implications of these concepts for actual individuals who inhabit real, lived bodies—both non-normative in their desires and their physical forms. This is especially true in discussions of a popular media object like video games, which have commonly depicted fat characters in discriminatory ways.[25] Exploring queer consumption as a video game mechanic is not intended to devalue the realities of people who are queer or fat (or, as in my own case, both) but rather to respect their embodied experiences as important ways of knowing, seeing, and valuing various elements of video games as a medium.

COMPARING *KATAMARI DAMACY* AND *DONUT COUNTY*

From the perspective of design, *Katamari Damacy* and *Donut County* appear to have much in common. The two titles were produced many years apart, by entirely different teams, and in different national contexts. Yet from the time that the first announcement appeared about the video game that would become *Donut County*, journalists and reviewers have compared the game to *Katamari Damacy* as its unofficial predecessor. In 2012, the video game news website *Polygon* published an article about an early iteration of *Donut County*, then called *Kachina*, with the title "IndieCade Selection *Kachina* Has Shades of *Katamari Damacy* and One Intriguing Hole." The article's author, Michael McWhertor, who had played a demo of the game at the independent games festival IndieCade, begins the piece by addressing these similarities: "[*Donut County*] designer Ben Esposito is open about the visual and gameplay similarities between his game . . . and *Katamari Damacy*. Both games feature simple, colorful characters and items that grow bigger in scale as players gobble up more stuff from the world. In *Katamari* games, players control a sticky ball. But in [*Donut County*], they control a hole."[26] Though much changed between that early iteration of *Donut County* and the final version of the game, which Esposito released in 2018, the fundamental parallels between *Donut County* and *Katamari Damacy* that McWhertor points out remain. The two games

25 Todd Harper, "Portrayals and Pitfalls of Fatness in Games" (presentation, Game Developers Conference, San Francisco, CA, March 3, 2015).

26 Michael McWhertor, "IndieCade Selection Kachina Has Shades of *Katamari Damacy* and One Intriguing Hole," *Polygon*, October 8, 2012, https://www.polygon.com/2012/10/8/3476056/indiecade-selection-kachina-has-shades-of-katamari-damacy-and-one.

share saturated, soft-edged aesthetics; they are both populated with playfully designed everyday objects; and their core mechanics—"gobbling up stuff," whether as a ball or a hole—are strikingly similar. Yet the value of comparing *Katamari Damacy* and *Donut County* runs deeper than identifying these points of commonality. Indeed, it is the fact that these two games *seem* so alike that allows us, when reading them in juxtaposition, to draw out the crucial differences in their design and, by extension, their implications for issues of culture, identity, and queerness.

The original *Katamari Damacy* was released in 2004 for the PlayStation 2 video game console by the Japanese development studio Namco. Game designer Takahashi Keita is widely credited as the creative force behind the game, although it is valuable to question narratives that foreground the work of individuals (typically straight, cisgender men) in the creation of video games developed by collaborative teams. In addition to its unusual mechanics, two of the many features that make the original *Katamari Damacy* unique are its striking visual style, which is reminiscent of surrealist and Dadaist collage art, and its high-energy, pop-inspired musical soundtrack. In her brief but wide-reaching book on *Katamari Damacy*, which looks at the game's production and the artistic influences that shaped its design, Laura E. Hall describes how the game initially faced sales challenges because reviewers were not sure how to classify *Katamari Damacy* according to traditional video game genres.[27] However, its popularity among a growing international fan base eventually made *Katamari Damacy* a large-scale success in both Japan and North America. Since 2004, Namco has developed a number of sequels and adaptations of the original *Katamari Damacy* for alternative and later-generation gaming platforms. The ongoing life of the franchise demonstrates that *Katamari Damacy* still holds an important place in the cultural landscape of video games. For the purposes of this analysis, however, I will focus on the original *Katamari Damacy* game.

In *Katamari Damacy*, players take on the role of the prince: a tiny, perky, silent character with an oblong head (or hat; we never really know) who is tasked with creating bigger and bigger "katamaris." A Japanese word preserved in its transliterated form in the North American localization of the game, *katamari* translates roughly as ball, mass, or lump. The player's objective in each level is typically to create a katamari large enough that the prince's father, the flamboyant King of All Cosmos, can shoot it into space and turn it into a star, slowly replacing the stars that the king recently destroyed while drunkenly stumbling around the night sky. The player begins with a small, bumpy ball no bigger than a golf ball, rolling it around levels strewn with an eccentric array of objects (see Figure 1). The bigger the ball grows, the larger the objects that the player can roll up. Since the player's katamari starts small, they can initially only pick up tiny items, like thumbtacks and matches. However, as the katamari grows—and as the game allots more time for individual levels—players can gather items of an exponentially larger scale. By the end of an early level, a player's katamari may only grow big enough to roll up a household pet. By the game's final sequence, however,

27 Laura E. Hall, *Katamari Damacy* (Los Angeles: Boss Fight Books, 2018).

Figure 1. Players begin *Katamari Damacy* (Namco, 2004) levels with a small, sticky ball. Screenshot by author.

a player can create a katamari so large that it rolls up skyscrapers, then whole islands, and eventually even the clouds from the sky. Each of these items is glommed unceremoniously onto the growing, rolling mass. This is key to what Hall calls the "pure anarchic fun" of *Katamari Damacy*'s gameplay.[28]

Donut County emerges from a different production paradigm and cultural context. The game was released in 2018, nearly a decade and a half after *Katamari Damacy*, by an independent American designer in conjunction with a comparatively small video game publishing company. Though *Donut County* is modest in scope—it takes about two hours to play and is available on PC and a selection of consoles—designer Ben Esposito spent six years developing it, notably longer than other video games of comparable scales. Along the way, the game took on many forms. Esposito created the first version of *Donut County*, then called *The Pits*, for a 2012 game jam: an event in which developers rapidly prototype new games.[29] Later in 2012, as mentioned above, Esposito demoed the game, by then called *Kachina*, at IndieCade. The first official trailer for *Donut County* appeared in 2014. In 2015, three years before its release, the game won a Story/World Design Award at the Independent Games Festival. Reports about previews of the game at events like the Game Developers Conference rolled in throughout 2016 and 2017.[30]

28 Hall, 2.

29 Jason Tanz, "How a Videogame God Inspired a Twitter Doppelgänger—and Resurrected His Career," *Wired*, October 19, 2012, https://www.wired.com/2012/10/ff-peter-molyneux/; and Michael McWhertor, "Donut County Is Like a Reverse *Katamari* Inspired by Bruce Springsteen and Fake Peter Molyneux," *Polygon*, August 11, 2014, https://www.polygon.com/2014/8/11/5992923/donut-county-kachina-ben-esposito.

30 Alec Meer, "Next Year's Indie Giants Today: IndieCade 2015 Winners," *Rock Paper Shotgun*, October 28, 2015, https://www.rockpapershotgun.com/2015/10/28/best-indie-games-2015/.

By the time the game was finally available for sale in 2018, *Donut County* had generated considerable buzz as one of the most anticipated indie video games of recent years. This long buildup speaks to the considerable amount of time that went into crafting *Donut County*—and arguably over-crafting it, as I discuss below. It also helps explain the charged (and at times erotically inflected) anticipation that circulated around *Donut County* as would-be players awaited its release.

While *Katamari Damacy* focuses on gameplay with only short, interstitial moments of storytelling, *Donut County* spends considerably more of its time on narrative. The game's two main characters are Mira, a young woman of color, and BK, a raccoon. Mira and BK work together at a local donut shop, which is set against the backdrop of a city skyline that is clearly an homage to Los Angeles. Trouble starts when BK, who is supposed to be using a mobile application to deliver donuts, instead uses the app to open holes beneath customers' houses, causing their belongings and even customers themselves to fall into a cavernous pit. In each level, players move the hole around the home (or workplace) of one customer. The narrative frame of the game, which also serves as a hub for these levels, is a conversation that takes place inside the pit. There, BK, Mira, and all of the customers whose homes BK has ruined sit around a campfire amid the rubble. Though initially defensive, BK comes to realize over the course of the game how his actions have harmed others. In the game's second half, BK and Mira set off to defeat the Trash King, the villainous raccoon behind the mobile application that has allowed BK to create such havoc. In the game's final sequence, BK and Mira, having vanquished the Trash King and acquired a hot air balloon, send all of the characters who were swallowed up by BK's holes back up to the surface.

Despite *Donut County*'s emphasis on characters and story, however, it is the mechanic of the all-consuming hole that has dominated the popular imagination around the game. This can be seen, for example, in the title of the *Polygon* article mentioned above, which describes the game that would become *Donut County* as having "one intriguing hole." As a bit of sexual innuendo, this reference to the game's "hole" is simultaneously playfully erotic and potentially homophobic, suggesting that the implicit connection between *Donut County* and the sexual body should be a source of humor. In later writing on *Donut County*, this fascination with the embodied suggestiveness of the hole continues to surface. We can see this, for instance, in Laura Hudson's *Verge* article titled "*Donut County* Is a Game about Swallowing Los Angeles and Realizing You're an Asshole. That's the Central Theme of the Game."[31] *Swallowing* and *asshole* stand in interesting relation to each other here. Hudson's title fittingly blurs the divide between hole, player, human body, the erotic, and the abject. It suggests that the player-character is at once a mouth receiving oral sex (swallowing) and an anus. This rhetoric reflects a general, low-key sexual aura that has surrounded *Donut County*, a game that appears otherwise unrelated to sex or sexuality. Such language

31 Laura Hudson, "*Donut County* Is a Game about Swallowing Los Angeles and Realizing You're an Asshole," *The Verge*, September 1, 2018, https://www.theverge.com/2018/9/1/17806888/donut-county-game-la-los-angeles-ben-esposito-interview.

nods toward the unspoken yet palpable fact that a game about playing with and as holes cannot help but have intriguing sexual implications. At the same time, it mirrors the precarity of this queer potential and foreshadows the ways that a video game's queer mechanics might, as in the case of *Donut County*, be used to support decidedly un-queer ends.

QUEER ELEMENTS IN *KATAMARI DAMACY*

Though this article focuses on how *Katamari Damacy* and *Donut County* model mechanics of queer consumption (to varying degrees of effectiveness) and thereby engage with queer experience through design, these video games also contain representational elements that can be interpreted queerly. As scholars of gender and critical race in video games have argued, it is important to consider questions of whom and what video games represent alongside an analysis of their mechanics and interactive structures so that we can understand them as computational objects with cultural meaning.[32] Indeed, my interpretation of these games' mechanics understands them as fundamentally coloring and colored by the visual and narrative contexts in which they appear on-screen. Together, these mechanics and representational elements, along with related considerations of the games' receptions, form what could be termed an *assemblage of queer meaning*—as adapted from T. L. Taylor's concept of the "assemblage of play" in video games.[33]

Of these two games, *Katamari Damacy* has the more obvious representational connection to queerness—though even these representational elements are far from the types of overt, "inclusive" LGBTQ content that many have called for in mainstream video games.[34] Much of the queer imagery in *Katamari Damacy* circulates around the figure of the King of All Cosmos. Before the opening title of the game appears, *Katamari Damacy* presents players with the image of a dark night sky, which brightens to reveal the king rising over the horizon of a field of cows. As if the game is celebrating his arrival, rainbows shoot out of the hillside like searchlights (see Figure 2). Throughout the game, whenever the king transports the prince back from Earth to the sky—where the king examines the balls of objects that the prince has rolled up—the king opens his mouth and lets out a royal rainbow, a wide shaft of saturated colors that beams the prince into space. These colorful spectacles are candy-like and "lush," to recall Chess's term. They associate the king with queer iconography: the vibrant rainbow that heralds his appearance and pours forth from his lips.

From his clothes to his movements, the king's body also drips with queer signifiers. He wears a large, sparkling, multicolored headpiece that matches his flowing purple cape, recalling the visual language of dandyism and drag.

32 Jennifer Malkowski and TreaAndrea M. Russworm, "Introduction: Identity, Representation, and Video Game Studies beyond the Politics of the Image," in *Gaming Representation: Race, Gender, and Sexuality in Video Games*, ed. Jennifer Malkowski and TreaAndrea M. Russworm (Bloomington: University of Indiana Press, 2017), 1–17.

33 T. L. Taylor, "The Assemblage of Play," *Games and Culture* 4, no. 4 (August 2009): 331–339, https://doi.org/10.1177/1555412009343576.

34 Bonnie Ruberg and Amanda Phillips, "Not Gay as in Happy: Queer Resistance and Video Games," *Game Studies* 18, no. 3 (2018), http://gamestudies.org/1803/articles/phillips_ruberg.

Figure 2. The King of All Cosmos appears in a flash of rainbows in *Katamari Damacy* (Namco, 2004). Screenshot by author.

Glitz, decadence, and feminine touches characterize his costumery. His skin-tight shirt, which shows off his muscular physique, contrasts with his ornate, oversized ruffled collar. He wears a gold crown to suggest his status as king but also gold rings, a gold bracelet, a gold necklace, and a chunky gold belt. Even his features suggest a queer, if comical, erotics. His chin is dramatically cleft into two globes that resemble firm buttocks. In the game's opening scene, the king stands larger than life at the center of the screen; looming over the pasture of baffled and enthralled cows, he spreads out his arms with dramatic flair in a stiff yet graceful gesture reminiscent of ballroom vogueing. As he begins to rise upward into space, and his body passes by the player's gaze, the outline of a prominent codpiece bulges noticeably from his crotch. Filling up the screen, the king's exaggerated genitals set a queer tone for the rest of the game that follows.

Queerness also manifests both in the way that the king speaks and in his relationship with the prince. The king is the main mouthpiece for the game—the prince himself never talks—and the humor of his chatty, self-aggrandizing commentary often lies in his implied gender and sexual non-normativity. For example, he wistfully considers the idea of starting a diary to write down his feelings, a feminine-coded proposition. His comments also suggest that the king is something of a "size queen." The king, and by extension the game, is preoccupied with measuring the player's katamaris. If the katamari is big enough, the king will proclaim his nearly sexual excitement at the sight of the impressively large ball. The king himself is a strikingly big figure. At times, he delivers these teasing remarks while looming over the tiny prince, who stands directly beneath his father's enormous, bulging crotch, suggesting an erotic tension between the two. The king is not just any queer figure, though. He is specifically a queer dad. *Katamari Damacy* is clearly invested in the relationship between the king and the prince—or what the king himself refers to as the "father-son bond." This is far from a heteronormative picture of parenthood, however. The King of All Cosmos offers a compelling if unlikely alternative vision of the queer daddy in video games: one who is both sexy and strange, domineering and often disappointed, yet caring, a desirous figure whom the player seeks to please.[35] Indeed, within the diegesis of *Katamari Damacy*, this longing for approval from the queer father is the hunger that drives the creation of the katamaris and, by extension, the play of the game.

KATAMARI DAMACY'S MECHANICS OF QUEER CONSUMPTION

Katamari Damacy offers the first of two models for how queer consumption might be expressed through elements of video game design. The game's core mechanic, rolling around a ball that grows increasingly large as it picks up items, is all about consuming. The purpose of the gameplay is to accumulate and engulf items, sucking them up into the body of the katamari, which expands in diameter, literalizing Stockton's image of grand lateral growth.[36] One of the characteristics of this model of queer consumption is that the katamari always remains hungry—that is, always capable of taking on more items and more girth. The game does impose arbitrary time limits on levels, which in turn limit how big katamaris can grow, but the ball itself never becomes "full." Without designed constraints, it could go on eating forever. In this way, *Katamari Damacy* offers up the insatiable ball as a model of queer consumption that defies dictates of reason and reasonableness. As it moves through each level, gobbling up a dizzying array of larger and larger objects, the katamari recalls Probyn's description of the shared qualities of sex and eating. As the ball grows larger and larger, quickly dwarfing the tiny prince, it seems to be driven by a set of desires all its own: the longing of "surfaces [seeking] out contact with other surfaces."[37] Indeed, this is how the katamari consumes: through the stickiness of surfaces, which causes new objects to glom onto old objects, thereby constantly expanding and changing the exterior surface (or skin) of the katamari.

This insatiability drives both the tension and the allure of *Katamari Damacy*'s gameplay. Generally speaking, players cannot collect all items in a level. No matter how many objects they collect, when the timer goes off, more remain strewn around them. In this way, the game fosters a sense of yearning: a desire for that which remains uneaten. When playing, one has the sense that, given enough time, the katamari could grow so large that it would roll up the entire world. Indeed, this is precisely what *Katamari Damacy* allows players to do in the game's final sequence, where they can create a katamari that reaches a nearly unfathomable scale. In this last level, which has

35 Queer game studies scholar Braidon Schaufert has argued that video games such as the popular *Dream Daddy: A Dad Dating Simulator* (Game Grumps, 2017), which purports to represent the romantic lives of gay men, have in fact deradicalized the daddy figure and put him in the service of homonormative notions of family. Braidon Schaufert, "Daddy's Play: Subversion and Normativity in *Dream Daddy*'s Queer World," *Game Studies* 18, no. 3 (2018), http://gamestudies.org/1803/articles/braidon_schaufert.

36 Stockton, "If Queer Children," 232.

37 Probyn, *Carnal Appetites*, 63.

Figure 3. In the final level of *Katamari Damacy* (Namco, 2004), the katamari can pick up enormous objects. Screenshot by author.

no time limit, players begin with the same tiny katamari as in other levels. Yet here, their balls ultimately grow so large that they can pick up an awe-inspiring buffet of objects that previously seemed too enormous to contemplate consuming: elephants, cargo ships, skyscrapers, and whole islands (see Figure 3). The pleasure of this level is its sheer excess. Once so tiny it could not pick up a scurrying mouse, the katamari has now become an enormous mass—monstrous, powerful, and thrilling. In this climax, the game delivers on the long-tantalizing prospect of unrestrained consumption. It also serves as a powerful suggestion that if queer worldmaking is the capacity to create worlds, then queer consumption may be the capacity to eat them up.

Katamari Damacy is dotted with elements that suggest an awareness that its mechanics are queerly reminiscent of eating. References to food and consumption appear throughout the game, and a number of these disrupt scenes of heteronormativity. In most levels of the game, the player starts inside what appears to be a family home, on top of a dining room table. Many of the first objects that a player can pick up, when their katamari is still very small, are food. Positioned at the center of this domestic tableau, the player rolls up chestnuts, mandarin orange slices, and, appropriately, pieces of candy. This first area of the level, which the player plays through multiple times over the course of the game, uses an array of items to make explicit the connection between food and games. Interspersed among the food items are objects representing digital and analog games, such as video game cartridges and dice. At the end of each level, when the King of All Cosmos arrives to assess the katamari, the game gives players a breakdown of which categories of objects they have collected. After playing through the game's first level, which introduces the player to the core mechanics of the game, the top category of items the player is likely to have collected is "snacks," followed shortly thereafter by "games."

This blurring of gameplay and eating has transgressive implications in *Katamari Damacy*. At times, characters in the game describe the katamaris themselves as if they were food, calling to mind the allure of abjection and pleasures that are distinctly non-normative. In one series of levels, players roll up objects themed around zodiac sign constellations. The level for the constellation Cancer, which is shaped like a crab, is overrun with scurrying, twitching crabs. By the end of the level, the player has amassed a writhing lump of frantic crabs of various sizes. When the king measures the ball, he proclaims, "Whee, that looks delicious! But also slightly disturbing!" He counts the number of crabs and notes approvingly, "This could fill the tummy." If we understand queer consumption as eating (or desiring to eat) in the wrong ways, this moment in which the king salivates over the comical, repulsive ball of crabs becomes a scene of queer hunger made possible by the player's successful engagement with the game's mechanics.

Importantly, the consumption mechanics of *Katamari Damacy* not only are insatiable but also do not straighten things up, such as by picking up objects to make the play space tidier. Much to the contrary, rolling around homes and towns with a growing katamari sends people running and items flying, creating an increasingly enormous mess. This mess takes many forms. The katamari itself is messy: not a round, smooth sphere but a lopsided mass of jutting objects that rolls unevenly through the terrain. As the ball grows in size, it also messes with the technical elements of the game. When it rolls up against obstacles, the ball often "clips"—a form of glitching in which one object appears to pierce and stick out the side of another. Indeed, messiness is a key component of how *Katamari Damacy* performs its worldbuilding and level design. Littered on the floor around the family table where the player starts the game, for example, are a dozen open tubes of lipstick. Why are these lipsticks here? This mess extends beyond any logical explanation. It exists for the sheer (queer) pleasure of rolling through it.

In this way, *Katamari Damacy* offers a model of consumption that inverts the "consuming mechanics" that Chess describes in casual match-three games. The pleasure of consuming in *Katamari Damacy* lies not in tidying things up (e.g., organizing objects into matching sets and clearing them from the screen) but precisely in messing things up. To create these opportunities for messiness, the game's design must itself remain messy. *Katamari Damacy* is not designed around precise calculations about which items players pick up when and where, how they should move through a level, or what story—however loosely defined—their progress through that level should tell. Instead, *Katamari Damacy* leaves its mechanics loose, messy, ecstatic, and chaotic, an approach to designing opportunities for in-game interactivity that we could see as itself queer.

QUEERNESS RE-NORMATIVIZED IN *DONUT COUNTY*

Like *Katamari Damacy*, *Donut County* also has representational elements that could be interpreted as queer. Importantly, though, these elements are ultimately re-normativized, paralleling the re-normativization of the game's mechanics of queer consumption. As discussed, the very premise of *Donut County* and its "one intriguing hole" has erotic implications. Indeed, the

Figure 4. The donut atop the shop where BK and Mira work with its prominent hole in *Donut County* (Annapurna Interactive, 2018). Screenshot by author.

hole emerges as a point of fascination throughout the game, both for the characters and for the game's visual focus. In one scene in the pit beneath Donut County, BK attempts to convince the characters whose homes he has swallowed up that he has simply been "delivering donuts." Mira asks, in response, "What exactly do you think donuts ARE?" Chimes in Roma, a small rabbit-like creature, "Who can say?" After all, Roma muses, "What is a donut without a hole?" The opening sequence of the game represents an earlier instantiation of this interest in the hole. We see a scene of a donut shop, which is shaped like a coffee mug with a large, upright, pink-frosted donut on top (see Figure 4). Slowly, the camera zooms in, as if to emphasize the enormity of the donut. Yet, instead, the camera zooms in on the hole itself. This emphasis on the hole continues during gameplay. Though the player technically takes on the role of BK, the raccoon only appears on-screen in a small heads-up display. Consequently, the hole comes to function as the character that players see themselves controlling on-screen. If we understand this image of the hole as fundamentally embodied and erotic, then we can interpret *Donut County* as initially leaning into its queer implications by playing up this focus on the hole.

Donut County also connects queerness and consumption in myriad ways. The game has its own queer ideas about food and eating. For example, it often conflates the acts of eating and being eaten. When a customer orders a donut to eat, BK deploys a hole that eats the customer. A number of the characters have food-related names, such as Morsel. These names play on the fact that the characters have become food for the hungry hole. Other examples of eating in the game make food seem distinctly unappetizing or simply weird. One of the characters swallowed up by BK's holes owns a soup shop. The level that takes place at the soup shop is crawling with cockroaches. To progress through this level, the player must fill up the hole with hot soup and use it to boil the cockroaches alive. At other times in the game, eating is used as a manifestation of intimate and arguably queer relationality. Two characters who are brothers, Salt and Pepper, reconcile after a fight by bonding over their shared love of eating the lava from inside lava lamps. "I shouldn't have smashed your lava lamp," says Pepper. "And I shouldn't have ate the lava. It was wrong of me." Salt replies, "Pep! It's alright dude. The lava is the best part." Previously in the game, these characters are described as "bird weirdos" who are so excited about watching videos of birds that their interest, other characters imply, may be worrisomely sexual. Here, the air of erotic transgression that surrounds Salt and Pepper is transferred onto their own relationship as brothers. Having fought, they reestablish their intimate connection through their mutual passion for eating a substance that is not food. Eating, intimacy, and the abject join in a queer bond.

However, the figure with the most queer potential in *Donut County* is BK himself. Fittingly, BK's defining trait is a non-normative pleasure: his love of trash. Apparently, BK is one of many raccoons who have recently overrun the city.[38] In part, BK's passion for trash is simply an expression of his urban raccoon nature. However, for BK, trash has become more than something he desires; trash also serves as the lens through which he sees the world. To BK, all the objects that humans own are already trash. Every item that the player swallows up in BK's holes gets subsequently listed in a "trash-o-pedia," where it is labeled with descriptive text written from the point of view of an irreverent raccoon. A small, potted, aloe-like succulent comes with the caption "Child's safety cactus"; the description beneath a suitcase reads "Climb inside for a free ride." If all the objects in *Donut County* are already trash, then the hungry hole functions not so much as the hole that eats things up as the hole that throws things away. Or perhaps, more queerly, it is the hole that eats trash. This connection between food, trash, and human waste is made explicit in a scene in which BK sits in the bathroom with his smartphone and performs a donut delivery while on the toilet (see Figure 5).

As befits a queer figure such as BK, what the raccoon finds stomach-churning is not trash but displays of heteronormative affection. Sitting in the hole beneath Donut County, characters Nicky and Roma, a married rabbit couple whose level is a carrot-shaped home overrun by scores of frolicking bunnies, nuzzle one each other by the campfire. Noticing this, Mira exclaims warmly, "It's really cute that you two are so in love." By contrast, in the conversation that ensues, BK makes it clear that he does not approve of this lovey-dovey performance of heterosexual pairing:

BK: This is extremely gross.
Mira: You're gross.
BK: No, I'm NOT gross.

38 *Donut County* presents itself as a parable of urban gentrification, with the raccoons described in terms that clearly parallel visions of wealthy outsiders gobbling up urban space and displacing current residents. However, this interpretation of the game becomes muddied by the racial overtones of the raccoons, who are depicted as lazy, dirty, dark-faced hooligans whose growing presence destroys "nice" neighborhoods. This suggests that the narrative of *Donut County* might be more aptly considered a playable vision of racism and white flight.

Figure 5. BK "delivers a donut" from the toilet in *Donut County* (Annapurna Interactive, 2018). Screenshot by author.

Mira: You love trash.
BK: You love trash too!! Everyone here loves trash!! Why else would you all make so much of it?

For BK, the kind of heterosexual romance associated with marriage and reproduction is far more repulsive than trash. In place of heteronormativity, trash itself becomes the object of love. Thus, through BK, *Donut County* seems to offer a vision in which the normative world and its straight desires—represented by the quaint, friendly settings of the game's levels and the people found within them—are themselves rendered queer: revealed to have been "trash" all along.

Yet *Donut County* ultimately re-normativizes the queer implications of these representational elements. By the game's final sequence, when BK and Mira restore order to Donut County, most of its characters have relinquished their quirks and queerness. Epitomizing this ambivalence, even BK ultimately gives up his love for trash and cleans up his act by learning to respect private property. Just before sending him up out of the pit and back to his home, BK asks the character Coyote whether he would like to come work at the donut shop with him. "We're going clean," says BK. "I promise." At first, *Donut County* seems to offer a critique of capitalist consumerism by intentionally mislabeling people's possessions as trash.[39] Yet BK's disavowal of the pleasures of trash and his move toward the legitimacy of "going clean" are accompanied by an embrace of neoliberal reverence for individual ownership, undermining the game's earlier critiques. Mira implores BK to make amends by "giv[ing] people back their things." When he does so, BK redeems himself in

39 *Katamari Damacy*, too, was intended as a critique of consumer culture. Allegra Frank, "*Katamari Damacy* Was Way Darker than You Thought," *Polygon*, June 22, 2018, https://www.polygon.com/2018/6/22/17493942/katamari-damacy-keita-takahashi-wattam-ps4.

the eyes of his community. In *Donut County*, respecting others means respecting the sanctity of their possessions.

This speaks to one of many differences between *Donut County* and *Katamari Damacy*. *Katamari Damacy*, too, could be imagined as a game about the pleasures of trash. As they are eaten up by a rolling ball, items in *Katamari Damacy* become part of a trash heap–like mass that will itself be thrown away—or, more literally, shot out into space. Yet, whereas *Donut County* concludes with the unmaking of trash and the reestablishment of consumerist norms, *Katamari Damacy* pushes trash to far queerer ends, allowing the player to grow the trash-body of their katamari to superlative proportions and indulge the exuberant queer desire encapsulated in BK's earlier exclamation, "Everyone here loves trash!!"

DONUT COUNTY'S UNFULFILLED QUEER POTENTIAL

While *Donut County*'s mechanics seem to have much in common with *Katamari Damacy*'s, they offer a different model for how queer consumption could be rendered into video game play. Both the balls of *Katamari Damacy* and the holes of *Donut County* literalize Stockton's notion of queer growth as grandly lateralizing, growing wider as they consume. Indeed, both games emphasize this lateralization through secondary elements, such as the in-game camera. For example, the first full level of *Donut County*, "Potter's Rock," begins with a tight zoom on a collection of small objects found at the potter's house, including a coffee cup and some ceramic jugs. As the hole swallows up these items, each object falls in with a pleasant, rubbery bounce and disappears into the pit below. Once all of the items in view have been swallowed, the hole grows larger. Simultaneously, the in-game camera zooms out to reveal more of the level. Eventually, the hole grows large enough for the player to consume the potter and his home, stripping all objects from the scene and leaving behind an empty lot. In this sense, consumption becomes a way to lateralize both the body, in the form of the hole, and the visible world that the body inhabits.

Yet visibility is also at the crux of one of the key differences between the mechanics of queer consumption found in *Katamari Damacy* and *Donut County*. While *Katamari Damacy* is about amassing a large, highly visible ball of objects, *Donut County* is about swallowing objects up and whisking them out of sight. Items disappear into the hungry hole of *Donut County* as into the belly of an invisible creature. This leaves the queerly consuming body eerily implied and unseen—or else we could say the consuming body is the ground itself, with the hole as its gaping mouth. In this model of queer consumption, materials (food, objects, people, and communities) are eaten but not digested. The items and characters that are swallowed by BK's holes appear to land in the pit unharmed. Later, they are regurgitated—that is, sent back up to the surface—whole. To an extent, this represents an inversion of the way that consumption works in *Katamari Damacy*. As it picks up items, the katamari becomes a stomach in reverse, accruing objects along its outer surfaces. By contrast, in *Donut County*, absence rather than visual excess becomes the mark of queer consumption. However, while there is certainly transgressive potential in the idea of swallowing up scenes of normativity, this mechanic of consumption is ultimately put in the service of making things tidy rather than messing them up. Reminiscent of Chess's description of match-three games in which players try to clear the screen, *Donut County* prompts players to clear away all objects in a level, removing signs of mess and leaving a clean, empty level behind.

This tidiness, which takes a number of forms, is the downfall of the game's queer potential. Through what we might think of as overly "tidy" or heavy-handed design, *Donut County* re-normativizes its mechanics of queer consumption. This re-normativization manifests, for example, in the game's level design. Whereas in *Katamari Damacy* levels are haphazardly packed with a bizarre and seemingly endless array of items, the levels of *Donut County* are small, comparatively sparse, and carefully crafted. Each scene is constructed with precision, like a diorama. With some notable exceptions, these scenes typically consist of one main building and its surrounding yard, in which the game's developers have placed an uncluttered collection of relatively logical items, many of which serve a pragmatic purpose for solving the game's puzzle elements. For this reason, among others, *Donut County* lacks the sense of chaos and disorder found in *Katamari Damacy*.[40] Because of its precise level design, *Donut County* has none of *Katamari Damacy*'s vertiginous sense of wildly shifting scale or rapid, gluttonous consumption. It similarly eschews the queer glee that *Katamari Damacy* takes in the absurdity and excess of an Earth that, as the King of All Cosmos states, is "truly full of things."

This puts serious constraints on what *Donut County*'s underlying queer mechanics can accomplish. Without a sufficiently overflowing world of objects to eat and enough room for playful destruction, the "intriguing hole" can only ever be a figure of hunger and not insatiability. As the gameplay of each level comes to an end, the holes of *Donut County* seem sated by meager objects and individual homes. Such limitations also manifest in the holes themselves. Even when they have reached their largest, the holes in *Donut County* hardly appear capable of (or interested in) eating up the world and, by extension, the hegemonic heteronormativity that characterizes it on a grand scale. Occasionally, the game does tease players with the possibility of eating to excess. In one level, players have to release a hot air balloon that has gotten stuck on Interstate 405, a Los Angeles freeway notorious for its traffic. Once players have completed the task, the game allows them to linger in the level, using the growing hole to gobble up rows of oncoming cars (see Figure 6). Yet this destructive indulgence only lasts a few moments, and the traffic is quickly consumed—leaving the hole seemingly full but players' longing for queer forms of consumption frustratingly unfulfilled.

Despite its promisingly queer premise, *Donut County* loses faith in the simple, transgressive pleasure of playing as a hungry hole before the game has even begun. Almost all of the game's levels incorporate additional, one-off mechanics that are matched to puzzle elements. In one level, for example, players move the hole around to collect snakes. The snakes' tails then stick out of the hole, and the player can use them to hit chickens. In such

40 This difference can also be attributed in part to the games' contrasting musical landscapes. Music and sound design give *Donut County* a placid feel, in contrast to *Katamari Damacy*'s frantic, upbeat vibe.

Figure 6. *Donut County* (Annapurna Interactive, 2018) players have the brief opportunity to gobble up traffic. Screenshot by author.

moments, *Donut County* deemphasizes the experience of embodying the hole and instead attempts to offer clever ways that a hole can be transformed into other things. From a queer interpretive perspective, then, it is unfortunate that the very thing that seemed to imbue *Donut County* with queer potential—its design—is also the thing that stifles that potential. At the outset, the game appears to promise gameplay that is "libidinal, captivating, repetitive, time wasting, [and] self-destructive," as Stockton writes.[41] Yet *Donut County* quickly molds itself into a far more traditional puzzle game, one that sidelines the mechanics of its own hungry holes and the queer longings that they embody.

THE LIMITS OF QUEER GAME DESIGN?

Katamari Damacy and *Donut County* offer two models for how video game mechanics might be used to reflect forms of what I have called here queer consumption. In this sense, these games offer a valuable illustration of how digital media can communicate queer meaning through their interactive elements as well as their representational content. Considered together, these games show not only that video games can be designed using queer game mechanics but also that there are multiple ways for video games—as a rich and varied medium—to engage with and reflect on such experiences. At the same time, this analysis challenges those who work at the intersection of queerness, games, and play (including myself) to consider how design can be both a site of queer potential and a limiting or even re-straightening force within video games. As Edmond Chang has argued of video games *FrontierVille* (Zynga, 2010) and *World of Warcraft* (Blizzard Entertainment, 2004), a number of mainstream video games that appear to contain LGBTQ characters and romances are still structured according to heteronormative

41 Stockton, "If Queer Children," 232.

gameplay mechanics.[42] The case of *Katamari Damacy* and *Donut County* extends and complicates critiques like Chang's by showing how even a game built around a fundamentally queer design element can be re-normativized. At times, as this article suggests, it may in fact be the lack of design that creates opportunities for queer meaning in digital media. That is, when a video game is designed more loosely, more messily, and with less precision, it allows more space for players to experiment with chaos and approach the game world as a sandbox for exploring queer possibilities.

Understanding video games and their queer mechanics in this way allows us to approach the interplays between queerness and digital media from new perspectives, such as by attending to how design resonates with queer experience far beyond the intentions of digital media creators. Indeed, in 2019, a new video game with echoes of *Katamari Damacy* and *Donut County* captured the hearts of many queer and trans players: *Untitled Goose Game* (House House, 2019).[43] Like *Katamari Damacy* and *Donut County*, *Untitled Goose Game* is about a non-human entity wreaking havoc on a quaint, normative community. Rather than gobbling up objects, however, the goose moves objects out of place, snatching them away from irritated villagers who are trying to go about their daily business in a small British town. Since its release, the goose from *Untitled Goose Game* has become a symbol of resistance, appearing in countless memes and on signs protesting everything from the dismantling of transgender rights to Brexit.[44] As journalist Ana Valens notes, *Untitled Goose Game* has struck a chord with queer players because "[the] Goose engages in play whereas the rest of the world engages in work, structure, labor. Demolishing this labor—the village itself, as seen at the end of the game—upsets everyone in the village, and yet, it won't stop the Goose. It's a story of queer resilience."[45] I close by pointing out the connections between *Katamari Damacy*, *Donut County*, and *Untitled Goose Game* to highlight how these questions of queer design can matter to queer players in strikingly real, immediate, and material ways. Even when their queer potential remains unfulfilled, the models of queer consumption that the video games discussed here propose are powerful precisely because they offer us alternative ways of playing through and playing with our own radical hungers as queer people in the world.

Bo Ruberg is an associate professor in the Department of Film and Media Studies at the University of California, Irvine. Their most recent book is *Sex Dolls at Sea: Imagined Histories of Sexual Technologies* (MIT Press, 2022).

42 Edmond Y. Chang, "Love Is in the Air: Queer (Im)Possibility and Straightwashing in *FrontierVille* and *World of Warcraft*," *QED: A Journal in GLBTQ Worldmaking* 2, no. 2 (Summer 2015): 6–31, https://muse.jhu.edu/article/585653.

43 Heather Hogan, "'Untitled Goose Game' Is an Adorable Fifteen-Dollar F*ck You to Authority," *Autostraddle*, October 1, 2019, https://www.autostraddle.com/untitled-goose-game-is-an-adorable-fifteen-dollar-fck-you-to-authority/.

44 Alistair Jones, "The Horrible Goose Was the Unexpected Hero of the UK's People's Vote March," *Kotaku*, October 22, 2019, https://www.kotaku.com.au/2019/10/the-horrible-goose-was-the-unexpected-hero-of-the-uks-peoples-vote-march/.

45 Ana Valens (@acvalens), "The Goose engages in play whereas the rest of the world engages in work, structure, labor. Demolishing this labor—the village itself, as seen at the end of the game—upsets everyone in the village, and yet, it won't stop the Goose. It's a story of queer resilience," Twitter, October 23, 2019, 5:44 a.m., https://twitter.com/acvalens/status/1186986702168055809.

Naomi DeCelles
IN TRANSLATION: Lotte Eisner

A Critic at Large: Lotte Eisner at the *Film-Kurier* (1927–1933)

ABSTRACT
Of the nearly nine hundred articles Lotte Eisner published during her five and a half years at the influential German trade paper *Film-Kurier* (August 1927–March 1933), fewer than a dozen have been translated into English, and no comprehensive catalog or collection of these articles exists. Following a biographical sketch contextualizing Eisner's journalism in her larger career trajectory, this installment of "In Translation" presents ten articles by Eisner on film aesthetics, industry regulation, and visual culture.

Born in 1896 into an upper-middle-class, assimilated German Jewish family, Lotte Eisner was a bright student and the recipient of a broad humanistic education, which culminated in a PhD in art history in 1924, at a moment when graduate education was rare for women, particularly in the humanities. Working as a freelance art and literary critic for the *Literarische Welt* and *Berliner Tageblatt* from 1926 to 1927, Eisner soon found herself immersed in the artistic and political ferment of interwar Berlin film culture. In 1927, despite her initial misgivings about seriously engaging with popular culture, she became the first professional female film critic at *Film-Kurier*, the leading German trade journal of the period. From her position on the *Film-Kurier* editorial staff from 1927 to 1933, Eisner participated in the key debates about film aesthetics, censorship, and industry regulation.

In late March 1933, after the Nazi Party newspaper, the *Völkischer Beobachter*, published specific threats on Eisner's life and the editorial board of

Naomi DeCelles, "A Critic at Large: Lotte Eisner at the *Film-Kurier* (1927–1933)," *JCMS* 61, no. 3 (Spring 2022): 129–152.

the *Film-Kurier* was purged, Eisner was forced to flee to Paris. Between odd jobs as a nanny, translator, and researcher, she continued to write about film there for several publications edited by fellow Germans in exile. During the Occupation, Eisner was interned at a prison camp for political dissidents and enemy aliens in southwestern France. She escaped and lived as a fugitive in unoccupied France until the end of the war, eking out a living on the margins of society under a *nom de guerre* she would continue to use on and off until the mid-1960s. After the war, she returned to Paris, where she began a new career at the Cinémathèque Française as chief curator, translator, and scholar. Throughout the 1950s, 1960s, and 1970s, Eisner published and lectured prolifically. Late in life, she mentored and befriended a transnational cohort of filmmakers associated with the New Wave movements in France, Germany, Latin America, and the United States, including Margot Benacerraf, Juleen Compton, Werner Herzog, Jonas Mekas, Sohrab Shahid Saless, and Wim Wenders. Eisner's imprimatur was particularly vital to New German Cinema; filmmaker Werner Herzog has emphasized her advocacy as critical to the reception of their early work, describing Eisner as the movement's "collective conscience."[1]

Today, Eisner is known primarily for her postwar scholarship on Weimar-era German film. In the last years of her life, her reputation was shaped by influential narratives propagated by colleagues, friends, and Eisner herself about her work as a curator at the Cinémathèque Française and her role as a mentor to the young filmmakers who congregated there. In the years since her death, Eisner's incisive and robust engagement of European and US history via film culture and the impact of political turmoil on her own life and work have been obscured by the emphasis placed on her later years in the personal testimonies of her friends and colleagues.

Film scholars working in the German-, French-, and English-language secondary literature have paid minimal attention to Eisner's interwar work, and no comprehensive assessment of her legacy has been published to date. The factors that have contributed to such neglect are multiple, including issues of language and accessibility and the politics of disciplinary boundaries. Anglophone film scholars have dealt primarily with Eisner's midcentury film history, *The Haunted Screen: Expressionism in the German Cinema and the Influence of Max Reinhardt* (1952; first translated into English, 1969), and her monographs on Fritz Lang and F. W. Murnau.[2] Apart from these books and a small subset of the numerous articles she published in the postwar

1 I discuss Eisner's relationship to Herzog and Sohrab Shahid Saless in detail in "Mediating Displacement: Lotte Eisner's Exile on Film," *Quarterly Review of Film and Video* 37, no. 4 (2020): 384–397. Herzog describes Eisner's influence on the New German Cinema group in dramatic terms: "Lotte was one of the most important film historians the world has ever seen. . . . So she alone had the authority, insight and the personality to declare us legitimate, and it was vitally important when she insisted that what my generation was doing in Germany was as legitimate as the film culture that Murnau, Lang and the other Weimar cinema filmmakers had created all those years previously." Werner Herzog and Paul Cronin, *Herzog on Herzog* (New York: Farrar, Straus and Giroux, 2002), 152–153.

2 Lotte H. Eisner, *The Haunted Screen: Expressionism in the German Cinema and the Influence of Max Reinhardt*, trans. Roger Greaves (Berkeley: University of California Press, 1969); Lotte H. Eisner, *Murnau* (London: Secker and Warburg, 1973); and Lotte H. Eisner, *Fritz Lang*, trans. Gertrud Mander (London: Secker and Warburg, 1976).

period, the majority of Eisner's publications have never been made available in English translation. For peers of Eisner's, such as Rudolf Arnheim, Hans Feld, and Siegfried Kracauer, the publication of single-author collections and critical editions of their German journalism in translation has promoted generations of scholarship engaging with their ideas. Contemporary research in media historiography and the intellectual history of film studies has shown the interdependence of film critical discourse; industry advocacy groups; regulation and taxation agencies and boards; and the various producers, distributors, and exhibitors working within the interwar German film industry. Sustained analysis of her interwar journalism reveals that Eisner offered contemporaneous, novel, and nuanced contributions in all of these areas, contributions that can complicate and enrich our understanding of the political, social, and economic investments of interwar film educators, academics, trade journalists, industry regulators, makers, and exhibitors. Furthermore, reading Eisner's journalism and scholarly publications together suggests that she anticipated contemporary media industries studies and media historiographical work on useful cinema, reception, taste cultures, and the effects of industrial economics on genre and style.

The articles translated here represent some of the primary areas of Eisner's film reporting, though other important threads—including theater, art, literature, and fashion coverage—are not included. I selected these particular articles to demonstrate several things. First, Eisner's range as a writer was broad, and she offered numerous original insights on topics that have subsequently been of substantial interest to scholars, including film technology, exhibition, labor, policy, aesthetics, and medium specificity, as well as visual culture, gender, and class. Second, Eisner published at the *Film-Kurier* under at least ten pen names, and her career there was interrupted by ascendant Nazism. Perhaps the single greatest factor in the historiographical neglect of Eisner's work and legacy has been the fragmentation of Eisner's corpus along linguistic, disciplinary, and historical lines. Each subset of her writing—her doctoral work, her interwar journalism, and her scholarly publications and archival work in the postwar period—has tended to be taken up in isolation from the broader, sixty-year trajectory of her public writing.

Proceeding chronologically, eight of these pieces showcase Eisner's approach to film as an industry, art form, and cultural expression. Some come from *Film-Kurier*'s "Glashaus" (Glass house) column, which ran behind-the-scenes sketches of and reporting about current productions. Eisner's "Glashaus" pieces contributed to what she would later describe as her on-the-job education in film, and they offer evocative, humorous sketches of the action on set. Over time, Eisner's commentary became more expert and her interest in film style and aesthetics more nuanced. In two early samples, Eisner discusses set design, labor, and choreography on the sets of *Haus Nummer 17* (*Number 17*, Géza von Bolváry, 1928) and *Vom Täter fehlt jede Spur* (*Berlin After Dark*, Constantin J. David, 1928). These pieces evince her already-keen interest in the mechanics of profilmic mimesis, trickery, and craft. Eisner describes a third studio visit in the 1928 article "Kulturfilm im Werden" ("*Kulturfilm* in Development"), which connects to a deep vein of her *Film-Kurier* work on the aesthetics, regulation, and exhibition of the

Kulturfilm, a genre encompassing a wide range of documentary filmmaking, including what is today known as "process genre," useful cinema, advertising films, and prestige feature documentaries.[3] This forceful article advocates for increased investment by major studios in the production of sound and silent documentary; in it, Eisner argues that the feature-length documentary is a key component of the production and exhibition on which sustainable, diverse, public cinema-going culture depends. Although Eisner would later disparage her *Kulturfilm* coverage in harsh terms, the five samples here suggest a complex negotiation at the juncture of advocacy, aesthetic critique, and policy analysis.[4] In contrast to the better-known commentary offered by peers such as Arnheim and Feld on the regulation and aesthetics of *Kulturfilme*, Eisner's analysis of the regulatory and creative aspects of documentary was informed by a granular understanding of the economics of production, distribution, and exhibition, as well as the conviction that the aesthetic potentialities of documentary film were multifarious and, in her view, woefully underexplored. (This conviction is particularly evident in "Der Künstler und seine Technik" ["The Artist and His Technique," 1931], "Kino-Sonntag in Amsterdam" ["Cinema Sunday in Amsterdam," 1928], and "Dilemma des Kulturfilmproduzenten. Wem soll er es recht machen?" ["The Dilemma of the *Kulturfilm* Producer: Whom Should He Please?," 1930].) A consistent theme of Eisner's coverage was her advocacy for experimentation with film form. In "Neue Kräfte im Tonfilm: Chancen für Weill und Brecht" ("New Forces in Sound Film: Opportunities for Weill and Brecht," 1930), we see a vociferous expression of this belief and an abiding fascination with questions of medium specificity and the novel problems and opportunities presented by sound film technologies.

The two pieces included here on non-film subjects are representative of Eisner's interwar cultural criticism and exemplify her unique contributions to period discourses on the mobilities of gendered, racialized, and class-bound bodies under the rubric of modernity, which have since been studied at length. The first, titled "Sieben im Autobus" ("Seven on the Bus," 1928), takes aim at both the objectification of women and the patriarchal assumptions at the root of Kracauer's vaunted critique of visual culture, capitalism, and the Tiller Girls dance troupe.[5] The second, titled "Spanischer Frühling: Jacobinermützen in Barcelona" ("Spanish Spring: Phrygian Caps in Barce-

3 Eisner's coverage includes a years-long engagement with *Kulturfilme* focused on the production of goods and fine art—under the rubrics of *Reklame-* and *Industriefilme* and the *Schaffende Hände* series by Hans Cürlis—a body of film that Salomé Aguilera Skvirsky nevertheless describes as a "heretofore unacknowledged and untheorized transmedial genre," in *The Process Genre: Cinema and the Aesthetic of Labor* (Durham, NC: Duke University Press, 2020).

4 In her memoirs, Eisner claims that she was assigned the *Kulturfilm* coverage as a result of her junior status upon her arrival at the *Film-Kurier*. Lotte Eisner, *Ich hatte einst ein schönes Vaterland* (Heidelberg: Wunderhorn, 1984), 79. The title of Eisner's memoirs quote a Heinrich Heine poem that is conventionally referred to by its first line, which is translated, "I once had a beautiful homeland." Heinrich Heine, *Der Salon*, vol. 1 (Hamburg: Hoffmann and Campe, 1834).

5 Kracauer called the Tiller Girls "products of American distraction factories[,] no longer individual girls, but indissoluble girl clusters whose movements are demonstrations of mathematics." Siegfried Kracauer, *The Mass Ornament: Weimar Essays*, trans. Thomas Y. Levin (Cambridge, MA: Harvard University Press, 1995), 76–77.

lona," 1931), is an evocative commentary that begs to be interpolated into the rich literature on Jewish travel writing of the period penned by Arthur Holitscher, Egon Erwin Kisch, Joseph Roth, and others. As in "Cinema Sunday in Amsterdam," Eisner narrates "Spanish Spring" as a *flâneuse* with a sharp eye for detail, although her observations are couched in a deeply prejudiced frame of reference in terms of class, race, and nationality.

For as free as Eisner apparently was to wander in person and on the page—as a Jewish, German, middle-aged, gender non-conforming woman and as a professional journalist—in her writing, she nonetheless falls back on orientalist tropes to describe the market vendors in Amsterdam and the Spaniards in revolt.[6] In "Seven on the Bus," Eisner makes no attempt to inhabit the point of view of the women on the bus as they are ogled, mobilized (unwittingly, as far as we are told) in a critique of capitalism and visual culture, and assessed by their fellow passengers. Instead, Eisner stages the process by which these women are objectified by everyone else on the bus; the passengers with speaking roles in this caricature flatten the dancers into two-dimensional pin-ups and project onto them wistful, fearful images of their role and their power. They are the object of one man's nostalgic desire, while another, the "lady," takes comfort in her ignorance ("with a little triumph in her voice"), thinking that, since they aren't part of a dance troupe whose name she recognizes, they do not pose the moral or sexual threat she had initially feared. The conceit, of course, is that each of these passengers is mistaken in how they read these women. Brief as it is, Eisner's piece suggests a biting critique of the patriarchal optic within which each onlooker operates as they assess the worth of all eight women in the party.

At an oblique angle, Eisner's observations indicate how imbricated the Frankfurt School's brand of critical theory was with the society from which its most prominent proponents emerged, marked by prejudices that eluded their considerable powers of insight and rhetoric. In "The Little Shopgirls Go to the Movies," Kracauer claimed that his against-the-grain readings of contemporary films came from listening to the "rude secret" burping forth from seemingly innocuous films, the recurring tropes of which reveal "how society wants to see itself."[7] While Kracauer does tally variations in the reactionary pablum of the films under review, the butt of the joke is always the female spectator. Patronized, infantilized, and ultimately blamed for the retrograde politics of the films, the figure of the ingenuous woman in the movie theater is a trope of critical theory that follows a long tradition within continental philosophy of misogynist contemplation.[8] Eisner, who described herself as a

6 Nicholas Baer has identified a similar "essentialist, Orientalist" impulse in "Lotte H. Eisner, A New India Film: *A Throw of Dice* (1929)," in *The Promise of Cinema: German Film Theory, 1907–1933*, ed. Anton Kaes, Nicholas Baer, and Michael Cowan (Berkeley: University of California Press, 2016), 63. In several other film reviews from the *Film-Kurier* days, her chapter on *Tabu* in *Murnau*, and in at least one film review from the mid-1950s, Eisner leans on dehumanizing language to describe non-European people, invoking tropes devised by brutal colonial regimes of power and trade while also offering unreservedly critical remarks on the depredations and atrocities perpetrated by those same colonial enterprises.

7 Kracauer, *Mass Ornament*, 294.

8 Kracauer's shopgirls of 1927 condense the traits of what Max Horkheimer and Theodor W. Adorno later dubbed the "dupes" of the culture industry as well as the

misogynist in numerous interviews and her memoirs, nevertheless points out contemporaneously with Kracauer's pieces on the Tiller Girls and women at the movies that his critique of the constitutive role of the fetishized female form in industrial capitalist aesthetics rests on a doubled objectification of women.[9]

In addition to complicating conventional wisdom about the significance of Eisner's work and legacy, the selections translated here suggest generative points of connection and exchange with contemporary film studies. This body of writing represents an ambitious, omnivorous effort on Eisner's part to understand the teeming media ecosystem of the interwar period, to grasp the effects of industry regulation on media aesthetics, and to seriously engage with useful cinema and below-the-line labor. As a corrective to presentist impulses in contemporary media studies, and as an unfamiliar perspective on a key period of the field's early development, Eisner's early work presents an opportunity to place questions of gender, class, affect, and historiography at the center of field inquiries moving forward.

Lotte Eisner

translated by Naomi DeCelles

NUMBER 17 AND A CHIMNEY THAT OUGHT TO SMOKE

Whitechapel in the studio. Narrow shafts of light, smoking chimneys. Crooked, angular houses with decrepit rooftops. [Set designer] O. F. Wendorff sourced bona fide roof tiles from the Berlin slums. The authenticity of the criminals is not likewise guaranteed. For the moment, only one of these gents is present: Fritz Greiner. Collarless, as befitting a respectable crook, and with a purple, smudgy stubble, ostensibly four days' worth. Is it in Fox's ominous *Haus Nummer 17* [*Number 17*, Géza von Bolváry, 1928] that he's pitched his shady headquarters? The very house into which people enter and mysteriously disappear, per Benno Vigny and Adolf Lantz's liberal adaptation of J. Farjeon?[10]

Diagonally opposite, a dilapidated shack with empty window frames. Somebody hurries to the slumbering chimney, which is, uncooperatively, not smoking on cue. You wonder: by what means is the chimney supposed to smoke? Your curiosity is sated: incense sticks stand in for fire. Then, Géza von

horoscope-reading Angelenos of Adorno's screed against irrationalism, *The Stars Down to Earth and Other Essays on the Irrational in Culture* (London: Routledge, 1994).

9 See, for examples, Heike Hurst, Dorothea Muenk, and Uscica Perabo, "Film . . . das ist so populo! Gespräch mit Lotte Eisner von Heike Hurst, Dorothea Muenk, Uscica Perabo," *Frauen und Film* 11 (March 1977): 29–37; the documentary *Lotte Eisner in Germany* (S. Mark Horowitz, 1981); and Eisner, *Ich hatte*, 159.

10 Fox Film Co. distributed Géza von Bolváry's 1928 film *Haus Nummer 17*, which was an adaptation of a 1925 Joseph Jefferson Farjeon play, *Number 17* (Farjeon also published a novelization in 1926 under the title *No. 17*). The English release title of Bolváry's film was *Number 17*, not to be confused with Alfred Hitchcock's later adaptation, *Number Seventeen* (1932).

Bolváry-Zahn calls out his "Go on" and "Come along!" and Lien Dyers, the junk man's little daughter, climbs, slim silk-stockinged legs first, out of the empty window frame and sneaks across rooftops and gutters to the mysterious neighboring house.[11] Craighall Sherry, the junk man, father, fence, and police informant with a Lon Chaney face, means to do the same. But when he clambers out, a piece of wall plaster bites the dust. At the camera, Eduard Hoesch groans about the white patch in his otherwise perfectly dirty Whitechapel until a painter quickly repairs the damage. Father and daughter disappear into the house next door.

Is it due to the latent perfidy of objects that now, after the take, the chimney smokes in such a picturesque way?[12]

ORIGINAL SOURCE: Lo-Ha., "Glashaus. 'Haus Nr. 17' und ein Schornstein, der rauchen soll," *Film-Kurier*, February 15, 1928.

MURDER IN THE BIG CITY

On the ruins of the *Metropolis* set at Ufa, Jacek Rotmil built the big city street set for the big deal crime picture *Vom Täter fehlt jede Spur* [*Berlin After Dark*, Constantin J. David, 1928]. The night sky and a chill set the scene. The asphalt is mirror-like, having just been sprayed down. Cars and people wait for the liberating cue that will call the movie to life.

Entrance to the Elysium Entertainment Palace. Posters, lights. Porters and elevator operators in fancy livery in front of the wide glass doors. In a corner with wooden scaffolding and crates, the upper half of the establishment in subtle miniature, a subway entrance with reverse script, to be reflected by the Schüfftan process.

A genuine cop is standing in front of C. J. David, the director, painstakingly giving his report on traffic and vehicle choreography. The signal: "Attention—High Beam Lights On—Action!"—and the city's bustle begins.

Pedestrians cross the wet asphalt, hurrying to the subway. Cars with improperly bright headlights whiz by. Giant buses, which appear to put an end to all lagging, laboriously make their way through, cross too early, have to double back again. Meanwhile, the wild shout, "More cars— — —move!" rings out, or: "Who's the idiot standing around over there again!"

At last, everything smooths out, people and cars portraying the suitably dense crowd of an evening thoroughfare, that symphony of the metropolis conducted by the traffic cop. In the meantime, the wet asphalt has slowly been glazed with black ice. The crew sprinkle it with sand. Someone passes a bottle of cognac around among the frozen spectators. The very prudent thaw their hands on hot Vienna sausages.

Cozy gentlemen stand around dispensing counsel: the homicide squad. Bona fide detective chief superintendents [*Kriminalräte*] and detective super-

11 Eisner quotes Bolváry in English.

12 Eisner invokes a phrase—*die latente Tüche des Objekte* (the latent perfidy of objects)—coined by Friedrich Vischer in *Auch Einer: Eine Reisebekanntschaft* (Stuttgart and Leipzig: Eduard Hallberger, 1879). She reprises the reference in the revised edition of *L'écran démoniaque* (Paris: Le Terrain Vague, 1965), 27, and in *Haunted Screen*, 23, vis-à-vis the uncanny under the sign of German Expressionism.

intendents [*Kriminalkommissare*] ensure that the murder and the pursuit of the murderer are depicted "true to form." Nobody wants a Sherlock Holmes cigarette ash diagnosis, so cheesy and pat, miraculously grasping the lone revelatory trace. This is why [Ernst] Stahl-Nachbaur, the film detective, likes to be lectured by his "colleagues," who in turn witness the film and debate as if it were a genuine murder mystery. — — — —

"Turn up the headlights!"—The picture's homicide squad car pulls up, skidding on the ice. The doorman at the Elysium rushes, gesticulating, toward Stahl-Nachbaur to report the murder, footage that has been already shot. Crowds of people jostle in excitedly; everyone wants to have been there. The cops form a cordon. — — —

The lights go out. Freezing extras stand in the dark. And the cars drive off the big city set out into the real big city.

ORIGINAL SOURCE: Lotte Eisner, "Glashaus. Mord in der Großstadt," *Film-Kurier*, February 22, 1928.

SEVEN ON THE BUS

Seven darling pin-up girl faces, beneath felt caps of every color, are laughing.[13] Seven adorable little rosy-lipped mouths chatter incessantly. Seven cheerful voices flutter unselfconsciously about the bus. In the broad, throaty English of the U.S.A. The whole bus is thrilled by such laughter and unselfconsciousness. All gentlemen gaze benevolently upon the seven darling pin-up girl faces under their felt caps of every color. Pleased by the seven rosy-lipped chatterboxes.

"You see," says the literary fellow in horn-rimmed spectacles to the fat man with the briefcase, "one can hardly distinguish among them. Seven, each like the next one. The *Girl* as the prototype of the collective man!"[14]

The fat man with the briefcase smiles courteously in helpless incomprehension. He, like everyone else behind him, cranes to catch a bigger eyeful of the darling pin-up girls. But all they glimpse is the troupe's commander in chief. A scrawny, miserable-looking chaperone with an old man's face.

"The virtue of the Tiller Girls is guarded," says one with experience, knowingly, to another. A set of Tiller Girls? Or some newly imported troupe from America? The words "Ziegfield [*sic*] Revue" are overheard, and all the men stare, fascinated, at the seven darling pin-up girl faces beneath their felt caps of every color.

13 *Postkartengesichter* (postcard faces) suggests an idealized femininity, something like the so-called Vargas Girls pin-up images; their creator, Alberto Vargas, illustrated some of the iconic Ziegfeld Follies publicity pin-ups in the 1910s.

14 In Eisner's original, "*Girl*" is in English, reflecting a period convention by which certain English-language loanwords connoted modernity, foreignness, and consumerism. Lynne Frame relates these loanwords to Weimar-era discourse on human typologies and gender performance in the service of an "anthropological project of appraising the German population, especially in terms of its relationship to metropolitan modernity." Frame observes that "[w]omen often stood at the center of these analyses," as the focal point for anxieties about social, political, and economic change. Lynne Frame, "Gretchen, Girl, Garçonne? Weimar Science and Popular Culture in Search of the Ideal New Woman," in *Women in the Metropolis: Gender and Modernity in Weimar Culture*, ed. Katharina von Ankum (Berkeley: University of California Press, 1997), 13.

Ziegfield [*sic*]! — — —

At some point, their scrawny chaperone rises, and the seven darling pin-up girls rise: Here's our stop! All the men goggle after them. To peep at those seven darling pin-up girls on the sidewalk, with their unbelievably impossible legs.

"So, not dancers after all," says a lady to her companion, a little triumph in her voice. "So, not dancers after all," murmur all the men to themselves, crestfallen.

"Boarding-house girls," sighs the fat man with the briefcase.

The literary fellow with the horn-rimmed spectacles peers censoriously; "A first pass at the collective man, at any rate," he concludes.

The bus gets on its way. Somewhere in the distance, seven darling pin-up girls stride along down the street on their impossible legs.

ORIGINAL SOURCE: Lolott., "Sieben im Autobus," *Film-Kurier*, April 14, 1928.

CINEMA SUNDAY IN AMSTERDAM

Uncontrived Film. On Sundays there is a market in the Jodenhoek [Jewish Quarter]. A fantastic, garish market, in the Oriental style, here beneath the cool brick houses of the North. A timeless market, hardly changed in three or four hundred years. Unlikely types. There's a quack doctor, looking straight out of a Dutch Renaissance genre painting the way he hawks his remedy for smoker's teeth here, in the land of tobacco.[15] He screams in a coarse Dutch, a barbaric French, filled with dramatic imagery. He passes around glass vials full of a red liquid for measuring the blood pressure of the nicotine-addled, scaring bystanders with a rotten set of dentures made of decaying wood. With much less fuss, a greasy Black man a few paces farther on is selling toothpaste from Canada. With a flourish—*Ladies and gentlemen*—he flashes his own pearly whites.[16] The Dutch are matter-of-fact people. A vigorous, visible proof such as this easily trumps whatever claims alchemy and hocus-pocus might hazard. You gawk at the zealous prophet and buy the toothpaste of the new world.

Mishmash of the Races. This hodgepodge of nations seems perfectly natural. There are the small, nimble Japanese men attempting to sell appallingly inauthentic Japanese cups, *made in Germany*.[17] A fellow countryman in western garb leans over, and they exchange a look and some quick, soft words, amused by the swindle and European stupidity; they are still very foreign and unfamiliar with this market of the Orient. They are foreign and unfamiliar even to the young man in the stall next door; with his round gestures and beautiful, melancholy fairy-tale eyes like Ernst Deutsch's, he sells a pair of secondhand pumps to a petite, blonde maiden in a Volendam bonnet, to replace her clattering wooden clogs. "*Haute nouveauté*" is printed on a tat-

15 Eisner describes the man as belonging in an *altholländischen Jahrmarktbild* [old Dutch festival painting]. Genre painting of the "low" style, taking peasants and rural life as its subject, is familiarly identified with Pieter Bruegel the Elder.

16 "Ladies and gentlemen" is in English in Eisner's original.

17 "Made in Germany" is in English in Eisner's original.

tered piece of cardboard.[18] An old man with a sorrowful face and a sorrowful nose is selling frock coats and corsets of dubious whiteness. *Haute nouveauté.* A Persian man in a tall fur hat is carefully weighing the cloth of the frock coats, his wallet grasped tightly in his left hand.

Chaplin's Old Shoes. The unlikeliest things are sold here, and here find their buyers. Leather patches for shoe soles, bent gramophones, oceanscapes in gold frames, silk petticoats long brittled with age. Brooches; stacks of old magazines; dried fruits from California that look like pieces of coal, for treating a sore throat; ancient boots of a deformed Chaplinesque model; poisonously colorful bonbons, amidst coffee pots without spouts; rusty pieces of iron; armchairs oozing their own upholstery. Screaming, haggling people, voices vying. Shuffling feet as people jostle in closer. Occasionally, sports champions jaunt up the aisle, a spring in their step; they, too, are strangely timeless, their caps and sweaters only spots of color in a natural variegation. Pausing to gawk, filled with boyish curiosity, sailors from the French warship *Somme* stroll through the crowd, with childish red pompoms atop their caps. Stretched across the Jodenbreestraat [Jewish Broad Street] are the fishmongers. Women selling vegetables and fruit sit sprawled over baskets. The lushest still life of a fertile country. There is a pungent smell of dried fish, cheese, and old clothes.

Cinema on the Jodenbreestraat. By the afternoon, the hustle and bustle of the market has disappeared. On Jodenbreestraat, the same people as this morning are standing around in groups. They seem more rested and, one could almost say, more Sunday-ish. They stand in the street, as if a life on the sidewalk and the banks of the canals were the most natural thing in the world, out in front of the open doors of their junk shops. By contrast to this morning's Jodenhoek, with its Oriental impression, the afternoon brings with it an Italian feeling. At two o'clock, the cinema on Jodenbreestraat opens. Larger than one would have expected for this neighborhood, the building's colorful design is not so different from that of some cinemas in northern and eastern Berlin. Only the music, somewhat cacophonous in its surfeit of percussion, is reminiscent of this morning's market.

There's a double feature program with two mainstream American films, a rainy newsreel, and a variety number featuring cyclists. It betrays nothing of the exoticism of the colorful street outside. The program is played as quickly as possible, even though the runtime was supposed to be three hours. If it weren't for the people, all the same characters from this morning, you might be disappointed. Youths with Ernst Deutsch's eyes. Broad, motherly women with large combs in their thick buns. Old men with their sorrowful faces, sorrowful noses. And young girls, their hair already bobbed, unusual looking in their thinness and the narrowness of their eyes, set in their beautiful, angular faces. They sit attentively, a little stiffly—it is an unfamiliar, peculiar world they glimpse. And they experience this unfamiliar, peculiar world with the affecting, devout doggedness of a people for whom miracles once happened.

18 The phrase *haute nouveauté* is transliterated "high novelty," connoting something along the lines of "latest fashions."

Nary a one—so lively a moment ago on the street—speaks to another during the changeovers.

Ten Cinemas Together. In the middle of the business district lies a dangerously narrow street, practically an alley: the famous Kalverstraat. Store after store, mostly clothing shops. Colorful announcements everywhere, although the sales are over. On many of these wares, the price in guilders is also given in dollars, shillings, francs, and reichsmarks. Here, the watchword of the moment is international. A vividness suffuses the air. Film posters plastered brightly cheek by jowl, always just clichés taken from movie scenes. It feels as though every other storefront along this street is a cinema. Of Amsterdam's twenty-six cinemas, ten can be found on Kalverstraat and its tributaries, the Nieuwendijk and the Reguliersbreestraat, alone. Naturally, given the close quarters, they're hardly movie palaces. Their façades barely distinguished from adjacent commercial buildings, these cinemas often have deep, low entrances, reminiscent on the whole of our smaller theaters. Apparently, among Dutch movie theaters, only the Ufa theaters obey a standard decorative principle.

One Line, Two Policemen. In front of the large cinemas, lines begin to crowd. People waiting to buy tickets are guarded by two good-natured policemen in straw pith helmets standing well into the street. After entering, however, nobody pushes; everyone quietly finds their seats. Incidentally, the ticket prices at the larger theaters range from about 2.50 to 2.60 guilders [*f*]. On Sunday afternoons, the so-called matinee, the most expensive seats cost around *f*1.25. And the smaller cinemas, like those in the provinces, lower the evening prices from *f*1.00 to *f*0.30.[19]

Smoking . . . *Not* Prohibited! A large cinema on Reguliersbreestraat, built in 1921. Its pre-Jugendstil excess of color is not to our taste. But the Amsterdamers are proud of it. Has Holland, the home of J. J. P. Oud's clean lines, not yet found a form for its cinemas?[20] The interior with its two high, steep tiers seems far more like a theater auditorium. However, one must be glad for the room's high ceilings, since they diffuse the cigarette smoke—already unbearable in the smaller cinemas by the third and fourth Sunday screenings—for smoking is very much permitted in all Dutch cinemas.

Loquacious Titles. The program is played somewhat more slowly here—it is still done at a faster clip than in our big cinemas—although this time there isn't a whole double feature to get through.[21] But the shorts program—with Standaart organ accompaniment—takes up much more time than it does in our cinemas.[22] Even the newsreel consists of two parts. One is the American

19 In 1928, *f*2.50 was about US$1.00.

20 Dutch architect J. J. P. Oud (1890–1963) was one of the leading adherents of the modernist International Style. Interestingly, he had already designed a movie theater by the time of Eisner's writing: the Cinema Schinkel (built in 1912, demolished in the 1950s) in his hometown of Purmerend.

21 The *Film-Kurier*'s readership was largely German; starting in September 1928, the paper served as the official organ of the Reichsverbandes Deutsches Lichtspieltheatersbesitzer (German Exhibitor's Union). Eisner's use of "our" here may have been even further localized to the cinemas of Berlin.

22 Standaart Orgel was a Dutch firm that produced and installed theater organs for

newsreel about world events; the other is a newsreel from Dutch cities, from Haarlem's Polygoonfilm. It features small local events from Utrecht, Delft, and Leiden: a poultry farm in Alkmaar, or the beginning of a bicycle race in Schiedam. Incidentally, Polygoonfilm is one of the few film companies in Holland that serves primarily as a "title factory," meaning that they create the very detailed Dutch intertitles for foreign films, which are often more loquacious than the originals.

"This and That." In the program, the next item is a "film hodge-podge." Cartoon shorts that seem to be half-advertisement, and things like that. Then, a film grotesque and the first vaudeville number are shown. Following that, a kind of newsreel called the "Cinéma Potpourri" commences, including "Kijkjes van hier en da" [Views from here and there] and "Ditjes und Datjes" [This and that]. However, after the "weekly" segment, only one "review" segment follows, as in America. This time, incidentally, it consists of segments of the Croeze-Bosman Pathé Revue, which are formally distinguished from the "Journaal" [Newsreel] only in that they elaborate in greater detail the individual events in various countries. After a second, almost too-long vaudeville number, the feature finally begins.

Interesting Things, Interestingly Shot. Not unlike the program at a large cinema in the Nieuwendijk, here again the "News of Holland" by Polygoon plus an issue of the American "International News."[23] This time, the American newsreel doesn't merely present the interesting actuality, but it does so in a way that makes the object of interest visually interesting too. The particulars are photographed at oblique angles, details thus emphasized, spotlight-like—the way that the Russians or [Walter] Ruttmann, for instance, do to such effect. For example: a parade sequence—which otherwise would have rehearsed the usual, boring template for the thousandth time—in which we cut, suddenly, to a close shot of the horses' legs, infinitely striding, propulsive hooves. Certain marching formations of troops are given a new aspect during the parade, carved out by the shot into a shape unique to them. These tricks are nothing new to the feature film, but they seem novel for a newsreel.

City Lights. You emerge from the cinema half an hour before midnight and are once again struck by the colorfulness of the street. Amsterdam knows not the magnificence of our illuminated advertising. But shining forth from cinemas, cafés, and stores, there is another, very modest kind: an illumination by the masses. On weekdays the street may seem to be deserted. But on these Sunday evenings, the city is strangely awake and strangely bright; anybody with legs is out promenading. The major-

---

cinemas in the Netherlands through at least the 1950s. In the 1940s, Dr. A. W. J. Standard Jr. immigrated to the United States and founded the Standaart Organ Company in Suffolk, Virginia.

23 The original reads, "Auch hier wieder die 'Hollands-Nieuws' von Polygoon und eine amerikanische International Nieuws." It seems likely that Eisner refers to the Hearst Corporation's silent International Newsreel, also called Universal International Newsreel and U-I Newsreel.

ity of them are very young men—all of them, as if by agreement, wearing gray caps, and only a few girls among them—mostly young, local boys, almost as if Holland had not been through a war, as if this were the country where Olympic youth could meet undiminished youth. They walk, here in the north, as if through a southern city. Music from open coffee houses and wine taverns spills out, punctuating the rhythm of colorful streets.

ORIGINAL SOURCE: Lotte H. Eisner, "Kino-Sonntag in Amsterdam," *Film-Kurier*, October 20, 1928.

KULTURFILM IN DEVELOPMENT: AT UFA IN NEUBABELSBERG

The *Kulturfilm* in Production—A Rare Sight, Indeed. Most people have an inkling that landscape films [*Landschaftsfilme*] and locality films [*Städtefilme*] are shot outdoors and that nature films are shot in zoos or out on expeditions.[24] Half an hour from Berlin, however, one has the opportunity to really get an insight into the laborious, careful detail work of *Kulturfilm* production, of which the greater public still knows far too little.

A Desk Piled High with Scripts. At its large campus in Neubabelsberg, Ufa has given over three areas to the *Kulturfilm* department for its workshops. The central node is a building with labs, work and projection rooms, and the archive. A second building, the menagerie, is home to the feathered and four-legged film stars. And a sort of shed houses the recording studio. In the central *Kulturfilm* studio, the desk is stacked high with models and well-organized notes. This is the office of Dr. [Nicholas] Kaufmann. This is where the scripts are conceived and worked out and where the intertitles get assigned. Three airplane pictures, already filmed, are awaiting their intertitles: the first, *Von der Schulbank zum Verkehrsflieger* [From pupil to commercial pilot, Nicholas Kaufmann, 1928], shows the training; the second one, *Vom Zeichentisch zum Verkehrsflugzeug* [*sic, Großflugboot*] [From the drawing board to the large flying boat, 1929]—by Hans Rudolf Meyer, the Zeppelin pilot from Ludwigshafen—illustrates the manufacturing process. And yet a third film, "Das Flugzeug als Kulturträger" [The airplane as cultural emissary], will demonstrate the culturally unifying function of aviation, which it shares in common with cinema and radio.

Seventy-Six Films. "And, as you see here," says Dr. Kaufmann, "we're planning a film called *Physikalische Spielereien* [Physics games, 1929]. We want to show the formation of crystals, or the structure of a soap bubble. Of course, we're also continuing to work on our biological cross-section films [*Querschnittfilmen*], in the same vein as *Motor des Lebens* [Motor of life,

24 *Landschaftsfilme* and *Städtefilme* of the period often served what Jeanpaul Goergen has described as the dual purpose of commercial and cultural propaganda: (1) to cultivate a sense of national identity and pride in German audiences and encourage business or commercial activity in the cities or localities featured and (2) to encourage tourism among foreign audiences. See Jeanpaul Goergen, "Urbanität und Idyll. Städtefilme zwischen Kommerz und Kulturpropaganda," in *Geschichte des dokumentarischen Films in Deutschland*, vol. 2. (Stuttgart: Reclam, 2005).

Nicholas Kaufmann, 1928] and 'Kraftprobe von Mensch und Tier' [Feats of strength by man and beast], as you see. There are just so many interesting ways to make comparisons among parallel processes. Like our film 'Mimik im Tierreich' [Mimicry in the animal kingdom], on the expressive capabilities of animals. And another on bizarre forms of locomotion. How many films are we making altogether? This production year, it's seventy-six films. Of those, forty-one are ready and thirty-five are in pre-production. All kinds, of course, from all areas of the natural sciences, medicine, geography and ethnography, industry and technology, agriculture and forestry, sports and games." Thanks to steady work at a fast clip, seventy-six films are already done or in production. Brick by brick, they're building a comprehensive oeuvre.

The World in Miniature. You descend into the labs. Mysterious jars and test tubes sit on tables. And aquaria, seeming to contain nothing other than a little algae. But here is a world in miniature, collected from a nearby lake or closest puddle of rain. Every few days, an "expedition" goes out, tearing up moss or sinking a strange canvas funnel into the pond scum, and schlepping its quarry back to the microscope. This is how the rotifers and other primeval, strange-looking creatures—more like plants than they are like animals—come before the microscope to be filmed. Over there, the most exciting stuff, events that often take days of patient waiting to unfold: the stentor-eating heliozoa, or perhaps the birth of a water flea.

The work requires a complicated apparatus. So many things to be considered! In order to keep the beam from frying the little animalcules, a row of water-filled cooling cuvettes stand between the lenses and the creatures being photographed. For double observations, a ninety percent silver-plated mirror is installed, which directs only ten percent toward the eye of the observer, and the rest is diverted toward the filmstrip for exposure.

Sitting on a table there is a little mound about the size of a cake pan. Resting atop a dark, mossy substrate, a tuft of light green moss. "You see," says Dr. [Martin] Rikli, who works here, "this, in a nutshell, is our film, 'Im Zauber des Liliputreiches' [The magic of the Lilliputian kingdom]."[25] A scant two square centimeters of moss encapsulates a whole swarm of life. And in that thimble-sized puddle, another unto itself. Together, the puddle and the mossy tufts provide the makings of a great film—eating and fighting, love and birth—a few things the miniature and human worlds have in common.

Slow Motion and Time-Lapse Revelations. Here, they do so much more than merely record things. Processes that until now scientists had been unable to observe in great detail are clarified: like the spread of rot, captured for "Und neues Leben wächst aus den Ruinen" [And from the ruins, new life grows], which shows that nature doesn't let a death go to waste. Dr. Rikli has invented a microscopic time-lapse photography for this purpose, and with it, he has enlightened the bacteriologists. The decaying fungi, like soldiers, form a veritable marching column; this finally explains their rapid spread.

25 This may have been a working title for *Waldeszauber* (Woodland magic, Martin Rikli, 1929).

"Slow motion has taught us a lot too," says Dr. Kaufmann. "That's how we learned that the mongoose readies its bite just before it attacks the rattlesnake; that is to say, there's a defined plan of attack."

Filmed under Water! Next door, most of the micro-equipment is missing. It is out on the Messina expedition, led by Dr. Schulz and Herta Jülich. This expedition planned to collect footage of deep-sea fish and the cultivation of lemons up above water, but the eruption of Mount Etna has been added to its brief. The slow advance of the lava flow will be filmed with great care, at each individual stage—to date, it has only ever been depicted in newsreels, in tiny clips—so as to provide new clues to science. Like the Dobruja expedition, which incidentally yielded seven individual films, the Sicilian expedition will—so you learn—be exploited to its fullest. This time, totally novel deep-sea footage will be collected.

"Up to now," Dr. Kaufmann explains, "the use of aquaria or glass-bottom boats has typically sufficed. But we've moved beyond that, because it restricts the range of camera angles, and in the boat, you can only ever shoot from above." A new underwater technique developed by the surgeon Krien—so you learn—makes it possible for the first time to film from all angles.

Box after Box. "But you must come see our archive," Dr. Kaufmann urges. As you pass by, you peek inside the splicing room. There stands Wilhelm Prager, at work on his film about Scheveningen, which intends to show the contrast between the fishing village and the elegant seaside resort.[26]

"It puts you in a very summery mood," Prager says, "just take a look at this beach scene." But you take your leave of Scheveningen and end up in the archive's card catalog room, the domain of Olga Adamara. A few librarians are sitting and writing busily, with crisply etched penmanship. They fill box after box of the card index with their slips of paper. Everything is divided into sections: Animal and Plant Kingdoms, Exotic Tribes, Shipping, and so many others. Rich materials, all numbered, easy to find and ready to be put to use in a new film, as Olga Adamara explains. And a little further on, the photo archive, in which the images are sorted by film.

The Landscape on Wheels. You head over to Wolfram Junghans's recording shed. On a few posts and a rolling set construction, he has created a very artful tropical world of earth and plants. Lianas grow on the uneven ground, and a few musty tree stumps poke out.

"This is our 'set' for the porcupine film," Junghans explains. "The paca—a South American rodent, you know—has just been filmed, as an extra." In fact, you *don't* happen to know; no doubt, you skipped class the day that zoology lesson was covered. But then, you find an odd fern cluster hung upon the side wall. Large fleshy leaves grasp tightly around its pot, a wild growth in and of itself.

In passing, you ask, "Also for the . . . 'set'?"

"Of course not!" cries Junghans, "that one is only for the African landscapes." He can't bear the idea of falsifying anything about the set, because

26 Scheveningen is a Dutch fishing port and coastal resort destination on the North Sea.

his tiny world on wheels is a fully formed reality. But these ever-shifting settings are not so easy to create. The plants must have several days to establish themselves and, most importantly, to get oriented toward the lights. For shooting, they get a little rain in preparation, which is to say they get sprinkled with a mister for a more natural appearance. This is how the "buildings" grow here; often the results are much more convincingly realistic than the studio landscapes that mimic the outside world. But tomorrow, a new set may already be here: a completely prosaic German forest and meadowscape with a few carefully dug working tunnels for field mice and hamsters.

Bashful Movie Stars. Now for the most difficult part: getting the shot. Directors who complain about temperamental movie stars would do well to come see Junghans and his cameraman [Bernhard] Juppe. Heaven knows, it's no easy task to get these movie stars, clad in their own fur, armor, or plumage, to hit their marks and get them accustomed to the spotlight, lure them into the foreground, and coax them gently with a stick when—ever so timid before the camera—they try to hide. There's another strange stick among the props, a leather snake snare that looks very much like Douglas Fairbanks's Zorro whip: to be placed around the head of poisonous snakes and used to move them from here to there without endangering anyone.

Hector and Comrades. All 180 (!) of these unusual and individual movie stars and extras live across from their menagerie. Cage after cage against the walls, and next to them, large glass terraria. A warm, sweetish greenhouse air that smells of predators pervades the room. Extras and stars alike, none of them strangers to the camera, are known by their screen names.

"These, of course you'll recognize, are the two magpies from *Mein und Dein im Tierreich* [Mine and yours in the animal kingdom, Ulrich K. T. Schulz, 1929]," Junghans and Juppe tell you. "And here is a star of *Der Quastenstachler* [The porcupine, 1928].—No, the hamster is only an extra in 'Intimes aus den Mäusereich' [Secrets of the mouse kingdom]. And here we have the rats from *Spare in der Zeit* [A penny saved, 1930]."

But, naturally, there are also A-listers: the dormouse from "Vom Vielfraß zum Siebenschläfer" [From wolverine to dormouse], or the mussurana snake—which is non-venomous—that eats its venomous enemy, the lachesis, alive. And, of course, the snake-slayer: the mongoose. Who, it so happens, found his future mistress in the no-longer-so-unusual way: by way of a personals ad in the paper. For the time being, she is too young—still just a tender babe—and needs to do a little growing up first. But when she does, they'll star together in a family drama.

Despite the mongoose's heroic deeds, Hector is the favorite son. Nevertheless, sad to say, from time to time he must make do with bit parts. Hector is, of course, the crocodile: so christened by dint of his decidedly roguish, canine appearance. Only one shouldn't imagine Hector a ravenous beast. Hector is only about six or eight years old and about forty-five centimeters long, a sort of super-lizard, his temporarily diminutive mouth filled with charming baby teeth. In about sixteen years, Hector will assume his full stature of at least two and a half meters in length. "Will you have to build out an addition at that point?" you ask Wolfram Junghans.

You proceed, deep in thought about what you've seen, toward the exit. How much longer will the exhibitor continue to see in the *Kulturfilm* merely a tax loophole? All this useful, well-planned work will require a proper reassessment of its worth.

ORIGINAL SOURCE: Lotte H. Eisner, "Kulturfilm im Werden: Bei der Ufa in Neubabelsberg," *Film-Kurier*, December 8, 1928.

NEW FORCES IN SOUND FILM: OPPORTUNITIES FOR WEILL AND BRECHT

For those who take an interest in film, the sound film has created a new state of affairs. This is a generally recognized fact. However, it is still unclear whether the changeover to sound film brings with it a new take on film itself.

A different set of skills than were needed before will be brought to bear, for the simple reason that they have become necessary: the sound film—for which every beat becomes musically meaningful and every word becomes significant in its finality upon projection in an auditorium—needs the musician, and it needs the poet.

But not just any musician, not just any poet will have the aptitude for this. The question is . . . WHO IS UP TO THE TASK?

The parallel case of contemporary theater may indicate the way forward. For example, *Die Dreigroschenoper* [*The Threepenny Opera,* Bertolt Brecht and Kurt Weill, 1928], a work at the juncture of opera and drama, produced a new form for the stage: THE MUSICAL VOLKSSTÜCK.[27]

Needless to say, incorporating this new theatrical genre into the sound film won't be easy, because the sound film, as we're all now aware, is more than canned theater. The industry will need to commit the energies devoted to the improvement of sound film with all seriousness to the task of creating a new type of sound film: the musical film as *Volksstück.*

It will be impossible to overlook a musician like KURT WEILL any longer. *Die Dreigroschenoper* demonstrates what he has to offer to sound film: his music has a certain transparency to it in the way the voices are independently conducted; it is a form that unites clarity and simplicity with quality. These are imperative for the sound film, whose peril lies in ambiguity, sluggishness of the musical form, and in mushily arranged orchestration.

At the same time, *Die Dreigroschenoper* is a departure from the filmed operetta, from the filmed opera. For in this musical *Volksstück,* SINGING

27 The term *Volksstück*, sometimes translated as "people's play," denotes a type of German-language popular theater. Michael Patterson defines the genre as "rang[ing] from light-hearted dialect comedies, which entertained audiences in Vienna throughout the eighteenth and for most of the nineteenth centuries, to present-day serious studies of the contemporary lower class," adding that "[i]n many respects, the *Volksstück* has now been appropriated, superseded, and sanitized by television soap operas." See Michael Patterson, "Volksstück," in *The Oxford Encyclopedia of Theatre and Performance* (Oxford: Oxford University Press, 2003), https://www.oxfordreference.com/view/10.1093/acref/9780198601746.001.0001/acref-9780198601746-e-4118.

EMERGES FROM WITHIN THE SITUATION; the music is always built in dramaturgically in such a way that it organically belongs to the whole.

Besides the musician Weill, the sound film will need a poet. An obvious choice presents itself: the author with whom he often works for stage productions, BERT[OLT] BRECHT. Here, too, the value of his songs for the sound film lies in the singability of their language, in the pithiness and pungency of his dialogue's diction. The material is also important. His way of interpreting the events of our time, drawn from social conditions, in singular, lively form.

But Bert Brecht and Kurt Weill will have to be given the opportunity TO ADAPT, for they will need to work differently than they do in the theater. So, it is important to give them the chance not only to make a sound film but also, as part of this chance, to look around. A script by Bert Brecht, a score by Kurt Weill: these alone don't define a Weill-Brecht sound film production. If their work is to be fruitful, Brecht and Weill will have to make their own experiences. Consequently, they need to be given time and opportunity during production to experiment, to become familiar with the technical and dramaturgical aspects of the sound film. Kurt Weill, as we know, was approached to work on projects at the beginning of the sound film era. At the time, he set as a precondition to his commitment that the studio be OPEN TO EXPERIMENTS. This demand was not met at the time. Today's experiences with sound film have shown how important intensive preparatory work is. Weill and Brecht will have to create the possibilities for these preliminary studies today.

ORIGINAL SOURCE: —ner., "Neue Kräfte im Tonfilm: Chancen für Weill und Brecht," *Film-Kurier*, March 27, 1930.

THE DILEMMA OF THE *KULTURFILM* PRODUCER: WHOM SHOULD HE PLEASE?

Kulturfilm producers are faced with a dilemma; on the one hand, cinema audiences demand of the *Kulturfilm* an interesting style: that means using montage and not using too many intertitles (since nobody cares where precisely the village of X is located, and so on). On the other hand, however, the Lampe Committee demands that if a film is to be deemed educational, it has to report the facts with great thoroughness, neglecting no details of the locale.[28] And, heaven forfend montage sequences, for the Committee feels that their use means the film's subject cannot have been "exhaustively treated." Cinemagoers are bored by the punctilious films awarded Lampe Certificates, and the Lampe Committee refuses to recognize the films that are made in intentionally cinematically interesting ways as having educational merit. So, whom is the *Kulturfilm* producer to please?

28 As the director of the Central Institute for Education and Pedagogy from 1919 to 1931, Professor Felix Lampe (1868–1946) headed the so-called Lampe Committee, a panel of educators who evaluated the educational and artistic merits of films. One of the Lampe Committee's requirements for the award of their certificate of approval, which in turn qualified the film for an exhibitor's tax break [*Prädikat*], was that the film serve an educational, instructive purpose; another condition was that the film treat its subject exhaustively.

Many people will think that it is more important, and at the same time more profitable, to create a sophisticated *Kulturfilm* for theatrical release, especially since schools and other organizations have less and less money to spend on film. (The numbers don't lie: whereas two years ago, a *Landschafts-film* [scenic film] producer might print thirty copies of a given kind of film, today he prints only three.) But the *Kulturfilm* producer can't do without the Lampe Certificate. After all, can exhibitors be expected to run his *Kulturfilme* in matinees, or as shorts alongside a feature for that matter, if they have to pay taxes on them? Even the discounted "educational" or "artistically significant" films have little chance, unless they're truly extraordinary. Hence the maddening recursion whereby the *Kulturfilm* producer depends on the educational film tax break, which is contingent upon whether the film appeals to the Lampe Committee.

The Lampe Committee assumes that the educational film must stand in for the textbook, and therefore they demand the same things from the *Länderfilm* [travelogue] as from a geography textbook: exceedingly precise information about the location, detailed explanatory intertitles, exhaustive coverage of the topic, etc. Needless to say, the artistic direction of the film falls by the wayside.

Moreover—as a number of producers have confirmed—teachers don't ask for proof of the certification when they are ordering films for use in the schools. The Lampe Certificate therefore has only fiscal significance. If not for this, no producer would bother submitting their film to the Committee. Yet because of the tax decree of 1926, this ostensibly voluntary process has become an unavoidable financial necessity.

The only way to improve the quality of the *Kulturfilm*, then, is for the Lampe Committee to revise its standards. The Committee must not demand that film merely stand in for textbooks. It will be up to teachers to contextualize the material, to provide explanations and supplement the films during their screenings. Film must be permitted to preserve its visuality and to exceed the purely pedagogical. (Incidentally, such visual moments are more sophisticated than the so-called "moving shots" that the Committee members persist in favoring. The stills that the reviewers object to shouldn't be confused for diapositives. Often it is the use of static shots, intercut in the service of montage, that they object to.)[29]

If the Lampe Committee doesn't proceed with greater flexibility, nervous producers who are apprehensive about whether or not they'll be awarded a tax break—and who otherwise have little use for the Committee's certification of their films as "promoting public education" [*volksbildend*] or as "artistically significant"—will become warier than they already are of any artistic inclinations. Professor Lampe's successor will have to bear this in mind. These pedagogical constraints won't lower the quality of *Kulturfilme* alone; they will be imposed on sound film newsreels too. If the cinematic qualities

29 Eisner often lamented that the Lampe Committee took an unsophisticated approach to film aesthetics; here, she quarrels with their emphasis on moving or tracking shots over static camera framing, implying that the criteria by which stillness is being judged isn't informed by a real knowledge of filmmaking craft: that is, a static shot is different from a still frame.

of a film continue to be valued so little by the Committee's reviewers, to the point, indeed, that they even become grounds for criticism, there is a distinct danger that we will soon be left with impeccably tedious newsreels. *Kulturfilm* and newsreel producers will have to stand up for themselves.

ORIGINAL SOURCE: —ner., "Der Kulturfilm: Dilemma des Kulturfilmproduzenten. Wem soll er es recht machen?," *Film-Kurier*, December 20, 1930.

THE ARTIST AND HIS TECHNIQUE

The Vereins für Deutsches Kunstgewerbe [German Arts and Crafts Union] film series featured the eighth of Dr. [Hans] Cürlis's *Schaffende Hände* [*Creative Hands*] films.[30] The films in the *Schaffende Hände* series were meant to be screened independently of one another, to be an endless supply of *Beiprogramme* [supporting shorts programming] for movie theaters. That the films are so wonderfully evocative of the artist's creative process is due to the fact that they represent the actual creation of the work. With yesterday's film, however, Dr. Cürlis fell short of expectations; instead of a completed film, he presented a vague and disjointed assemblage of new and not-so-new reports on the artist's work, the intertitles in mismatched typefaces, lacking on the whole any hint of coherence.

Every single one of these films has its artistic value, but it is regrettable that they have not been combined into one organic whole. Indeed, if the Institut für Kulturforschung [Institute for Cultural Research] wants to make films for broader audiences, it needs to work with montage. The average viewer, unlike the art historian, will not want to watch long sequences in which an oil painting comes into being; he won't understand the subtle differentiations among the variations or be able to preserve in his mind's eye for the purposes of comparison a clear image of the earlier stages of composition.

To that end, a quick juxtaposition of the individual techniques is necessary, and a clear, straightforward explanation must be provided in the intertitles. And here, no doubt, Dr. Cürlis would wish for the ability to introduce audio. He explained yesterday in his brief introductory remarks that he lacks the funding to continue work on the *Schaffende Hände* series. A documentary series of such importance, such revelatory significance for the art of our time, must not be halted. Where is the cooperation and support—from Degeto [The German Society for Sound and Image], which could secure excellent archive films with these individual films, and from the university art history seminars—in this moment of need?

ORIGINAL SOURCE: —ner., "Der Künstler und seine Technik," *Film-Kurier*, January 8, 1931.

30 The *Schaffende Hände* series consists of over eighty short films (some now lost) about the artistic processes of various painters, sculptors, engravers, and artists working in other media, made between 1922 and 1969. The first film of the series was *Lovis Corinth* (Hans Cürlis, 1922).

SPANISH SPRING: PHRYGIAN CAPS IN BARCELONA

Aboard the Saarbrücken. Apropos of sea voyages: in addition to the joys of taking in the marvelous sea air and novel jargon (within three hours, even the most inveterate landlubber speaks in a highly nautical manner of disembarkation and depth sounding and can even tell starboard from port, since certain spots bear the red or green light), one also picks up, in such a wonderfully natural way, a little bit of geography and, with any luck, even a little history. Who, for instance, can truthfully say they know exactly where the Cape Finisterre is off the top of their head? And who knew that Bill's Ballroom in Bilbao really exists?[31] But the applied history that plays out before one's eyes is even better: it's like a newsreel minus the screen. One participates a little in the fate of the world, without distance and in detail, as if through a merry kaleidoscope, albeit—upon later careful reflection—plenty powerfully.

There is a revolution in Spain; so said the radio message on board the *Saarbrücken* just before we reached Barcelona. But it sounded no different then than it does when the newspapers tell us, "over in faraway Turkey . . ." And then suddenly, you're there in the harbor, and, as if on cue, a small but eager crowd rushes along, ready to demonstrate their revolution for the cameras. They wave the new red, yellow, and purple flag; their cries of "Viva la República!" are shouted with the sense that we aboard the steamer were all, at the very least, Henny Porten.[32] Rhythm, charm, and verve: the birthright of southerners.

Flags, flags everywhere. They appeared overnight; factories must have worked overtime to give a few old red-yellow-red flags their new crimson-purple stripe. The most determined have colored in their own paper flags, with blue always in place of purple. It happens quickly—the steamer beside us in the harbor, previously called the *King Alfonso* [*sic*, *Alfonso XIII*, renamed *España*], has already been painted over, and the street signs are rapidly being repainted. The revisionists work tirelessly: you can see for yourself that the goddesses of stone on the state house in the *Plaza de la Constitución* and in the *Audiencia* are already wearing tidily plastered red Phrygian caps. And nobody from public works is going to come to wash them off, either—it is explained with a grin—since it's a revolutionary holiday. A revolutionary holiday it may be, but there's not a drunk to be found anywhere, since the Catalonians, like most Spaniards, don't drink to quench their thirst; here, the notion of getting as "drunk as an Andalusian" is figurative at best. Even the monarchists in our midst aboard the *Saarbrücken* are enthusiastic: the revolutionary holiday, in all its there-will-be-no-washing-it-off glory, gives us one more day in Barcelona, that is,

31 Eisner refers to "The Bilbao Song," from Kurt Weill, Elisabeth Hauptmann, and Bertolt Brecht's 1929 musical comedy *Happy End*.

32 Eisner's meaning is somewhat unclear; it's possible she meant that the greeting they received was worthy of a star of at least Henny Porten's status (i.e., the *Saarbrücken*'s passengers got a celebrity's welcome), or she may be referring somewhat vaguely to one of the revolutionary crowd scenes in Porten's filmography. Porten (1890–1960) was a prolific actor and producer in the German film industry; by the publication of Eisner's article in 1931, Porten had been a major star for nearly two decades.

one more day for a visit to Montserrat, the *Gralsberg*.[33] A Lloyd car drives through the city, through the most colorful and romantic of all revolutions. Again and again, our car is stopped by new crowds of men in Phrygian caps—and its close cousin, the Catalonian *barretina*—all waving their flags in our faces. Proceeding leisurely enough, we are cheered to see people taking off their caps, and we wave. Then everyone claps their hands, and we drive through the crowd. Down south, they love symbols. In one tiny, provincial village, they place a portrait of King Alfonso under the car's wheels so that we can run it over. And just as at a bullfight, they've hung colorful rugs from the windows and balconies.

The sharply cut zigzag silhouette of "Saw Mountain," Montserrat, rises up from sun-greyed greenery, already scorched by the summer sun. In the distance, the snow-covered Pyrenees shimmer. Atop the fantastic stony crags like a giant's fingers, a strange vision of *Parsifal*: no Wagnerian operatics, but plenty of doves fluttering about. A hotel has opened up near the monastery, and from there, a funicular leads to the pinnacle, to the chapel of Sant Joan. Civilization does have its pluses: in the absence of this cable car, who would make such magnificent vistas possible?

The hotel also has a deeper purpose: in the monastery there is a miraculous image of the Black Madonna, who redeems unhappy marriages and makes the happy ones permanent. And so, in sage foresight, wedding parties make a pilgrimage up to her; young couples are married upstairs and must have their honeymoon there, and later, of course, the first child is baptized at Montserrat. Since love, as we all know, doesn't let historical events get in its way, we have five newlyweds upstairs at their festive wedding dinner, despite the revolution. A heavenly host of Spanish fashion is on display, tending to favor bright red and a very sweet pink. In her chapel, the wise Black Madonna stands, tall and mysterious, ten fresh bridal bouquets about her.

The Rambla, Barcelona's wide street with trees down its middle, has a terrific night life. All the vaudeville theaters and cinemas are closed for the holiday, but life's talkies are screening outdoors. Directors, you can learn a lot here. Cars whiz by, one after the other. Boys and girls within, picturesque with their flags, sashes, and caps. By now, they're a little worn out, yet as enthusiastic as ever. Amblers amidst them. Little clusters, polemicizing. Every few steps, a champion of the people, speechifying with sweeping gestures. Newspaper vendors have been descended upon by all. The newspaper *Liberdad* displays the revolutionary goddess in large format. Pictures of the revolutionary martyrs executed by General Berenguer hang everywhere. A Spanish summer's warmth. Cafés upon cafés. You sit outside on the cobblestones,

33 Richard Wagner's opera *Parsifal* opens with a scene set in the fictional "Montsalvat" in the "northern mountains of Gothic Spain." According to the libretto, the Holy Grail is kept at a castle on the "Gralsberg" (Grail Mountain), where it is guarded by an order of knights. This scene direction in the libretto has been taken by some as a reference to Montserrat and the Pyrenees, a notion Eisner plays with here and in her description of the "Wagnerian operatics" of Montserrat's fluttering doves: in the opera, the death of Kundry is marked by the appearance of a white dove, which flutters above the hero, Parsifal. Richard Wagner, *Parsifal: Ein Bühnenweihfestspiel* (Mainz: B. Schott's Söhne, 1879).

the colorful crowd flooding by, occasionally tossing up a mendicant beach-comber in our direction. Spanish liqueur tastes like sunshine, and there are wild strawberries garnished with oranges—a national dish—to be had. In the distance, the Marseillaise fades away.

Come morning, everybody is back to work. The bright streets are quieter. In the flower market on the Rambla, florist after florist, with summer flowers in the middle of spring. Barcelona in the daytime is a different place, the city of the 1880s. It is all magnificent, too magnificent, with its rock sugar Jugendstil buildings. And what's more, a mad architect planned to inaugurate a Catalonian Renaissance with a cathedral and palazzo composed entirely of organic shapes, which were never finished, and remain swollen and flabby, like raw dough [*ungehärteter Teig*]. To escape this proliferation of horrors in stone, you proceed into the cathedral's gloomily beautiful nave. From above, however, in the view from atop Montjuïc, Barcelona looks radiantly glorious, a gigantic, white fairy-tale city on the sea.

ORIGINAL SOURCE: Lotte H. Eisner, "Spanischer Frühling: Jacobinermützen in Barcelona," *Film-Kurier*, May 2, 1931.

WITH THE BEGINNING OF THE SCHOOL YEAR, CLASSROOM CINEMA RETURNS

Berlin, August 8th. School is back in session, and with it returns the problem of what is to be done with school cinemas [*Schulkinos*]. It's a difficult subject; ask around, and you'll find that nobody really knows how many there are today. This is because many of these school cinemas exist only on paper anymore, having withered away for lack of funding. New ones are no longer being established. Again and again, you hear the phrase "economic crisis."

Like Pen and Paper. School cinemas, one should always remember, are a vital component of instruction. They are as necessary as the atlas and textbook, the composition notebook and pen. Yet they have greater immediacy than any other teaching materials. Managed correctly, school cinemas needn't compete with movie theaters. If Parents Night events are to serve as effective fundraisers, good (silent) *Kulturfilme* that have been screened theatrically should be chosen.

Edicts from Above. The question of whether, despite the current economic situation, film could be made compulsory in schools has become, yet again, a pressing one. It is possible—as [Per] Kviberg, the *Kulturfilm* authority of Oslo, in Norway, has proven—to mandate the installation of school cinemas.[34] An intervention such as this would also, it should be noted, result in higher demand, thus regulating the costs of the apparatus and of production. It would be cheaper for schools to accomplish this if the edict were to come from above. (And if, as expected, narrow-gauge film proves its usefulness.)

Black and White. Narrow-gauge film has various advantages. It would be possible to screen films in the classroom itself; such an arrangement would

34 Per Kviberg (1881–1960) was a Norwegian educator and politician who advocated for the use of film in classrooms.

be less complicated than the usual way of screening films in an auditorium or school theater, given the time and preparation required for these types of projection. This would also entail fulfilling the demand—the need for which can't be overstated—for classroom projection screens: a white wall beside every blackboard.

An "Advocacy Committee." The *Bildspielbund* does what it can.[35] At the conference in Vienna, the problems relating to narrow-gauge film were discussed at length.[36] The eleventh *Bildwoche* [Picture Week], which takes place in Berlin from October 7–10, will be another venue for discussing this problem.[37] It would be best to engage authorities beyond teaching staff with this gathering. One suggestion, from an interested party: in addition to the expert committee of state councilors [Werner] Völger and Dr. [Walther] Günther, an advocacy committee concerning school cinema must be organized.[38]

No Administrative Turf Wars! Mind you, this institution should not—it is emphasized—conflict with the *Bildspielbund*. It would be an office for authorities that, once established, should work hand in hand with the *Bildspielbund*. The teachers could—it is explained—take their requests to the *Bildspielbund*, and the new department would work to address them.

The Right Man . . . In a Germany characterized by innumerable associations and cumbersome bureaucracy, skepticism about the establishment of a new administrative authority is to be expected. If, however, this new administrative authority really were the missing link, and establishing it neither interfered with the work of the *Bildspielbund* nor strained the budget, if the right man for the job could be found, then we'd be in a position to discuss it. The primary concern remains helping the school cinema.

ORIGINAL SOURCE: L. H. E., "Wenn die Schule beginnt—kommt auch das Schulkino," *Film-Kurier*, August 8, 1931.

Naomi DeCelles is a film historian and author of *Recollecting Lotte Eisner* (University of California Press), a feminist historiographical critique of the legacy and significance to film studies of the historian, journalist, and archivist Lotte Eisner.

35 The Deutsche Bildspielbund (German Association for Image Use) was a lobby founded by Walther Günther in 1921 to promote the use of film in schools; in 1924, the organization merged with the Bilderbühnenbund deutscher Städte (roughly, the Film Projection Association of German Cities) to form the Bildspielbund deutscher Städte (roughly, the Image Use Association of German Cities), which advocated for municipal funding for non-profit theaters throughout Germany and increasing integration of educational film into classrooms.

36 Eisner covered the third Internationale Lehrfilmkonferenz (International Educational Film Conference), held May 26–31, 1931, for the *Film-Kurier*.

37 The Deutsche Bildwoche were yearly conferences at which educators met to discuss the use of film in classrooms and educational film policy.

38 Filmmaker Werner Völger succeeded Felix Lampe in 1931 as head of the Bildstelle des Zentralinstitut für Erziehung und Unterricht vom Preußischen Kultusministerum (roughly, the Image and Film Library of the Central Institute for Education and Teaching within the Prussian Ministry of Culture).

Edited by Eszter Zimanyi and Emma Ben Ayoun

IN FOCUS

Humanitarian Immersions

Eszter Zimanyi and Emma Ben Ayoun

Introduction

Since the mid-2010s, humanitarian organizations, journalists, and artists have increasingly been turning to virtual reality (VR) and immersive filmmaking for its ostensibly unprecedented ability to conjure empathic feelings that lead to humanitarian action.[1] Technology companies and charitable institutions alike have touted immersive storytelling's "potential for good"; prominent examples include the United Nations High Commissioner for Refugees virtual reality program, UNICEF's Augmented Reality/Virtual Reality for Good initiative, and Oculus's VR for Good project.[2] These initiatives emphasize the power of immersive media in a variety of instructive contexts, including medical training and diagnostics, physical and psychological therapy, interactive historical education modules, and philanthropic fundraising for humanitarian causes.[3]

Scholars including Kate Nash, Mandy Rose, and Sasha Crawford-Holland have attended to the possibilities and pitfalls of experiments in immersive media within the context of documentary filmmaking; however, these analy-

1 In this dossier, immersive filmmaking refers not only to 360-degree virtual reality films viewed through a headset but also to media projects that require participants to make decisions in order to advance a narrative and to films that create immersive sensations through their (often extended) duration.

2 See "Augmented Reality/Virtual Reality for Good," UNICEF, accessed September 15, 2021, https://www.unicef.org/innovation/XR; and "VR for Good," Oculus, accessed September 15, 2021, https://www.oculus.com/vr-for-good.

3 Taking just the Oculus VR for Good initiative as an example, as of September 22, 2021, recent updates under the "Stories" section of the initiative's website include "VR for Safety—Mine rescue teams discover a new tool for training," "VR for the E.R.—Preparing for emergencies before they happen," "VR for Heritage—A tribal past finds its future," and "VR for Action—Travelling While Black explores black America past and present." See "VR for Safety," https://www.oculus.com/vr-for-good/stories/mine-rescue-teams-discover-a-new-tool-for-training/; "VR for the E.R.," https://www.oculus.com/vr-for-good/stories/preparing-for-emergencies-before-they-happen/; "VR for Heritage," https://www.oculus.com/vr-for-good/stories/a-tribal-past-finds-its-future/; and "VR for Action," https://www.oculus.com/vr-for-good/stories/traveling-while-black-explores-black-america-past-and-present/; all accessed September 22, 2021.

Eszter Zimanyi and Emma Ben Ayoun, "Introduction," *JCMS* 61, no. 3 (Spring 2022): 154–159.

ses primarily focus on immersive media's visual components.[4] In the context of VR filmmaking, scholars such as Adam Daniel, Sarah Jones, and Steve Dawkins have drawn attention to the spectator's ability to enact a sovereign gaze within 360-degree spherical images, leaving other bodily sensations un(der)accounted for.[5] Although immersive nonfiction media depends in part on the believability of virtual environments, the fantasies at play in immersive media—which attempt to make viewers feel that they have participated in something real—are not only about creating convincing ocular illusions. They are also about generating persuasive haptic sensations and legible bodily responses from viewers. As such, the embodied experience of engaging with and navigating these environments demands sustained attention from media scholars studying immersive nonfiction. This is especially pertinent within the context of humanitarian media, which aims to inspire direct action from viewers and to foment wide-scale social change. What political and ethical concerns arise when rendering humanitarian crises not merely visible but also *tangible* for public consumption?[6]

In recent years, industry specialists, journalists, and early adopters of VR have heralded VR filmmaking as an unparalleled breakthrough in narrative storytelling, overshadowing an important element of its lineage: nonfiction media's long history of experimentation with interactivity and immersion.[7] In the context of traditional cinema spectatorship, *immersion* has traditionally been defined as the loss of one's self to the narrative; however, Alison Griffiths defines immersion as "the sensation of entering a

4 See Kate Nash, "Virtual Reality Witness: Exploring the Ethics of Mediated Presence," *Studies in Documentary Film* 12, no. 2 (2018): 119–131, https://doi.org/10.1080/17503280.2017.1340796. See also Mandy Rose, "The Immersive Turn: Hype and Hope in the Emergence of Virtual Reality as a Nonfiction Platform," *Studies in Documentary Film* 12, no. 2 (2018): 132–149, https://doi.org/10.1080/17503280.2018.1496055; and Sasha Crawford-Holland, "Humanitarian VR Documentary and Its Cinematic Myths," *Synoptique* 7, no. 1 (2018): 19–31.

5 Adam Daniel, "Inhabiting the Image of *Collisions*: Virtual Reality Cinema as a Medium of Ethical Experience," *fusion journal* 14 (2018): 6–15; and Sarah Jones and Steve Dawkins, "Walking in Someone Else's Shoes: Creating Empathy in the Practice of Immersive Film," *Media Practice and Education* 19, no. 3 (2018): 298–312, https://doi.org/10.1080/25741136.2018.1520538.

6 Lisa Nakamura has argued that, due in no small part to the limited demographics of VR's target audiences, users, and developers, VR regularly offers "common gendered fantasies of empowerment that rely upon mastery and subjugation of virtual non-male, non-white bodies and space." The problems inherent in mediated simulations (and representations) of bodily difference and suffering are, of course, not exclusive to VR technologies, but as Nakamura reminds us, "VR 2.0 titles about refugees and other objects of pathos that situate the viewer outside the point of view of a foreign body invite the user to confuse immersive viewing with access to the actual experience of an-other." In this dossier, we extend her arguments toward questions of the relationship between immersivity, embodiment, and control. See Lisa Nakamura, "Feeling Good about Feeling Bad: Virtuous Virtual Reality and the Automation of Racial Empathy," *Journal of Visual Culture* 19, no. 1 (2020): 47–64.

7 See, for example, Chris Milk, "How Virtual Reality Can Create the Ultimate Empathy Machine," TED, March 2015, https://www.ted.com/talks/chris_milk_how_virtual_reality_can_create_the_ultimate_empathy_machine; Mark Anderson, "Can Tear-jerker Virtual Reality Movies Tempt Donors to Give More Aid?," *The Guardian*, December 31, 2015, https://www.theguardian.com/global-development/2015/dec/31/virtual-reality-movies-aid-humanitarian-assistance-united-nations; and Paul Darvasi, "Five Ethical Considerations for Using Virtual Reality with Children and Adolescents," KQED, August 17, 2016, https://www.kqed.org/mindshift/46103/five-ethical-considerations-for-using-virtual-reality-with-children-and-adolescents.

space that immediately identifies itself as somehow separate from the world and that eschews conventional modes of spectatorship in favor of a more bodily participation in the experience."[8] Following Griffiths's attention to bodily participation, we conceptualize nonfiction, humanitarian immersive media as media that makes a documentary claim to the real while seeking to directly mobilize spectators' bodies through the use of interactive and engrossing tactics.[9] Throughout this introduction, we consciously engage the language used in promotional materials and interviews by the creators of many of these works—language that is often steeped in histories of exclusion and a very abstracted, and limited, understanding of VR's typical viewer. The fact that the majority of VR exhibition takes place in broadly inaccessible spaces—such as museums and festivals—means that the audiences who get to experience these works are imagined to be not only able-bodied but also correspondingly privileged in their modes of access to new technologies and artistic works.

We define *humanitarian media* broadly to include projects engaged with both human and environmental concerns; likewise, our conception of nonfiction media includes contemporary digital projects that use personal testimonies and statistical data to ground their virtual representations of real-world characters and locations. Through this framework, our dossier re-centers and historicizes embodiment across maps, gallery installations, interactive web-based projects, and contemporary VR filmmaking in order to ask how immersive nonfiction media engage, discipline, destabilize, and erase the spectatorial body. What types of humanitarian responses can nonfiction media provoke when viewers are tasked with mastering (virtual) spaces through a mastery of their own bodies?

The ethical implications of immersive nonfiction media, particularly virtual reality, have received a great deal of attention in recent years, both within media studies and beyond. In a 2018 special issue of *Studies in Documentary Film*, Jamie McRoberts, Kate Nash, Miriam Ross and Alfio Leotta, Mandy Rose, and Kim Munro considered, respectively, virtual reality's ability to invoke "sense of presence," its relationship to practices of witnessing and tourism, and the ways it has been marketed and distributed as a vitally *new* technology, a tool for generating empathy, and a representative of a particular kind of hope for the future.[10] Legal scholars such as Woodrow Hartzog and Frederic Stutzman have also examined the ways that existing social values are built into new technologies as well as the troubled (ethical and

8 Alison Griffiths, *Shivers Down Your Spine: Cinema, Museums, and the Immersive View* (New York: Columbia University Press, 2008), 2.

9 While documentary scholarship has largely shifted toward analyses of subjectivity, reflexivity, and hybridity in nonfiction media, we emphasize a "claim to the real" here because contemporary VR and immersive media projects often insist on their indexical relationships to the physical world in order to market themselves as nonfiction, even when they are created entirely through computer-generated imagery. We elaborate this point further in our essay "On Bodily Absence in Humanitarian Multisensory VR," *Intermédialités: Histoire et théorie des arts, des lettres et des techniques (Intermediality: History and Theory of the Arts, Literature and Technologies)*, no. 34 (Autumn 2019): 1–28.

10 See Kate Nash, ed., "Virtually Real: Exploring VR Documentary," special issue, *Studies in Documentary Film* 12, no. 2 (2018).

political) boundaries between virtual and real worlds.[11] Media psychologists and internet researchers have also considered the degree to which immersive technologies can influence a user's sense of embodiment and subjectivity and, more recently, how these changes might cause shifts not only in immediate behaviors but also in longer-term social attitudes.[12] Across each of these inquiries, researchers ask what is ultimately a habitual set of questions that accompany innovations in media form: What hegemonic legacies remain, and what possibilities—for the transmission of information, for the mediation of human relations—might be newly available?

This In Focus dossier works to move beyond the discourses of empathy and witnessing that have dominated scholarly, popular, and humanitarian approaches to immersive media. We consider the historical lineages that have led to the contemporary "humanitarian VR" movement in order to better understand how and why VR is often celebrated as an exceptional or singular empathy machine.

Through a range of international case studies, both historical and contemporary, our contributors examine the fraught relationship between embodiment, trauma, truth claims, and knowledge production within nonfiction and documentary forms. Their essays consider not only how attempts to cultivate immersivity and interactivity have long been a part of humanitarian nonfiction media-making but also how these media objects elicit particular performances of humanitarianism and (re)construct ideal viewers as well as ideal citizens. They further consider the potentially productive political and ethical engagements with humanitarian questions that can emerge from cultivating embodied knowledge instead of, or in tandem with, visual evidence.

The dossier opens with two case studies that historically and politically situate experiments in immersive humanitarian documentaries. In "Modern Time: Abbas Kiarostami's Immersions, from Sponsored Documentary to Slow Cinema," Simran Bhalla traces connections between immersivity and humanitarian aims to a set of Abbas Kiarostami's early state-sponsored documentaries, which encourage bodily self-discipline as a form of civic behavior—behavior that, in turn, is framed as a humanitarian endeavor. Bhalla then examines Kiarostami's posthumous film, *24 Frames* (2017), to argue that Kiarostami's independent work, while significantly more abstract and experimental, continues to demand bodily management from spectators through its immersive tactics. By considering the relationship between pedagogical/state media, gallery installations, and theories of immersion, Bhalla shows that both Kiarostami's educational-institutional and independent films reorient the viewer's relationship to time through duration and repetition, demonstrating how nonfiction films attempted to cultivate immersion long before VR technology became accessible to the public.

Alison Griffiths's essay, "Virtual Reality and the Cartographic Imagination,"

11 Woodrow Hartzog and Frederic Stutzman, "Obscurity by Design," *Washington Law Review* 88, no. 2 (2013): 385–418.

12 See James J. Cummings and Jeremy N. Bailenson, "How Immersive Is Enough? A Meta-Analysis of the Effect of Immersive Technology on User Presence," *Media Psychology* 19, no. 2 (2016): 272–309; and Mila Bujić, Mikko Salminen, Joseph Macey, and Juho Hamari, "'Empathy Machine': How Virtual Reality Affects Human Rights Attitudes," *Internet Research* 30, no. 5 (2020): 1407–1425.

explores the shared aesthetics of, and enduring tropes across, medieval cartography and contemporary ethnographic VR filmmaking. She contends that, much like VR, medieval maps served as vessels for humanitarian and civilizing discourses, encouraged bodily intervention, and invited the viewer into a relation with the world that, while alluring, necessarily relegated the images and communities being represented to a symbolic space—the space of otherness. Griffiths argues that neither representational mode can make claims to objectivity or heightened empathy; by prioritizing the spectator's interactions and identifications, these technologies work in the service of an imperialist logic that aims above all to transform the world into a visible and knowable entity.

We then move into two provocations on contemporary humanitarian immersive media. In "War and Humanitarian Aesthetics: Notes on Modular Immersion," Christian Rossipal presents a series of case studies in which humanitarian and military organizations, most notably the Red Cross and the United States Army, developed immersive media projects to raise awareness about the horrors of warfare, treat post-traumatic stress disorder in army veterans, train personnel, and improve the mental well-being of Syrian refugees, among other goals. Across all of these projects, he argues, VR's immersive quality, and more specifically its ability to engage the spectatorial body on a pre-linguistic and non-representational level, is what makes it at once exceptionally effective and exceptionally dangerous. Rossipal's essay reveals the extent to which, under neoliberal governance, the binary distinction between peacekeeping and militarizing discourses is a false one; indeed, he reveals immersive media to be a particularly salient site for their convergence.

In our essay, we analyze the web-based interactive documentary *Migration Trail* (Alison Killing, 2017) to consider how the project's real-time narrative, which unfolds over the course of ten days, attunes viewers' bodies to the temporalities of irregular migration journeys. Thinking against the frameworks of urgency and immediacy that pervade humanitarian nonfiction media, we explore what possibilities *Migration Trail* offers through slowness. Whereas the humanitarian immersive media described by Rossipal plunges the viewer into a virtual environment where intervention is a primary aim, *Migration Trail* denies its users the ability to participate in its narrative in any direct or meaningful way. We explore the ways in which the project invokes the shifting sensations of waiting and uncertainty experienced by both migrants and the community members from whom they are separated to consider the recuperative possibilities of humanitarian immersive nonfiction media.

Closing out the dossier is an interview with multidisciplinary artist and educator Aggie Ebrahimi Bazaz. Her films and installations engage narratively with questions of citizenship, identity, and social justice and in many ways operate within a humanitarian framework. However, Bazaz experiments with form in order to work against those documentary conventions that reinforce existing social hierarchies. Bazaz details her working process, in particular her interest in co-creation and what she terms "critical reflexivity" as well as the ways that she situates her own work within documentary theory.[13]

13 See Aggie Ebrahimi Bazaz and Liz Miller, "Invited and Implicated: Toward Critical Reflexivity in Non-fiction VR," *Digital Radical*, Center on Digital Culture and Society,

In exploring spectatorial embodiment in immersive media alongside documentary's history of bodily engagement, we hope to foster a generative, multidisciplinary conversation that extends existing discourses about nonfiction media's role in not only cohering humanitarian subjectivities but also training—or mobilizing—bodies for action. The essays contained herein provoke exciting encounters across different historical and national contexts, media forms, and theoretical approaches. What they share is a commitment to interrogating the ways we both live inside our technologies and are continuously transformed by them.[14]

Eszter Zimanyi is a postdoctoral fellow in cinema and media studies at the University of Southern California. She has published in *Feminist Media Studies*, *Visual Anthropology*, and *Media Fields Journal*, among others. Her research interests include migration and refugee studies, global media, and documentary.

Emma Ben Ayoun is a PhD candidate in cinema and media studies at the University of Southern California. Her dissertation, titled "Sick Cinema: Disability, Disease and the Moving Image," works at the interstices of film theory, disability studies, and visual studies.

University of Pennsylvania Annenberg School of Communication, June 18, 2020, https://www.asc.upenn.edu/research/centers/center-on-digital-culture-and-society/the-digital-radical/Invited-and-Implicated.

14 The impetus for this dossier grew from the 2019 Society for Cinema and Media Studies panel we co-organized on "Embodying the Humanitarian in Immersive Documentary and VR." We are incredibly grateful to our panelists Pooja Rangan, Juan Llamas-Rodriguez, and Marit Kathryn Corneil for engaging with our ideas and inspiring new ones.

Simran Bhalla

Modern Time: Abbas Kiarostami's Immersions, from Sponsored Documentary to Slow Cinema

Abbas Kiarostami's educational film, *Beh tartib ya bedoun-e tartib* (*Orderly or Disorderly*, 1981), features four sequences of Tehran's citizens engaging in quotidian activities. In the first, a group of schoolboys descends the stairs to the schoolyard after class. In the second, they line up to drink water from the school water fountain. In the third, they board the school bus. The fourth sequence focuses on drivers negotiating a busy Tehran cross street. For each activity, we see how city life proceeds if citizens are orderly or disorderly. The orderly version of doing things saves everyone time, whereas in the disorderly versions, no one is able to complete their duties. This sense of time loss is experienced by the audience, who see the results of activities completed in an orderly fashion but are left waiting by disorderly citizens who fail to realize their goals.

Beh tartib ya bedoun-e tartib is one of many films Kiarostami made for Kanoon, or the Iranian Center for the Intellectual Development of Children and Young Adults, the government organization that employed him for several years before he became an independent filmmaker. These non-profit films were made to encourage and, indeed, model good citizenship. This essay examines Kiarostami's state-sponsored instructional documentaries as pre-digital examples of pedagogical media that animate modes of bodily

Simran Bhalla, "Modern Time: Abbas Kiarostami's Immersions, from Sponsored Documentary to Slow Cinema," *JCMS* 61, no. 3 (Spring 2022): 160–166.

conduct, in service of purportedly humanitarian or civic goals. I argue that Kiarostami's use of a time-based, and time-bound, medium's immersive potential aided viewers in their bodily adaptations to new temporal conditions. This history also contextualizes Abbas Kiarostami's immersive use of duration in later independent films, such as *24 Frames* (2017).

Many of the sponsored films were produced before the Islamic Revolution of 1978–79, when Iran was still a constitutional monarchy ruled by Mohammad Reza Pahlavi. His wife, Farah Pahlavi, founded Kanoon. The Pahlavi regime's concerted interest in modernization is evident in the lessons and aesthetics of their state-sponsored films. Scholars of colonialism and documentary such as Peter J. Bloom argue that photorealistic imagery of social and public health problems, particularly ones perceived to originate in unmodern practices, helped to justify colonial interventions on a humanitarian basis. Such images link caring citizenship at home with civilizing missions and methods abroad.[1] Here I propose that developing nation-states such as Iran likewise configured their state-sponsored educational films in terms of their humanitarian purpose, by tying citizens' bodily conduct to their own good health and well-being. Indeed, the Shah of Iran writes in his autobiography that films help communicate scientific and medical knowledge to the masses, demonstrating "new ways for helping ordinary people everywhere."[2]

Institutional media pedagogy also has a long relationship to theories of immersion. Museums construct immersive exhibitions and project educational IMAX films, militaries use virtual reality programs for training, and interactive digital projects aim to educate participants about histories and communities.[3] Immersion as a pedagogical and epistemological method is also foundational in anthropology and ethnographic research. In anthropology, *immersion* has historically referred to a researcher's ability to absorb themselves in the field linguistically, socially, and professionally as a participant-observer in order to deepen their knowledge and perspective of the subject being studied. Anthropologists such as Margaret Mead popularized this method of cultural learning—of living with the subject, in one sense or another—which now informs some modes of *immersion* in media pedagogy.[4]

Immersive pedagogical modes rely on duration, repetition, and the temporality of embodied activities. The instructional films I focus on here, *Do rah-e hal baraye yek massaleh* (*Two Solutions for One Problem*, 1975) and *Beh tartib ya bedoun-e tartib* (both directed by Abbas Kiarostami), also engage in repetition and the evocation of "real time" to communicate various forms of bodily conduct to their audiences. They do so by demonstrating the full duration,

1 See Peter J. Bloom, *French Colonial Documentary: Mythologies of Humanitarianism* (Minneapolis: University of Minnesota Press, 2008).

2 Mohammad Reza Pahlavi, *Mission for My Country* (London: Hutchinson, 1961), 168.

3 See Alison Griffiths, *Shivers Down Your Spine: Cinema, Museums, and the Immersive View* (New York: Columbia University Press, 2008); Sasha Crawford-Holland, "Virtual Healing: Militarizing the Psyche in Virtual Reality Exposure Therapy," *Television & New Media* 20, no. 1 (2019): 56–71; and research projects such as Kristy H. A. Kang, *City Stories: Mapping the Spatial Narratives of Singapore's Landscapes*, http://citystories.sg.

4 Minette Hillyer, "Camera Documents Made at Home: Visual Culture and the Question of America," *Film History* 27, no. 4 (2015): 46–75.

or every necessary step, of various activities. In doing so, they also reveal how individual bodily movements impact groups and environments.

In using formal structure to emphasize temporality, these films share an impulse with another genre of film: slow cinema. Scholars have also identified other immersive qualities in slow cinema's contemplative long takes and static shots, enveloping soundscapes, and hapticity. They claim that these qualities can generate intimacy and that their meditative nature creates its own mode of heightened engagement.[5] Works of slow cinema often feature sequences that mimic the temporality of everyday life or present duration in ways that invite viewers to feel the passing of time. Hence Matilda Mroz draws on Henri Bergson's writing on duration as something materially experienced to argue that the immersive nature of Lucile Hadžihalilović's *Innocence* (2004) is based on its evocation of how its characters experience time. Similarly, Kiarostami's films depict the "protracted, lived duration" that Mroz contends is immersive.[6]

Salomé Aguilera Skvirsky advances the idea that media representing labor might be considered immersive. While Skvirsky more commonly uses the term *absorption*, she does not find meaningful distinction between the two terms as regards the viewer's experience. She writes that *absorption* represents "what I take to be a common experience of immersion when one is faced with processual representation."[7] Repetitious tasks and sequences are also prominent in works of slow cinema, such as films by Chantal Akerman and Béla Tarr. These, too, rely on creating "rhythms" or temporalities in order to absorb the viewer.

These theories of slow cinema and process media—which can share durational and demonstrative qualities—should together inform our reading of Kiarostami's early nonfiction films. The films include processual elements and depict how individuals or groups experience time while engaging in daily activities in order to communicate time to the audience. Indeed, all Kiarostami's films take pleasure in the details of both local environments and manual activities, often evoking what Skvirsky terms "kinesthetic identification," or empathy in the spectator.[8] Below, I demonstrate that the historical and industrial contexts in which Kiarostami worked are central to understanding how his films engage these identificatory modes of spectatorship.

State-sponsored films in developing nations often addressed anxieties about modernity, both implicitly and explicitly, and provided pedagogies for being modern and adjusting to new material realities. This frequently centered on new forms of public self-discipline, mostly concerning bodily control. One such important tool for modern conduct was time management. As the historian Cyrus Schayegh argues, in early- to mid-twentieth-century Iran, time had been "transformed into a commodity, to be filled with activity . . .

5 See Tiago de Luca and Nuno Barradas Jorge, "Introduction: From Slow Cinema to Slow Cinemas," in *Slow Cinema*, ed. Tiago de Luca and Nuno Barradas Jorge (Edinburgh: Edinburgh University Press, 2015).

6 Matilda Mroz, "Performing Evolution: Immersion, Unfolding and Lucile Hadžihalilović's *Innocence*," in de Luca and Jorge, *Slow Cinema*, 292.

7 Salomé Aguilera Skvirsky, *The Process Genre: Cinema and the Aesthetic of Labor* (Durham, NC: Duke University Press, 2020), 30 (emphasis mine).

8 Skvirsky, 41.

Traditional life, with its protracted conversations, breaks, delays, and slow motion, seemed out of tune with the exigencies of the new age."[9] Time management was important for new modes of transport, such as cars, trains, and buses; communication modes, such as the telephone; and work, as labor and education hours became increasingly regulated. Urban leisure activities—such as moviegoing—also relied on the ability to manage one's time. If time was well-organized, then both work and leisure would be productive.

Kiarostami's Kanoon films echoed popular social ideas in Iran concerning children's moral education, which themselves had emerged from mid-twentieth-century psychological discourses. By this period, psychology had become a popular medical field in Iran, utilizing specialized scientific understanding of human behavior both to address newly identified nervous disorders and the social problems they might engender as well as to provide advice to citizens on how to cope with new anxieties. Iranian psychological thought incorporated and reconciled ideas both from modern Western psychology and Iranian philosophy.

The Iranian psychological tradition that developed focused primarily on the qualities of willpower and attention. These discourses extended to parental instruction. Schayegh observes, "Authors stressed children's special psychological condition, examined the role played by instincts and willpower, and debated how the need for children's discipline could be harmonized with their willpower, that is, the associated freedom of action and independent personality."[10] Writers of psychological texts considered both schools and parents responsible for *parvaresh*, or the moral education of children. Kanoon, which had cultural centers throughout the country (including mobile libraries and cinemas), provided a space for parents to educate their children in moral and civic values. In addition to films, the center also produced books, tapes, and theater. Frequently, state-sponsored films integrated scientific knowledge with values of will and self-reliance, for example, instructing children about hygiene, wellness, and even sex education. Some Kanoon films, such as Kiarostami's film *Dandan dard* (*Toothache*, 1980), which concerns dental hygiene, operated in this mode of personal scientific instruction for children. Others focused more broadly on the moderation of moral behavior. These films were often set in schools, which demonstrated how good conduct was also civil conduct and showed how such conduct related to productivity and progress. As Schayegh notes, "Rationalism and reasoned argumentation would benefit pupils, and by extension, society as a whole."[11]

The form of Kiarostami's early short *Do rah-e hal baraye yek massaleh* embodies these communitarian values of logic and rationalism. Kiarostami's focus on action and reaction development models efficiency and economy through form, while the use of a scoreboard as a visual device emphasizes a mathematical understanding of behavior. In the film, Dara, a schoolboy, borrows a textbook from his friend Nader. When he returns it, the cover

9 Cyrus Schayegh, *Who Is Knowledgeable Is Strong: Science, Class, and the Formation of Modern Iranian Society, 1900–1950* (Los Angeles: University of California Press, 2009), 99.

10 Schayegh, 172.

11 Schayegh, 38.

is torn. In the first "solution," Nader takes revenge by tearing the cover of a book belonging to Dara, who in turn snaps Nader's pencil, and a cycle of serial property destruction ensues. The visual presentation of Dara and Nader's conflict is schematic. Each action takes place in one shot, filmed in medium close-up, with a corresponding reaction shot. The reaction shots draw attention to the boys' increasing agita; viewers can even observe their breaths becoming shorter and faster.

Meanwhile, an animated sequence shows viewers a tally of these offenses on a chalkboard. A disembodied hand writes each infraction on the chalkboard, suggesting an omniscient impartiality.[12] Finally, the film presents the second scenario, in which Dara notices that he has torn Nader's textbook and mends it with glue. The presentation is almost identical until the children resolve their problem and play outside. Here Kiarostami uses a wide establishing aerial shot to show viewers the dozens of schoolboys playing on the basketball court. He then cuts to Dara and Nader, situating them as part of a larger community in which they are participants and emphasizing their social responsibility.

In the first "solution," the film demonstrates the consequences of their disregard for each other's personal property (and, by extension, for each other's work). Not only is property destroyed, but things also devolve into a physical fight, and both boys are injured. In the second "solution," the film ends with the boys playing on the school's outdoor court with the rest of their peers. It clearly demonstrates the value of self-directed responsibility for oneself and to others and presents isolation as the consequence of antisocial behavior.

Skvirsky compiles viewer reactions to process media (focusing, in her initial example, on educational films), which register this media as immersive. She writes that "process narration," which involves elements of steps and repetition structured by narrative, is responsible for this sense of immersion. *Do rah-e hal baraye yek massaleh* was one of several of Kiarostami's instructional films to operate in the mode of permutations. These conclude, as with the examples Skvirsky provides, in narrative closure, as the viewer's curiosity is sustained through the result of an often recognizable set of actions.[13]

Beh tartib ya bedoun-e tartib presents a mediated version of this narrative form in which the director uses a clapperboard to signal new permutations of the same scene. These variations include shots of students calmly exiting a room in single file or pushing and shoving one another in an unruly manner. Another variation features a polite queue at the water fountain, in which each child parches their thirst with a full glass, versus an injurious rush in which the tank is knocked over, wasting water. As in *Do rah-e hal baraye yek massaleh*, Kiarostami uses exterior aerial shots to show the impact of individual conduct on a larger group of people, implying the larger

12 Though this film does not explicitly foreground the film technology involved in its production, as other Kanoon documentaries do, the animated sequence nonetheless gestures toward the possibilities of new technologies.

13 *Ghazieh shekl-e aval, Ghazieh shekl-e dovom* (*First Case, Second Case*, Abbas Kiarostami, 1979) expands on the same form—albeit with the inclusion of interviews with authority figures providing their interpretation of good and bad behaviors—though it also deviates from it in order to make a political argument.

social and humanitarian benefits of bodily management.[14] Another pair of scenes feature children boarding a school bus. Here, Kiarostami uses a time counter on screen to track how long it takes for children to board the bus when they are doing so in an organized versus a disorganized manner.[15] The viewer must experience this delay along with the individuals in the film. A shot of the boys rowdily boarding the bus focuses on the physicality of bodies pushing against one another. Their hands tightly grip the door as they strain to enter; they grimace and exclaim as others shove past them. One of the narrating voices comments on how long the disorganized boarding takes, and the other responds, "Well, it's supposed to take time. That's what we're trying to show."[16]

Beh tartib ya bedoun-e tartib provides a useful example to discuss how Kiarostami reflexively depicts the way in which modernity reordered one's visual and sensory environment. The rise of psychology in Iran had accompanied a perceived preponderance of mental health problems. Medical writings from the midcentury argued that "people are unprepared to adapt to the rapid progress of civilization" and that the "confused, noisy, and agitated" social conditions of the modern age were the source of an increase in anxiety and anti-social behaviors.[17] Cinema represented and negotiated the qualities of condensing speed and time that characterized emergent modernity and its discontents.[18]

Each scenario in *Beh tartib ya bedoun-e tartib* targets the individual's ability to understand and manage their body in relation to time—and particularly the economizing technologies of speed and mobility—and their impact on civil society. Kiarostami's later, slow films are freed of the imperative to educate viewers about conduct, yet they retain a similar attention to quotidian activities and their durations. These later films are also imbued with a developmentalist-humanitarian perspective. For example, in *Zendegi va digar hich* (*Life, and Nothing More . . .*, 1992), Kiarostami returns to Koker, Iran, where he made a previous film with local non-actors and which has since been devastated by an earthquake. Kiarostami casts an actor as a version of himself in this semi-fictional film that focuses on details of how real

14 The disembodied voices of the filmmakers reviewing the film reel amplify the aerial shot's connotations as a perspective of surveillance, emphasizing the state-sponsored film's governmentality.

15 Skvirsky invokes Alfred Hitchcock's theory of suspense, in which the example given includes the audience's attention to a clock ticking, their anticipation heightened by knowing that something will happen, or must be done, in a specific time frame.

16 The second half of the film concerns pedestrians at a busy intersection. Orderly scenarios demonstrate how, by obeying the signals of traffic lights, pedestrians can cross the street safely and vehicles can avoid accidents and delay. The film has a comic dénouement, in which the crew calls for an orderly take, but the drivers and pedestrians they are filming do not observe the guidance of stoplights or the traffic policeman. Kiarostami later made another sponsored documentary about traffic management, *Hamshahri* (*Fellow Citizen*, 1983), which focuses on the frustrating and long afternoon of a traffic policeman dealing with drivers who try to negotiate road rules.

17 Schayegh, *Who Is Knowledgeable*, 90.

18 See Leo Charney, "In a Moment: Film and the Philosophy of Modernity," in *Cinema and the Invention of Modern Life*, ed. Leo Charney and Vanessa R. Schwartz (Berkeley: University of California Press, 1996); and Miriam Hansen, "Benjamin, Cinema and Experience: 'The Blue Flower in the Land of Technology,'" *New German Critique*, no. 40 (1987): 179–224.

lives in the region were impacted by the earthquake. In 2001, the United Nations commissioned Kiarostami to film *ABC Africa* (2001), a documentary on an NGO working with Ugandan orphans, in which he appears. Here, he emphasizes the children's perspectives through contemplative camerawork and showcases their resilience through a focus on the persistence of mundane events.

Kiarostami's final (posthumously released) film, *24 Frames*, is certainly his slowest, consisting of twenty-four shots, largely of natural landscapes, each roughly four and a half minutes long. The shots are almost entirely still, with only short flickers of movement. As the critic Bilge Ebiri writes, "Understated and languid, these twenty-four segments . . . may at first feel more like environments than components of a movie."[19]

In reading *24 Frames* alongside Kiarostami's state-sponsored films and documentaries, we can identify a genealogy of his formal strategies and their relationship to embodied spectatorship and immersion, developed over the course of his diverse oeuvre. Although *24 Frames* does not elaborate on specific activities through multiple sequences or have a conventional narrative, it does rely on its audience coming to understand its themes through a firm temporal structure that includes both repetition and references to previous events or images in the film. For example, the first sequence is a gentle animation of Pieter Bruegel the Elder's painting *Jagers in de Sneeuw* (*The Hunters in the Snow*, 1565). Several other sequences feature animals congregating; in a few, gunshots disperse the creatures. The animals are computer animated, at times visibly so, but Kiarostami uses time to make the viewer believe in the environment. Hence they become startled when it is disrupted, from time to time, by unseen human intervention. Much of the film presents a surveillant's view on nature: the camera is concealed and unobtrusive, and the viewer must patiently watch for new details. Where Kiarostami's state-sponsored films work to acculturate the viewer to modern life in Iran, *24 Frames* asks instead that they adapt to the pace of the natural world, viewed from a distance. Instead of training the viewer to be a good citizen, Kiarostami concedes that the filmmaker—who has striven to humanize his subjects through sensitivity to duration and generosity with detail—remains a manipulator of natural time and space.

Simran Bhalla is a visiting assistant professor in communication at Tulane University. Her research interests include institutional films, experimental documentary, and global modernisms. She has published in *Iran Namag* and curated film series on Indian, Iranian, and Arab cinemas.

19 Bilge Ebiri, "*24 Frames*: The World Made Visible," *Current*, January 8, 2019, https://www.criterion.com/current/posts/6132-24-frames-the-world-made-visible. Ebiri also commented on social media that film may be immersive even for nonhuman viewers, capturing how his cat is "mesmerized" and "transfixed" by the film, opening up new avenues for thinking about immersive characteristics of film and other visual media.

Alison Griffiths

Virtual Reality and the Cartographic Imagination

The eye carries men to different parts of the world.
—Leonardo da Vinci[1]

While virtual reality (VR) scholars have not been blind to its aesthetic and spectatorial affinities across large-scale painting, panoramas, dioramas, stereoscopy, globes, cinema, IMAX, and 3D video, less attention has been paid to the influence of cartographic techniques from the medieval and early modern era of geographic exploration.[2] Without denying the obvious phenomenological differences between VR and cartography, cartographic techniques may be considered part of the long dureé of recombinant media that bring the world into visibility, practices of imaginary projection and reconciliation that serve as containers for civilizing and humanitarian discourses. Through the deployment of high-definition 3D cameras to record the world and optical technologies and data systems to reassemble it for users, VR draws meaning and is haunted by much earlier cartographic practices that interpellate users into subject positions that resonate in uncanny ways with medieval cartography. As liminal, multilayered, and disjunctive artifacts of the real and the imagination, medieval maps and humanitarian VR are discursive allies, trafficking in forms of embodied seeing, virtuality, and presence that

1 Leonardo da Vinci, cited in Samuel Y. Edgerton Jr., *The Renaissance Discovery of Linear Perspective* (New York: Basic Books, 1975), 92.

2 Alfio Leotta and Miriam Ross, "Touring the 'World Picture': Virtual Reality and the Tourist Gaze," *Studies in Documentary Film* 12, no. 2 (2018): 151. For introductions to VR, see Oliver Grau, *Virtual Art: From Illusion to Immersion* (Cambridge, MA: MIT Press, 2002); and Ken Hillis, *Digital Sensations: Space, Identity, and Embodiment in Virtual Reality* (Minneapolis: University of Minnesota Press, 1999). For a useful overview of VR's emergence, see Brooke Belisle and Paul Roquet, "Introduction: Virtual Reality: Immersion and Empathy," *Journal of Visual Culture* 19, no. 1 (2020): 3–10.

Alison Griffiths, "Virtual Reality and the Cartographic Imagination," *JCMS* 61, no. 3 (Spring 2022): 167–175.

allow access to reified worlds from a safe distance. This essay probes some of these correspondences, arguing that while technologies of virtual projection are effective in generating wonder and curiosity about the human condition, this comes at the cost of a deeper intellectual engagement.

Medieval maps were resplendently visual and included vignettes of Indigenous peoples, wildlife, cities, and religious figures; as cartographic scholar John Block Friedman explains, a map was more a "visual work of art and expression of contemporary cosmology and theology than it was an object of utility"—which is to say, a way of imagining the world through a particular mode of humanist and Christological thought.[3] Both medieval maps and VR invite viewers to picture themselves moving through the world, along visual pathways that could be traced with a finger or eye, projecting their bodies into virtual spaces that draw authority as much if not more from the imagination as from cartography or geography. No world map did this better than the *mappa mundi*, a world map that functioned as a metaphoric storage device for all manner of cosmological, religious, and geographical knowledge. *Mappae mundi* represented Latin Christianity as forging inexorably westward from Paradise in the east, to the Apocalypse in the west, a journey through time itself. Densely packed with encyclopedic knowledge and hearsay about what lay at the edges of the world, *mappae mundi* regularized vision, triggering a measure of interactivity through an invitation to touch or—depending on the method of display—walk around or over the map.

Medieval map makers exploited the *idea* of maps as sensual objects for imaginative projection and immersion centuries before VR pioneers envisioned them as a navigable geospatial technology.[4] Similar tropes of reification are deployed in each form: people transformed into pictograms or emblematic images that viewers cannot help but stare at and that invite bodily identification in relation to movement, travel, space, and difference.[5] Portolan charts, mariners' guides identifying coastal ports that also contained information about what lay inland—such as topographic features, tribal leaders, Indigenous people, and wildlife (both real and imagined)—also leveraged meaning from art as well as science. Geographic reality co-

3 John Block Friedman, *The Monstrous Races in Medieval Art and Thought* (1981; repr., Syracuse: Syracuse University Press, 2000), 1, 38.

4 The idea of film creating space for viewers to wander about and act like voyagers is by no means a new endeavor with Tom Conley, Giuliana Bruno, Anne Friedberg, Teresa Castro, Ken Hillis, Brooke Belisle, and others exploring similar questions. Belisle, for example, exposes the paradox of the whole world view in Google Earth VR and precursive worlding technologies such as globes and photographs of the "Blue Planet," while Bruno views cinema and exploration as virtually one and the same, similarly driven by a language of curiosity and a look that sees and seizes. See Giuliana Bruno, *Atlas of Emotion: Journeys in Art, Architecture, and Film* (London: Verso, 2002), 76, 79; and Brooke Belisle, "Whole World within Reach: Google Earth VR," *Journal of Visual Culture* 19, no. 1 (2020): 112–136, https://doi.org/10.1177/1470412920909990. (Belisle guest-edited this special issue on VR with Paul Roquet.) See Tom Conley, *Cartographic Cinema* (Minneapolis: University of Minnesota Press, 2006); Bruno, *Atlas of Emotion*; Anne Friedberg, *Window Shopping: Cinema and the Postmodern* (Berkeley: University of California Press, 1994); and Teresa Castro, *La pensée cartographique des images* [The cartographic thought of images] (Lyon: Aléas Éditeur, 2011).

5 See Thomas Fuchs, "The Virtual Other: Empathy in the Age of Virtuality," *Journal of Consciousness Studies* 21, no. 5–6 (2014): 152–173.

existed with the imagination in *mappae mundi* and portolans; both they and VR invite bodily intervention, whether that be walking around a medieval portolan chart spread out on a ship's map table—in order to read the toponyms and see the world the right side up—or reaching out for a phantom object in the space of VR; and in both we detect a tension between seeing as a source of knowledge and power versus seeing as a locus of disquiet or discombobulation. In VR, for example, the user's ability to absorb geographical information from a unitary subject position is threatened by an anxiety about being swallowed up by the world, while in the case of medieval maps, the user has a sense of dread about what lies at the edge of the map where human oddities, Indigenous people, and Judgment Day reside.

Like VR, medieval maps constructed "a global space for the reader [or viewer] to imagine and inhabit, pre-furnished with unique peoples, places, and things, both wonderful and grotesque, that could serve as nodes of mnemonic retention."[6] Phenomena that could not be fully explained and were widely debated among natural philosophers found a way onto the map; Indigenous peoples whose bodies had adapted in ingenious ways to different climates took up residency on the margins; and real and mythical animals were scattered here and there in images that might have been copied from bestiaries.

In order to explore the subtle ways in which medieval mapmaking foreshadows some of the governing rubrics of humanitarian VR, I compare and contrast an Italian portolan chart completed by Johannes Oliva in 1602 (identified as HM 40) and the *Vallard Atlas* (1547), one of the first world maps to depict the existence of Australia, to the VR experience *Nomads* (Felix & Paul Studios, 2016).[7] *Nomads* consists of three eight- to twelve-minute VR films set among Maasai pastoralists living along the Great Rift Valley in southern Kenya and northern Tanzania; Bajau Laut sea nomads of South East Asia; and pastoral yak herders from the Mongolian Steppes. Even though the *Nomads* trilogy is less explicitly engaged with humanitarian discourses than some other VR works, such as *Clouds Over Sidra* (Gabo Arora and Barry Pousman, 2015), its reference to climate change and Indigenous sovereignty resonates with humanitarian VR.

Oliva's portolan chart of the Mediterranean Sea and surrounding countries brilliantly exemplifies the hybrid and sensual quality of medieval maps; pictogramically dense, with vignettes of cities, banners, figures of sovereigns, and coats of arms, and spread across the northern and western coasts of Africa are depictions of wildlife, including an elephant, lion, and camel ridden by a Tunisian man (as well as mythical creatures such as unicorns; see Figure 1). Geographic accuracy is deemphasized in favor of an accumulative iconography of typicality, a trope that resurfaces in contemporary nonfiction VR. Accuracy of scale matters less than the spatial prominence of regional

6 John Wyatt Greenlee and Anna Fore Waymack, "Thinking Globally: Mandeville, Memory, and Mappaemundi," *Medieval Globe* 4, no. 2 (2018): 71.

7 For a history of portolan charts, see Tony Campbell, "Portolan Charts from the Late Thirteenth Century to 1500," in *The History of Cartography*, vol. 1, *Cartography in Prehistoric, Ancient, and Medieval Europe and the Mediterranean*, ed. J. B. Hartley and David Woodward (Chicago: University of Chicago Press, 1986), https://www.press.uchicago.edu/books/HOC/HOC_V1/Volume1.html.

tribal leaders who, armed with weapons and shields, stand poised to fend off invaders. These figures appear larger than the wildlife, as big or bigger than the cities and often represented as if frozen in action. Similarly, the palm trees and clumps of vegetation sprouting next to the feet of the animals not only unify the space but code it as habitable and capable of supporting a diverse ecosystem.

Toponymic information competes with the visual for our attention in this portolan chart, the pictorial drawing our eye away from the coastal edges toward the open interior, not unlike what we imagine lies beyond VR's entombed dome.[8] Oriented vertically toward the crucifixion at the top of the map, the coastline of the Mediterranean, Western Europe, Scandinavia, Africa, and the Middle East are positioned horizontally, suggesting that either the map or the human body must move in order for one to read the toponyms.[9] This provocation to alter one's body in space around the Oliva map aligns the portolan's embodied mode of spectatorship with VR; not only does it overcome cartography's sensory deficits by alluding to the physical nature of travel, but the visual vignettes entrust the reader's imagination with authoritative agency in the same way that VR makes viewers believe that our projection into the humanitarian space of crisis derives from the indexical power of the image and heightened sense of immersion. This agency is illusionary, though, since both the VR user and map viewer are inoculated from any actual threat, becoming vicarious witnesses to disaster or danger, and in the case of the medieval map that compels its viewers to walk around it, less bodily immersed than bodily *engaged*. The details construct an idea of place drawn more from the cultural imagination—what Helen Jackson calls "the poetics of lived space"—than an instrumentalized charting of the world.[10] Maps and VR are both in the virtual transportation business, exporting "the parlor to the field site and transforming the latter into an open-air museum," to quote C. Nadia Seremetakis.[11] Placing the Latin Christian world at the map's center, embodied by the imagined European spectator, is a intriguing corollary to VR's own omniscient, humanitarian witness. Substitute the parlor for the VR headset, and we have a perfect description of the looking relations of the *Nomads* VR experience.

8 For more on the role and different types of cartographic signs found in medieval maps, see Catherine Delano-Smith, "Cartographic Signs on European Maps and Their Explanation before 1700," *Imago Mundi* 37 (1985): 9–29.

9 According to Richard Pflederer, portolan charts were drawn onto the skin of a sheep (or a cow), the dimensions determined by the size of the animals, typically a meter wide and half as long and wide. The animal's neck, which was retained, provided space for either the author's inscription, the crucifixion, or some other image. Richard Pflederer, "Portolan Charts: Vital Tool of the Age of Discovery," *History Today* 52, no. 5 (May 2002): 20.

10 That being said, the southern European knights and North African tribal leaders with weapons drawn might have supplied the map user with useful intelligence about regional rulers. Helen Jackson, "Embodiment, Meaning, and the Augmented Reality Image," in *Image Embodiment: New Perspectives of the Sensory Turn*, ed. Lars C. Grabbe, Patrick Rupert-Kruse, and Norbert M. Schmitz (Darmstadt, Germany: Büchner-Verlag, 2016), 212.

11 C. Nadia Seremetakis, "The Memory of the Senses: Historical Perception, Commensal Exchange and Modernity," *Visual Anthropology Review* 9, no. 2 (Fall 1993): 13.

Figure 1. Portolan chart detail showing the northern coast of Africa (modern-day Libya, oriented sideways) and pictograms of real and imaginary animals. HM 40, Johannes Oliva, Italy, 1602, parchment, 32 rhumb line network. The Huntington Library, San Marino, California.

With the production values of a *National Geographic* special, the user-friendly human-interest appeal of a Margaret Mead Film Festival selection, and the social justice–based journalism of humanitarian VR, the *Nomads* trilogy exploits virtually every feature in the 360-degree VR toolkit. As a composite experience enlisting the signifying practices and ontological rubrics of cinema, gaming, theatrical performance, journalism, and large-format photographic installations, *Nomads* is exemplary in foregrounding several basic tenets of VR as a site-specific, geo-imaginary phenomenon. First, it constructs an uncanny sense of co-presence, similar to theater's breaking of the fourth wall, although unlike in theater, there's no collective shared experience but rather a pervasive sense of spectator isolation. Despite being stared at for what seems like an eternity at the start of *Maasai* (with no direct address), we stare back as if through the glass of a museum diorama. Stimulated by the heightened sense of the uncanny but unable to dislodge the sensation of being an interloper, we are eager to respond to social cues that invite more meaningful interaction but are unable to move save turn our bodies in endless circles to see what's behind us. Thus, we become so self-conscious of our looking—at least in my experience—that an intruder syndrome sets in, a feeling of having been dropped into another world. But how does this relate to the portolan chart's obviously less visceral sense of immersion?

First and foremost, it's important to recognize that immersion is not an all-or-nothing experience but rather, as Doug Bowman and Ryan McMahan argue, "a combination of many components . . . [along] a multidimensional continuum."[12] Given that presence encompasses such features as perceived social reality and pictorial realism, which are palpable even in such mediated forms of communication as reading a book, users of the HM 40 portolan chart might very well have perceived the bodies of people and wildlife on the surface of a map as an envisioning of what might be found there. As devices for an imaginary projection into virtual space, portolan charts and world atlases trigger something closer to a broad psychological definition of *presence* as "inner presence," akin to how we "sense" characters when reading a novel, rather than the notion of VR as an innately less mediated technology.[13] The logic of staring is also built into the viewing protocols of HM 40, as the reader's eye lands on each of the human figures, studying its pose, gesture, and attitude.

The *Vallard Atlas* is a stunning example of the visualization of geo-ethnographic information in the early modern period, a re-imagining of cartography beyond the limits of toponyms into an entirely new realm of the ethnographic imaginary (Figure 2). In the maps of India, Asia, the Malay Archipelago, and the northern coast of Australia represented in folio 2,

12 Doug A. Bowman and Ryan P. McMahan, "Virtual Reality: How Much Immersion Is Enough?," *Computer* 40, no. 7 (July 2007): 39. For a review of literature on presence and definitions of physical, social, and self-presence, see Kwan Min Lee, "Presence, Explicated," *Communication Theory* 14, no. 1 (February 2004): 27–50, https://doi.org/10.1111/j.1468-2885.2004.tb00302.x.

13 For more on the idea of presence as an evolved neuropsychological process, see Alessandra Gorini et al., "The Role of Immersion and Narrative in Mediated Presence: The Virtual Hospital Experience," *Cyberpsychology, Behavior, and Social Networking* 14, no. 3 (2011): 100, https://doi.org/10.1089/cyber.2010.0100.

Figure 2. *Vallard Atlas*, representing the East Coast of Australia, a disputed continent at the time. Dieppe School, unknown author, 1547. The Huntington Library, San Marino, California.

the lower edge of the map depicts a verdant land and home to Indigenous people who look noticeably different from the Europeans in the western part of Australia in the first folio. In both maps, however, figures of action are juxtaposed with figures in moments of intimacy and relaxation, and distance is connoted via the size of the images. Thus the *Vallard Atlas* elevates mapping as visual spectacle above its utility as geographic survey. The eschewal of cartography's toponymic fixity opens up possibilities for a far more sensory engagement with people qua people; the framing device of the map permits a form of emotional geography, a drawing of the self into space through the unleashing of narrative possibilities. The omniscient gaze of the map's spectator is transubstantiated for a different kind of spectatorial experience in which the user has control over the object and can choose if and when to look at another map.

The crucial question here is whether being immersed in a non-real space, cartographic or technologically mediated, helps us better appreciate cultural difference and humanitarian plight or whether presence, immersion's visceral penumbra, is so compelling that our sense of wonder or shock in the case of human suffering in humanitarian VR leaves little space for intellectualization of root causes. Courtney Baker's counter-model of "humane insight" is a useful rejoinder to the empathy machine ballyhoo surrounding humanitarian VR. Baker defines this insight as a look that explicitly acknowledges the humanity of the person being looked at rather than simply gazing at them as humanity spectacularized. Regarding race and the ethics of the gaze, Baker argues that looking is always an active gesture and that humanity can never be imagined in some absolutist sense, neither visually nor verbally. Her work challenges us to think about the history of cartography and VR as opportunities for self-monitoring our feelings, for being mindful of our reactions to the hyperbole around VR as a so-called compassionate technology.[14] Similarly, media theorist Roger Silverstone's theory of "proper distance" interrogates how mediation produces attitudes of belief and ethical awareness in the representation of humanitarianism. Silverstone thus brings a much-needed critical lens to VR's polyvalent mode of address and, by extension, the history of cartography.[15]

The creators of medieval portolan charts and atlases were experimenting with cartographic form in ways that evoke contemporary debates about VR as a nonfiction storytelling device. But whereas the fate of the portolan chart was sealed once use value trumped decorative figuration, VR developers are still trying to locate its killer app. Following *National Geographic*'s visual rhetoric, they venture into the realms of expedition cinema, photojournalism, and humanitarian video, terrain that, while relatively novel for the medium, has a

14 Courtney R. Baker, *Humane Insight: Looking at Images of African American Suffering and Death* (Champaign: University of Illinois Press, 2015), 5, 8–9; for more on the empathy debate and VR, see Lisa Nakamura, "Feeling Good about Feeling Bad: Virtuous Virtual Reality and the Automation of Racial Empathy," *Journal of Visual Culture* 19, no. 1 (2020): 47–64, https://doi.org/10.1177/1470412920906259.

15 Roger Silverstone, "Proper Distance: Towards an Ethics for Cyberspace," in *Digital Media Revisited: Theoretical and Conceptual Innovations in Digital Domains*, ed. Gunnar Liestøl, Andrew Morrison, and Terje Rasmussen (Cambridge, MA: MIT Press, 2003), 469–490.

fascinating history in medieval cartography. The embodied viewing protocols of medieval *mappae mundi* and portolan charts tie these hybrid cartographic experiences to humanitarian VR in fascinating ways, through a shared philosophical interest in projecting the reader or viewer into the geographic lifeworlds of Others.

Alison Griffiths is distinguished professor of film and media studies at Baruch College, City University of New York, and the Graduate Center. Griffiths's fourth book, *Nomadic Cinema: A Cultural Geography of the Expedition Film*, will be published by Columbia University Press.

Christian Rossipal

War and Humanitarian Aesthetics: Notes on Modular Immersion

In 2009, Swiss ex-artillery officer Christian Rouffaer, working for the International Committee of the Red Cross (ICRC), was tasked with documenting war crimes committed in video games, in a research project called "Playing by the Rules."[1] Rouffaer found that human rights law was frequently violated in games such as *Call of Duty* (Infinity Ward, 2003). This discovery was mocked in the press, with reporters declaring that the Red Cross was out to incite moral panic, could not distinguish between fiction and reality, and had "virtually lost the plot."[2] Bad press aside, the outcome of this rather bizarre episode is interesting if we consider how virtual reality (VR) and so-called gamification would later become key to the organization's media strategy, which lets us examine the convergence of humanitarian governance and immersive media.

To shift the sudden media attention to their favor and reach new target groups, the ICRC collaborated with Bohemia Interactive on the first-person shooter game *Arma 3* (2013), which simulates infantry warfare taking place in the near future on the islands of the Aegean Sea. The collaboration generated a new add-on for the game *Laws of War* (Bohemia Interactive, 2017), in which the player takes on the role of an international humanitarian aid worker instead of a soldier. Working for the fictional ICRC surrogate "Inter-

1 Charlie Hall, "How the International Red Cross Turned a PR Disaster into DLC," *Polygon*, September 19, 2017, https://www.polygon.com/2017/9/19/16330216/international-red-cross-pr-disaster-arma-3-laws-of-war-dlc.

2 Chris Berg, "How the Red Cross Virtually Lost the Plot," *Sydney Morning Herald*, December 18, 2011, https://www.smh.com.au/politics/federal/how-the-red-cross-virtually-lost-the-plot-20111217-1p05x.html.

Christian Rossipal, "War and Humanitarian Aesthetics: Notes on Modular Immersion," *JCMS* 61, no. 3 (Spring 2022): 176–182.

national Development and Aid Project," the player is tasked with clearing mines and cluster munition in the aftermath of a bombing campaign. The goal, according to the collaborators, is to foster a better understanding of international humanitarian law (IHL).

Bohemia Interactive is currently licensing a military-grade version of the underlying *Arma* game engine for VR training in the US Army and other military organizations around the world, where immersive media are widely used for training before deployment and to treat soldiers after they return (e.g., for post-traumatic stress disorder).[3] As Pasi Väliaho puts it, such military training and treatment function as a "merger between computer-generated imagery, biological psychology and the management of affectivity and memory, based on the foundational idea that affective responses and behavioral patterns are interiorized in the organism's neurophysiological circuits."[4] Väliaho further explains that military immersive media have less to do with embodiment or emotional responses on an individual level than with biopolitical governance on a collective level. In other words, the military's primary investment in immersive media is not curing individual soldiers of their trauma but rather managing how affective and behavioral patterns are distributed across a population. As we will see, immersive media from humanitarian organizations operate within this biopolitical domain too.

In 2018, the ICRC turned to immersive media for fundraising and advocacy, hoping to raise awareness and build empathy. To date, two immersive works funded by the ICRC have been released for download on mobile app stores: the interactive VR short film *The Right Choice* (Avril Furness, 2018) and the augmented reality (AR) app *Enter the Room* (Nedd, 2018). Based on the ICRC report on urban warfare, "'I Saw My City Die': Voices from the Front Lines of Urban Conflict in Iraq, Syria and Yemen," *Enter the Room* transforms the user's cell phone into a kind of portal: a three-dimensional doorway leading into a child's bedroom. Seeing the steady decay of the room and hearing air-raid sirens from outside, the user indirectly gleans the human costs of war.

Whereas *Enter the Room* does not show any humans onscreen and lets its user imagine the horrors of war, *The Right Choice* portrays both people and violence up close. Shot in Beirut using a war-damaged building as a set, the film includes staged but profoundly disturbing imagery. By consulting and casting Syrian refugees now resettled in Beirut, the filmmakers were able to achieve seemingly impeccable attention to detail and realism that is further emphasized through the film's high production value. *The Right Choice* depicts a Syrian family in their home while urban warfare unfolds right outside their building. Specifically, a man sweeps the floor in a ground-level apartment as his wife and their two young kids sit on a rug, doing daily chores. We observe the wife sewing and the children doing their homework until, suddenly, a bullet comes through the window and

3 Charlie Hall, "How the 101st Airborne Trains in Virtual Reality," *Polygon*, October 7, 2014, https://www.polygon.com/2014/10/7/6934741/how-the-101st-airborne-trains-in-virtual-reality.

4 Pasi Väliaho, "Affectivity, Biopolitics and the Virtual Reality of War," *Theory, Culture & Society* 29, no. 2 (March 2012): 66.

into the father's shoulder. The video freezes, and the viewer is asked to click "hide" or "run." If they opt to run, they discover this option is futile. The father collapses, a burst of live rounds penetrates the building, and the family panics and flees into another room. We soon hear gunshots in the distance, and the kids run back to the first room alone, where the VR camera has remained. Their return implies that both parents have been shot. The viewer is able to go back to make a different choice, but the outcome is nonetheless tragic. The piece ends with the statement: "For millions in warzones there is no right choice."

This simple, even banal, message is delivered in a straightforward way, but it is less clear why the ICRC would want to produce a shocking video to underscore such a point. What exactly is the purpose of investing in expensive VR technology and computer-generated imagery, such as glass that shatters in slow motion when the father is shot? Is it because a more conventional documentary image is not, as Susan Sontag puts it, "fearsome enough, and therefore needs to be enhanced; or reenacted more convincingly" to provoke empathy?[5] Christopher Nicholas, the ICRC's project lead on *The Right Choice*, seems to imply that this is indeed the case: "Virtual reality transports viewers from the comfort of their homes to the horrors of the battlefield in a visceral and powerful way. This film asks: What would you do if you came under attack? . . . We wanted to create a short and dramatic experience that was still compelling and realistic. We want people who aren't familiar with urban conflict to get a sense of what it looks and feels like."[6]

The tropes of *visceral*, *powerful*, and *compelling* experience are familiar for those studying the field of contemporary humanitarian aesthetics. The creative agency behind *The Right Choice* uses even more pointed language in their short synopsis: "Many don't realise that those living in conflict-affected cities are left without a choice. So we created a *shocking* VR film, dropping viewers into a home in the middle of a besieged city."[7] The piece is indeed shocking and effective in the sense that it slowly draws viewers in to then catch them off guard with the sudden shot through the window. This approach can be insidious, however, as the shock becomes familiar or wears off. As Sontag notes, even if images continue to shock, "they are not much help if the task is to understand."[8] Instead, they might induce secondary traumatization or "compassion fatigue."[9] While some empirical evidence suggests that shocking immersive media might be effective for fundraising or to temporarily spotlight an issue, Mary Anne Franks convincingly argues that "constant media coverage of human suffering does not provide the hoped-for antidote to human indifference; rather, it entrenches it. . . . Virtual reality not only provides society with the ability to view atrocities in realistic and compel-

5 Susan Sontag, *Regarding the Pain of Others* (London: Penguin, 2004), 82.

6 "War at the Front Door: A Virtual Reality Challenge inside Urban Conflict," ICRC, October 22, 2018, https://www.icrc.org/en/document/war-front-door-virtual-reality-challenge-inside-urban-conflict.

7 "The Right Choice," Don't Panic, accessed November 7, 2020, https://www.dontpaniclondon.com/project/the-right-choice/ (emphasis mine).

8 Sontag, *Regarding*, 117.

9 Mary Anne Franks, "The Desert of the Unreal: Inequality in Virtual and Augmented Reality," *UC Davis Law Review* 51, no. 499 (2017): 516–517.

ling detail; it provides the opportunity to view such atrocity over and over, on an endless loop."[10]

The idea of creating immersive images in the context of war is nothing new, of course, even if the technology and devices might be. In 1899, the second president of the ICRC, Gustave Moynier, noted, "We now know what happens every day throughout the whole world . . . the descriptions given by daily journalists put, as it were, those in agony on fields of battle under the eyes of [newspaper] readers and their cries resonate in their ears."[11] The notion that media consumers could know what happens "every day throughout the whole world" was a notable exaggeration, but Moynier's underlying assumption is telling. As Sontag puts it, "For a long time some people believed that if the horror could be made vivid enough, most people would finally take in the outrageousness, the insanity of war."[12] Indeed, this seems to still be the guiding assumption of the ICRC.

The ICRC conceived *The Right Choice* as an early test to find out if interactive media "has the potential to change someone's perception or incite behavioral change."[13] To get feedback, the ICRC conducted their own internal research in the form of pre- and post-viewing surveys. Responses from over five hundred completed surveys indicated viewers' heightened sense of "concern" directly following *The Right Choice*, but the final results were never published in an official research report because of the difficulty of deducing general conclusions.[14] Both the survey responses and the ICRC's hesitation to draw conclusions echo the findings of empirically oriented VR scholars, who lament the lack of research on longitudinal change, implicit attitudes, and other factors that might skew survey results.[15]

Much has been written about (im)proper distance, voyeurism, and the ethically flawed notion of VR inherently being an empathy machine.[16] In addition to such issues, however, the ICRC actualizes the less examined idea of directly modulating behavior with humanitarian immersive media—the behavior of both those who witness from a distance and those who live or work in war-torn regions. The ICRC is currently researching how immersive media can be used as a tool for behavioral change, not only with public-facing projects like *The Right Choice* but also internally.[17] While the aim with the former is mainly to increase donations and to affect public engagement and policy-making, the latter has to do with operational uses such as training for the field and educating militaries.

10 Franks, 517.

11 Cited in Sontag, *Regarding*, 27.

12 Sontag, 21, 82.

13 "War at the Front Door."

14 From the author's email exchange with Christopher Nicholas at the ICRC, October 22, 2020.

15 Mila Bujić, Mikko Salminen, Joseph Macey, and Juho Hamari, "'Empathy Machine': How Virtual Reality Affects Human Rights Attitudes," *Internet Research* 30, no. 5 (2020): 1407–1425.

16 Franks, "Desert of the Unreal," 509–514.

17 "ICRC Researches Virtual Reality as a Behavior Change Tool," ICRC, June, 29, 2019, https://blogs.icrc.org/inspired/2019/06/29/virtual-reality-tool-influence-behaviors/.

Other international humanitarian actors—including the United Nations High Commissioner for Refugees, Amnesty International, and Médecins Sans Frontières (Doctors Without Borders)—have sponsored VR productions similar to *The Right Choice*, but the ICRC is quite unique in that it has not only commissioned VR works but also built its own production facilities. The ICRC founded a dedicated Virtual Reality Unit in 2013, headed by Rouffaer. A central aim of the unit is to develop virtual environments with more efficient gamification for the training of new ICRC personnel, but they also use immersive media to educate warring groups on international law. ICRC delegates bring 3D renditions to meetings with armed factions and authorities in order to show evidence of possible violations and to educate on international treaties like the Geneva Convention.

Other humanitarian projects, such as Building Resilience Through Heritage (BReaTHe), created by the University of Bradford in partnership with the global aid organization Mercy Corps, use strategies similar to those of the ICRC and bring immersive media technology to populations affected by war. BReaTHe notably uses virtual reality as part of "psychosocial programming" for Syrian refugees: the project aims to help refugees create a cultural connection to their war-torn homeland, enhance mental well-being, and build "personal and societal resilience" using 3D models along with immersive photography and video.[18] When the VR equipment is brought to camps in Jordan, refugees can enter virtual museums or visit locations and see landmarks now destroyed.

While BReaTHe underwent a rigorous ethical approval process, consulted with local stakeholders, and offered psychosocial support from trained professionals on-site, other immersive media risk re-traumatizing precarious populations directly affected by war.[19] Regardless of their creators' laudable intentions, then, scholars need to carefully trace the wider biopolitical ramifications of such humanitarian interventions. Projects such as BReaTHe and those of the ICRC compel us to construct a critical and ethical framework that takes into account not only the representation of the distant, suffering other in humanitarian immersive imagery but also the ways in which immersive media are used for behavioral change and governance. As Väliaho argues, the governing function and potential "violence of this imagery may indeed originate not so much in what the images show but in their modular nature."[20] This kind of modular immersion (adaptive, modulatory, and cybernetic) could be compared to what Michel Foucault called "environmental intervention," which is to say, a mode of power that shapes the behavior and regulates the conduct of individuals by "modifying their adaptive and self-organizing capacities and conditions."[21]

18 "How Virtual Reality Is Helping Refugees in Jordan and Beyond," University of Bradford, June 18, 2019, https://www.bradford.ac.uk/news/archive/2019/how-virtual-reality-is-helping-refugees-in-jordan-and-beyond.php.

19 Franks, "Desert of the Unreal," 516.

20 Väliaho, "Affectivity, Biopolitics," 81.

21 Foucault cited and discussed in Pasi Väliaho, *Biopolitical Screens: Image, Power, and the Neoliberal Brain* (Cambridge, MA: MIT Press, 2014), 46.

In the context of immersive media and gamification, the process of environmental intervention involves a dual movement: environments are incorporated into the viewer's consciousness at the same time that their mind-body is being incorporated into the environment.[22] According to Väliaho, the key battleground in the context of immersive media and warfare concerns the brain's reality emulation, not "interpretation of the external world but, rather . . . the media technological regulation of basic affect programmes and the endogenous imagery they produce."[23] In other words, the governing function of immersive media is to a large extent independent from symbolic depiction and even individual cognition. To that end, operational (re-)training in the military seeks to bypass higher faculties and targets a pre-linguistic and non-representational level of mind-body inscription.[24] By aiming to shock, change behavioral patterns, and psycho-socially reprogram users of immersive media, humanitarian organizations are increasingly operating within this domain too.

With the brain as primary target of intervention and capture, neural plasticity becomes a central focus of governance under neoliberal societies of control. Much like the dual incorporation of immersive media, neural plasticity involves "a process through which the nervous system adjusts to changes in the internal and external milieu."[25] In the context of war—particularly the sheer violence and shock it generates—the brain is subjected to a "destructive plasticity" that can radically alter the constitution of the subject.[26] Destructive plasticity is not limited to war zones, however; some scholars argue that the neoliberal cerebral subject is constantly underpinned by and subjected to "the forces of metamorphosis, destruction—and death."[27] Immersive humanitarian media under neoliberalism are likewise entangled with the biopolitical emergence of life as well as the necropolitical "subjugation of life to the power of death."[28]

Under neoliberal governance—and, in particular, when liberal nation-states wage war—biopolitics and necropolitics cannot be separated. Even if the purported mission of a military organization is construed as humanitarian and peacekeeping, "[p]eace becomes the extension of war through the discourse of security," as Michael Dillon explains.[29] According to Dillon, this implies that "[l]iberal peace is a necropolitics of security which makes permanent war against life on behalf of life."[30] By extension, humanitarian

22 See Gordon Calleja, *In-Game: From Immersion to Incorporation* (Cambridge, MA: MIT Press, 2011), 169.

23 Väliaho, "Affectivity, Biopolitics," 76.

24 Väliaho, 69, 77.

25 Warren Neidich, "From Noopower to Neuropower: How Mind Becomes Matter," in *Cognitive Architecture: From Bio-Politics to Noo-Politics*, ed. Deborah Hauptmann and Warren Neidich (Rotterdam: 010 Publishers, 2010), 547.

26 See Catherine Malabou, *Ontology of the Accident: An Essay on Destructive Plasticity*, trans. Carolyn Shread (Cambridge: Polity Press, 2012).

27 Väliaho, "Affectivity, Biopolitics," 84.

28 Achille Mbembe, "Necropolitics," trans. Libby Meintjes, *Public Culture* 15, no. 1 (Winter 2003): 39.

29 Michael Dillon, "Security, Race and War," in *Foucault on Politics, Security and War*, ed. Michael Dillon and Andrew W. Neal (Basingstoke: Palgrave Macmillan, 2008), 176.

30 Dillon, 177.

organizations also operate within the general necropolitical domain, which itself is intimately tied to neural plasticity and "neuropower."[31]

If we consider the ICRC or BReaTHe in light of the complex interrelations outlined above—between humanitarianism, biopolitics, necropolitics, and neural plasticity—it becomes clear that what is at stake is not merely the image of the suffering other, or even representational politics more broadly. Rather, these organizations operate in a sphere of political physiology in which the boundary between the political and the somatic is blurred. The mind-body is the primary locus of mediation and target of capture. Much like in the military, the objective is to change affective and behavioral patterns. Regardless of the good intentions of humanitarian organizations, this warrants a careful attention to new forms of power. Consequently, humanitarian immersive media pertaining to war necessitate a renewed media critique that considers operational aspects and that dispenses with dualist conceptions of mind and body, that goes beyond representational politics to take into account the entanglement of images, media, and bodily matter(s).

Christian Rossipal is a PhD candidate in cinema studies at Tisch School of the Arts, New York University. He is also part of the Culture and Media program at NYU's Department of Anthropology. His research interests include migration, minor cinemas, and necropolitics. Christian is a member of the artist-activist collective Noncitizen.

31 Neidich, "From Noopower to Neuropower," 545–546.

Eszter Zimanyi and Emma Ben Ayoun

Virtually Wandering the *Migration Trail*

On November 20, 2017, artist and architect Alison Killing launched a ten-day-long, web-based multimedia narrative addressing Europe's so-called migrant or refugee crisis. Billed variously as documentary, journalism, and interactive storytelling, Killing's project, titled *Migration Trail,* draws upon data visualizations, maps, and social media to recreate the journeys of two fictionalized irregular migrants: Sarah, a nineteen-year-old Syrian woman, and David, a thirty-year-old man from Nigeria.[1] In separate storylines, these two characters make their way to Europe via the Eastern and Central Mediterranean routes, respectively.[2] Sarah's and David's experiences are visualized on a two-dimensional map of the world. Their stories unfold through written text messages sent by the characters to their loved ones through Facebook Messenger.

Each day, *Migration Trail*'s users are pinged with updates from Sarah or David on their web browsers and cell phones and can check the virtual map to see where either character is at any given moment. The characters' progress, however, feels decidedly slow. Sarah's and David's movements adhere to the length of time migration journeys take in reality; for example, it takes one hour and fifty minutes of *Migration Trail*'s run-time for Sarah to cross by

1 The project can be experienced at https://www.migrationtrail.com. The International Organization for Migration defines "irregular migration" as the "movement of persons that takes place outside the laws, regulations, or international agreements governing the entry into or exit from the State of origin, transit or destination." See "Key Migration Terms," International Organization for Migration, accessed September 15, 2021, https://www.iom.int/key-migration-terms.

2 The Eastern Mediterranean route takes migrants from Turkey to Greece. From here, many migrants and refugees seek to continue their journeys toward Western Europe either by connecting to the Western Balkan route (a land route that traverses Southeastern and Central Europe) or, if they have the means, by flying to their desired destination country. The Central Mediterranean route takes migrants and refugees from North Africa to Italy.

Eszter Zimanyi and Emma Ben Ayoun, "Virtually Wandering the *Migration Trail*," *JCMS* 61, no. 3 (Spring 2022): 183–188.

boat from Izmir, Turkey, to Lesbos, Greece. Similarly, if the characters spend a night at a squat or safe house, they remain in place on the map for seven to eight hours. If they are sleeping, they likewise do not send messages to their family members. As users, we find ourselves suspended in wait during these communicative gaps; at times, the project easily fades into the background of our daily lives, and at others, rapidly arriving messages thrust *Migration Trail*'s narrative back into our consciousnesses. While the user is able to rewind *Migration Trail* to revisit an earlier point in time, they cannot fast-forward or speed up the characters' journeys.

Killing argues that her refusal to condense the project's run-time makes its narrative more "urgent and immediate" than traditional documentaries and news reports, because *Migration Trail*'s viewers "find out about events right as they're happening."[3] This insistence on making humanitarian crises ever-more urgent and immediate for distant viewers pervades both documentary and immersive media practices. As Pooja Rangan cogently argues, documentary filmmaking grew out of a "modern ethical imaginary [of] emergency thinking" that "institutes a humanitarian order of priorities in which saving endangered human lives takes precedence over all other considerations" and favors "action over thinking, ethics over aesthetics, and immediacy over analysis."[4] Emergency thinking similarly undergirds the growing number of interactive and virtual reality (VR) experiences that aim to immerse participants within crisis situations—whether they be war zones, attempted illegalized border crossings, or scenes of police brutality—in order to elicit emotional and bodily reactions.[5] Yet, despite Killing's claim, *Migration Trail* eschews many of the formal, aesthetic, and narrative choices that would instigate emergency thinking.

Therefore, in this essay, we choose to think against Killing's framework to ask what her project makes possible by way of its slowness and limited interactivity. We read *Migration Trail*'s attempts to incorporate itself into the daily rhythms and screen habits of its users as a provocative re-thinking of media immersivity, one that opens a new set of questions around spectatorship, participation, and temporality in humanitarian media. The felt experience of media boundaries, their appearances and dissolutions, takes on a new resonance in immersive media with humanitarian aims. This is particularly true when the humanitarian crisis being represented involves another set of boundaries and their bodily effects, such as national borders and the myriad other socioeconomic barriers, both visible and invisible, that migrants and refugees face worldwide. Killing's multi-platform digital

3 Allison Meier, "An Interactive Story Follows Two Migrants on Their Journeys to Europe," *Hyperallergic*, December 7, 2017, https://hyperallergic.com/413919/migration-trail-online-interactive-story/.

4 Pooja Rangan, *Immediations: The Humanitarian Impulse in Documentary* (Durham, NC: Duke University Press, 2017), 3.

5 Eszter Zimanyi and Emma Ben Ayoun, "On Bodily Absence in Humanitarian Multisensory VR," *Intermédialités: Histoire et théorie des arts, des lettres et des techniques (Intermediality: History and Theory of the Arts, Literature and Technologies)*, no. 34 (Autumn 2019): https://doi.org/10.7202/1070876ar. See also Mandy Rose, "The Immersive Turn: Hype and Hope in the Emergence of Virtual Reality as a Nonfiction Platform," *Studies in Documentary Film* 12, no. 2 (2018): 132–149, https://doi.org/10.1080/17503280.2018.1496055.

narrative attunes users' bodies to the temporalities of irregular migration. By delimiting and refusing users' direct participation in shaping Sarah's and David's actions, it also allows for an ongoing encounter with migrant subjectivities that instigates what Aggie Ebrahimi Bazaz, in this dossier, describes as a critical, reflexive immersion.

Though *Migration Trail* is advertised as an immersive experience, it does not physically envelop its participant through a headset, nor does it dominate the environment in which it is situated, as large-scale immersive installations do. The project does not inherently demand total absorption or any specific activity on the part of the user. *Migration Trail*'s interactive map is accompanied by eleven, supplementary podcast episodes exploring the experiences of contemporary refugees and migrants in further detail. There are no steps or decisions participants must take to move through the narrative; rather, the map dutifully updates throughout each day regardless of how often one chooses to open it. The characters, Sarah and David, are represented as small, circular data points that inch slowly across the map, trailed by a dashed line that tracks their movements from place to place. They thus remain visually abstracted throughout the experience; we never see Sarah or David in embodied form, nor are we shown any photographic or video material of the places they transit through. In this way, the project refuses the lure of gameplay, the ideology of intervention, and the voyeurism of the twenty-four-hour news cycle that broadcasts dramatic footage of migrants in distress on loop for distant viewers to consume.

In a panel on the right-hand side of the map, we are provided background information and data about a chosen character and their environment: we can see their cell phone battery life change throughout the day, the speed and method by which they are traveling, their last known location, and their direction of travel. This data is individualized and narrativized through the character's messages, which are logged within the same informational panel. The text messages are also visually represented as notification bubbles on the map, such that each time the character sends an update, geographic locations are marked with the number of communicative actions the character makes at that site. Clicking on these message bubbles brings up the texts sent from that location, so that areas of the map are inscribed with different emotional registers relayed by the character, be they excitement, fear, worry, or relief.

Migration Trail builds suspense through unpredictable patterns of communication from its characters. Sarah's and David's ability to send texts depends on their access to mobile and Wi-Fi service. As a result, the characters sometimes go silent for hours, reflecting the gaps in connectivity real-world migrants experience. The project shows us only one side of their conversations; we receive Sarah's and David's messages but not their family members' responses, leaving us guessing as to how often their family members may be trying to make contact. Sarah and David are often apologetic in this regard, explaining they had no service or hid their phone for safety. In this way, *Migration Trail* attunes our bodies to the shifting sensations of waiting and uncertainty experienced by both migrants and the loved ones from whom they are separated. The project inserts itself into users' routine practices of checking their phones for text messages and generates gradually increasing anxiety with its slowness. The longer Sarah and David go without sending an update, the more likely it is that users feel compelled to repeatedly, and futilely, refresh *Migration Trail*'s map.

Once the experience begins, the site consistently updates itself over the allotted ten days, even if the user closes the project's associated browser window. As users, we find ourselves habitually returning to the map to search for new information as we wait for Sarah and David to send updates, despite there being, or perhaps because there is, no way for us to reach out to or converse with these characters. We check on their progress by moving our cursors across the map, exploring the shifts in our characters' environments and emotions. Our interaction with the project is limited to zooming in and out of the frame. Doing so reveals new layers of data, from wind speeds at sea and the level of internet connectivity in any given area to information about common migration routes to Europe, travel restrictions and visa requirements, and the specific locations of reported migrant deaths at sea. Moving within the map also activates sonic elements that enhance *Migration Trail*'s claim to immersivity. Zooming all the way into the character's location reveals sounds that the character hears, from the lively chatter and clanking of pans in the kitchen at dinnertime to the heart-stopping soundtrack of ocean waves pounding against a rubber dinghy and a coast guard helicopter flying overhead during an unauthorized sea crossing. Though *Migration Trail* refuses to reproduce the kinds of graphic images of trauma and mass death that viewers have grown accustomed to seeing in news and documentary footage, the characters' text messages are deeply intimate, sensorially rich, and evocative. David's texts to his brother, for example, frequently reflect the weight of trauma on his body: he reports that he is seized with fear upon seeing the water, recounts the odors and itching that accompany days on end without bathing, and conveys his awareness of his hair and beard growing, his leg swelling, and blisters forming on his feet. Together, *Migration Trail*'s descriptive text messages, sound design, and durational narrative create a compelling and immersive experience that plays with users' expectations about where and how they can participate, and who or what they are entitled to see.

Migration Trail constructs this immersive experience by appropriating the visual form of the tracking map to narrativize statistical data about unauthorized migration to Europe. Its immersivity operates along two axes: duration and infiltration of the user's everyday bodily habits. In her work on geolocative technologies, Brenda Smaill locates the spectatorial pleasures of tracking maps precisely in the act of "repeated and intermittent engagement" rather than total absorption or identification; the interactive map is enjoyable precisely because one leaves it and returns to it.[6] Smaill's objects of study—maps that reflect the movements of sharks and rising sea levels—are certainly different from Killing's, but the tracking of ecological crisis is also meant to

6 Brenda Smaill, "An Ecocritical Approach to Documentary Interactivity: Spatial Technologies in a Film Studies Frame," *Studies in Documentary Film* 12, no. 3 (2018): 173–189, https://doi.org/10.1080/17503280.2018.1498622.

invoke urgency, the need to act now, and an awareness that it might already be too late. In Smaill's case studies, the mapping of ecological data visually renders emergency by evidencing measurable changes in environments over time: when viewers witness animations of rising sea levels, for example, they understand that coastal cities will soon be underwater. Yet, in humanitarian media focused on people, urgency is most often communicated through first-person accounts of traumatic events, in which victims' testimonies about the horrors they have experienced (attempt to) animate viewers' collective drive to act. What to make, then, of *Migration Trail*'s intentional slowness, its refusal to visually represent its characters as embodied beings, and its denial of direct intervention in its narrative?

Migration Trail's liveness and the urgency of the situations it represents co-exist uneasily with the user's ability, and pragmatic need, to engage and disengage at will. This duality is in some ways reminiscent of the split identified by Elaine Scarry in her work on emergency; in states of emergency, she writes, there is often an "unspoken presumption . . . that either one can think or one can act" and that, because the need for immediate action is what constitutes the emergency as such, "thinking must fall away."[7] For Scarry, this opposition is a false and dangerous one, as it disregards the role that habit plays in forming emergency responses. "Habit," she writes, "yokes thought and action together."[8] Habit thus brings embodiment back into the picture: habit is embodied, pre-reflexive, but also suggestible, subject to change. If we imagine that the user of *Migration Trail* habitually checks their phone throughout the day in response to flickering notifications, then does the project merely, as Wendy Hui Kyong Chun has argued, "personalize crisis" via the theater of social media?[9] We would argue the contrary: *Migration Trail* infiltrates and disrupts the habitual, defamiliarizing both the mediums at hand (e.g., the cell phone, the computer, the map) and the humanitarian crisis being mediated.

For Bazaz, critically reflexive documentary projects evoke a contemplative state in viewers that disrupts the emergency thinking reproduced so often in humanitarian nonfiction media. She argues that critical reflexivity, on the part of creators, and reflexive immersion, on the part of spectators, aim to "activate critical faculties in the viewer" and, we suggest, to rupture the presumably stable identity of the spectator, negating the false sense of proximity to—and empathy with—the Other that (immersive) humanitarian media typically celebrates.[10] Critical, reflexive immersion acknowledges the distance between the viewer and the documentary subject represented and repeatedly draws viewers' attention to their own practices of and desires for looking. *Migration Trail* similarly disrupts our desires to not only look at but *intervene* in the actions of others. Unlike other interactive documentaries, *Migration Trail* does not ask its users to make a series of high-stakes decisions

7 Elaine Scarry, *Thinking in an Emergency* (New York: Norton, 2011), 13.

8 Scarry, 69.

9 Wendy Hui Kyong Chun, "Crisis, Crisis, Crisis, or Sovereignty and Networks," *Theory, Culture & Society* 28, no. 6 (2011): 95, https://doi.org/10.1177/0263276411418490.

10 Aggie Ebrahimi Bazaz, personal conversation with authors, July 10, 2021.

and watch their consequences instantly play out.[11] Yet, by attuning us to the temporalities of migration—to the dizzying shifts between long periods of waiting and disconnection and the sudden changes in our characters' environments that force their immediate action—Killing's project pushes us to become aware of how the decisions we make are embedded within a network of choices that all affect one another. By coupling the interactive map, a tool for spatial and temporal orientation, with an insistently one-sided conversation, Killing pulls the *Migration Trail* user out of the frame at the precise moment when action seems most necessary. Like fully immersive VR experiences that erase the user's view of their own body, *Migration Trail* makes both its users' and characters' bodies into unstable and visually absent entities, provoking a set of anxieties around choice—or its felt foreclosure—that brings users into a renewed understanding of their own agency and responsibility to those around them.

Eszter Zimanyi is a postdoctoral fellow in cinema and media studies at the University of Southern California. She has published in *Feminist Media Studies*, *Visual Anthropology*, and *Media Fields Journal*, among others. Her research interests include migration and refugee studies, global media, and documentary.

Emma Ben Ayoun is a PhD candidate in cinema and media studies at the University of Southern California. Her dissertation, titled "Sick Cinema: Disability, Disease and the Moving Image," works at the interstices of film theory, disability studies, and visual studies.

11 See Christian Rossipal's essay in this dossier for several key examples of this dynamic.

Interview by Eszter Zimanyi and Emma Ben Ayoun

Against Immersion: An Interview with Aggie Ebrahimi Bazaz

Aggie Ebrahimi Bazaz is an Iranian American practice-based researcher and assistant professor of film production at Georgia State University. Her creative work, which emphasizes community engagement and participatory practice, includes live performance and virtual reality (VR) and multimedia installations. Bazaz explores issues of immigration, diaspora, and liberation, often with a reflexive eye toward the limits and capacities of media itself. Her 2019 film, *How to Tell a True Immigrant Story*, is a 360-degree documentary VR short made in collaboration with the residents of Saratoga County, New York. Bazaz's sensory film plays with the conventions of the documentary interview, staging an encounter between the county's affluent (and mostly white) communities and the immigrant laborers whose presence, though largely unseen, sustains such lifestyles. Bazaz's work thus reflects political potential and limits of immersive media's capacity to incite changes in felt embodiment and subjectivity, which was of particular interest to us as we put together this dossier. The interview below has been edited and condensed for clarity.

Eszter Zimanyi and Emma Ben Ayoun: *Can you tell us more about the process of completing* How to Tell a True Immigrant Story? *In the years since its production, have there been any changes in terms of human flows, technologies, or your own intellectual and creative process that have made you rethink how we tell immigrant stories?*

Aggie Ebrahimi Bazaz: *How to Tell a True Immigrant Story,* which I conceived and developed during a 2016 residency at the Skidmore College's John B. Moore Documentary Studies Collaborative (MDOCS) Storytell-

Interview by Eszter Zimanyi and Emma Ben Ayoun, "Against Immersion: An Interview with Aggie Ebrahimi Bazaz," *JCMS* 61, no. 3 (Spring 2022): 189–194.

ers Institute in Saratoga Springs, New York, is a short, experimental act of critical reflexivity in 360-degree VR. It applies strategies from documentary scholarship to our existing discursive frameworks pertaining to people and experiences categorized as "immigrant"—a category that includes myself, my brother, my mother, my aunt, and my grandmother. It is personally meaningful for me to ask, Who and what truths, nuances, and paradoxes might our standard cultural narratives around *immigrant* or *immigration* exclude?

The making of this film began from a discomfort with mainstream documentary's approach to immigrant stories. As an immigrant to the United States myself, I find the term *immigrant* to be a useful organizing principle but also one that inherently others. In order for it to exist, it must presuppose the category of *native*. It must create categories of belonging that may begin as questions of nationality but quickly transform into questions of self and psychology; it creates material and symbolic boundaries. The film argues that when we tell immigrant stories in documentary, we ask questions that are themselves a form of boundary-keeping: *Where are you from? Why are you here? Do you work?* Implied in these are questions like *Are you safe? Do you belong?* These are questions of incorporation and control.[1]

I think what's changed for me in the years since its production isn't so much a change but more a clarification. That is, with the good fortune I've had to think about the film alongside other research-based practitioners, I've developed a language for articulating and critically contextualizing a process and approach to documentary power that was previously a bit more intuitive.

EZ and EB: *To what extent is your work in conversation with discourses about immersion and its connection to empathy?*

AEB: Empathy brings us back to a question of power. We might see an analog for the empathy conversation in a liberal town like Saratoga Springs. Saratoga Springs is a predominantly white and affluent town in upstate New York. It has about 28,000 full-time residents but bursts with activity during the summer launch of the thoroughbred horseracing season. For more than 150 years, the Saratoga Race Course and all its offerings have brought the town countless spectators and a great deal of revenue every summer, as well as thousands of jobs.[2]

As you might imagine, the people whose labor upholds this foundational, vibrant economy are mostly folks of color from Asia, Mexico, and Central and South America, many of whom migrate into the United States via guest worker visas for six to nine months a year to "care for some of the world's most elite racehorses."[3]

1 See Trinh T. Minh-ha, "Mechanical Eye, Electronic Ear and the Lure of Authenticity," *Wide Angle* 6, no. 2 (1984): 58–62.

2 "Saratoga Generates Record Handle Topping $800 Million," Associated Press, September 7, 2021, https://apnews.com/article/sports-new-york-saratoga-springs-horse-racing-6baca6cf799f48a34a65c60a773a7c1d.

3 Krystle Nowhitney Hernandez, "The Oral Histories of Latino Immigrant Backstretch Workers at Saratoga Race Course" (master's thesis, Skidmore College, 2015), 4.

Almost all who work with the horses live and labor at the barns, across the street from the public racing venue in an area called "the backstretch." Housing at the backstretch is in barrack-style dormitories with communal bathrooms and no functional kitchens. For six months of the year, laborers live in this environment, with up to four people sharing one unit. They work seven days a week, rain or shine, because "animals need care every day, so work proceeds regardless."[4]

So, you have a predominantly white, upper-middle-class town benefiting from and allowed to exist in large part due to the immense, continual labor of mostly folks of color from across Latin America and Asia. This is nothing new, of course. But what's interesting and unique about Saratoga Springs are the ways in which the dominant culture grapples with this relationship.

One of the dynamics shaping relations in Saratoga Springs is benevolence, which also undergirds the humanitarian documentary impulse. There are, for example, plenty of people who volunteer at the racecourse, who give out free food and supplies, who take community members on outings or drive people to appointments. This is all useful; I don't at all mean to suggest it's not. But it does nothing to challenge existing social relations. In fact, it reinforces them through individual acts of kindness.

This is how I see the empathy framework. Documentaries that rely on empathy link their viewers—typically conceived as "educated middle and upper-middle class audiences"—to the subjects on screen through nothing more than "feelings, like caring, concern, sometimes outrage" and "make no structural analysis of the problems described and rarely [propose] solutions," as Jill Godmilow points out.[5] Sonya Childress goes further, noting that empathy's "overemphasis on attitudinal change toward individuals leaves less room for films that push audiences to grapple with the structures and systems that reinforce inequality."[6]

EZ and EB: *You describe* How to Tell a True Immigrant Story *as an "experimental act of critical reflexivity." Can you tell us more about how you conceptualize this term and what it responds to in the longer history of documentary filmmaking?*

AEB: Critical reflexivity is a term that Elizabeth (Liz) Miller has used in publications in which we've brought our two VR films into conversation with each other.[7] With this term, we refer to an approach to documentary methods that is guided not only by content but also by an iterative self-reflection on our processes. Social scientists conceptualize media as serving one of two functions: either media effect social change, or they further the social control of predom-

4 Hernandez, 28.

5 Jill Godmilow, "What's Wrong with the Liberal Documentary," *Peace Review* 11, no. 1 (1999): 92.

6 Sonya Childress, "Beyond Empathy," *Medium*, March 20, 2017, https://firelightmedia.medium.com/beyond-empathy-ad6b5ad8a1d8/.

7 Aggie Ebrahimi Bazaz and Liz Miller, "Invited and Implicated: Toward Critical Reflexivity in Non-fiction VR," *Digital Radical*, Center on Digital Culture and Society, University of Pennsylvania Annenberg School of Communication, June 18, 2020, https://www.asc.upenn.edu/research/centers/center-on-digital-culture-and-society/the-digital-radical/Invited-and-Implicated.

inant ideologies and social structures.[8] Critical reflexivity is one methodological framework for guiding documentary away from the latter and toward the former. It is the same approach all of the writers in this issue take to studying different media texts and exposing the ideologies underpinning them. These cogent, urgent media analyses you do, these insights into power and ideology, then inform and guide how filmmakers like Liz and I make media.

As other scholars have shown, critical reflexivity attempts to disrupt the ease with which "the indexical power of the [documentary] image" can be deployed to "regard—at a distance—other people's pain."[9] It also works to disrupt the display of traumatic moments for sensationalist value, which reinforce rather than challenge worldviews and norms. In such instances, the documentary image can "monopolistically impose itself on people as a kind of complete reality," thus colonizing the mind; participate in extraction or other forms of community damage; or create that peculiar viewerly comfort of retreating from the screen thinking, "thank God that's not me."[10] Through critical reflexivity, we find a pathway to intervene in documentary's sometimes unconscious immediations, diverting our attention away from reproducing content of "endangered human lives" and toward considering the "aesthetics and politics of representation."[11]

EZ and EB: *To what degree is embodiment—be it your subjects' or your participants'—central to your conceptualization of your creative work? And how does a shift in attention from visual evidence to embodied knowledge complicate the documentary tradition we have inherited?*

AEB: The shift in attention from visual evidence to embodied knowledge is akin, I believe, to a shift from *looking at* to *looking within*. I think it's clear in *How to Tell a True Immigrant Story* that my collaborators and I are not aiming for total mastery of mind, body, and environment.[12] First, because we are working in 360-degree video, the immersion that you experience in more gamified, high-tech, computer-generated environments, like the Red Cross films that Christian Rossipal writes about in this dossier, is completely unavailable to us. Also, many people watch *How to Tell a True Immigrant Story* on YouTube or in Google Cardboard. Even in a headset, though, people become aware of their bodies because of the structuring of the image. View-

8 J. David Slocum, "Film Violence and the Institutionalization of the Cinema," *Social Research* 67, no. 3 (2000): 649–681.

9 See Alison Griffiths's contribution to this dossier and Susan Sontag, *Regarding the Pain of Others* (New York: Picador, 2003), 13.

10 Haile Gerima, "Decolonizing the Filmic Mind: An Interview with Haile Gerima," interview by John L. Jackson, Jr., *Callaloo* 33, no. 1 (2010): 27; and Jill Godmilow, "Kill the Documentary as We Know It," *Journal of Film and Video* 54, no. 2–3 (2002): 4.

11 *Immediations* references Pooja Rangan's *Immediations: The Humanitarian Impulse in Documentary* (Durham, NC: Duke University Press, 2017); see Eszter Zimanyi and Emma Ben Ayoun, "On Bodily Absence in Humanitarian Multisensory VR," *Intermédialités: Histoire et théorie des arts, des lettres et des techniques (Intermediality: History and Theory of the Arts, Literature and Technologies)*, no. 34 (Autumn 2019): para. 23.

12 Throughout this interview, Bazaz uses the first-person plural to refer to the makers of *How to Tell a True Immigrant Story* even though she is credited as the sole director; this is a move on her part to emphasize the project's collaborative nature and the significant contributions made to it by other local artists as well as members of the community in which she filmed.

ers may, for example, see a stitch line or be frustrated by what imagery they'd expect and are not seeing. For us, these were all tools at our disposal, all ways of keeping viewers' critical faculties activated.

Through our resistance to hyper-realism and our interventions in the field of view, we wanted to create either a shock of recognition or a shock of defamiliarization, feelings which course through the body, erasing that feeling of bodily absorption and instead calling the viewer back into the piece but also into themselves. In these ways, we're in line with a framework of immersion that Simran Bhalla discusses as a "pedagogical and epistemological method."[13] We wanted the experience to be instructive, to reveal the symbolic boundaries disguised beneath grammars of benevolence.

EZ and EB: *Your projects are all immersive in different ways, and you have previously framed your work as part of a practice of reflexive immersion. Could you tell us more about what this means?*

AEB: When making *How to Tell a True Immigrant Story*, we were not interested in humanitarian immersion. Rather than suppress critical responses, we wanted to *activate* critical faculties in the viewer and *activate* a reflective position rather than give the (false) impression of proximity or "walking in someone else's shoes."

There are, however, scenes in the film that I would describe as *sensory*, scenes in which sensory qualities form a poetics. I'm thinking, for example, of the scene in which a mother and her two children walk through grass while one child asks, "Are we there yet?" I don't define this scene as *immersive* because it's not designed to convey a harsh reality but instead to abstract and defamiliarize reality. It obscures more than it reveals. The design of the scene prioritizes abstraction: texture, motion, and tone are all punctuated by the melodic voice of a young girl repeating her mom's assurance that "*Ya casi llegamos*" ("We're almost there"). The scene never attempts to locate where *there* is but to evoke a sense of placelessness through motion, point of view—the camera is positioned behind the family—and the tensions between the harshness of the grass and the tenderness of the family. This scene, too, is a collage, a stitching together of different types of footage: 360-degree footage mixed with DSLR material and handwritten text. So even though we're located somewhere inside tall grass, we are not immersed. And that's again a play with the viewer's desire for looking-in-on. This scene has some analogs to border crossing—the border being, as we know, a site of horror and spectacle, among other things. We wanted to interrupt the viewer's possible voyeuristic desire to *immerse* themself in border crossing and instead use poetics and abstraction to transport the viewer intellectually elsewhere (to thinking about other acts of looking, for example). We avoid and reject the promise of an unadulterated, hyperreal, wide-angle view and instead disrupt access, aiming in this way to make audiences aware of their "practices of [and desires for] looking."[14]

13 See Simran Bhalla's contribution to this dossier.

14 Zimanyi and Ben Ayoun, "On Bodily Absence," para. 30.

EZ and EB: *What potentialities for imagining different politics, policies, and futures might nonfiction immersive media allow us (if any)?*

AEB: Nonfiction VR is still so new that the productive possibilities of engaging it toward humanitarian questions are still making themselves known. But I am inspired by Courteney Morin's thoughts on how VR can be used as space for screen sovereignty for Indigenous filmmakers. Morin suggests that VR is uniquely suited to "reflect individual Indigenous philosophies and epistemes" because of its abilities to hold past, present, and future together at once; "deepen storytelling capacity"; and visualize spiritual realms in ways that indexical documentary images can't as easily do. As Morin writes, "the current state of VR allows for the invention of new grammars."[15] And to me, this is an exciting possibility. If cultural narratives "shape our values and behaviors," teaching lessons about "who belongs, what is valued, who and what matters," then cultural narratives are also foundational to necropolitics.[16] If VR allows us new tools and grammars for exploding such narratives, or even exploding our notions of what narrative is, then it can be an additional set of tools in our work to foster transformative social change.

Aggie Ebrahimi Bazaz is an Iranian American practice-based researcher and an assistant professor of film production at Georgia State University. Her work investigates immigration, belonging, citizenship, and documentary's adjacency to relations of power.

15 Courteney Morin, "Screen Sovereignty: Indigenous Matriarch 4 Articulating the Future of Indigenous VR," *BC Studies*, no. 201 (Spring 2019): 144.

16 Chi-hui Yang, "Documentary Power: A New Manifesto," International Documentary Association, January 31, 2019, https://www.documentary.org/feature/documentary-power-new-manifesto.

Edited by Laura Isabel Serna

BOOK REVIEWS

Reviewed by Bren Ram

Data Selves: More-than-Human Perspectives

by Deborah Lupton.
Polity Press.
2020. 208 pages.
$64.95 hardcover; $22.95 paper; also available in e-book.

It is not a new idea to suggest that our twenty-first-century technologies of data collection are changing who we are. The idea of selfhood—already under scrutiny by philosophers and information studies scholars alike—is even more precarious in a world of gene indexing, facial recognition, browser tracking, and similarly invasive media. Fortunately, Deborah Lupton's *Data Selves: More-than-Human Perspectives* goes much further than rehearsing such well-known threats to personal sovereignty. Ambitious and multidisciplinary, it outlines what amounts to a new theory of media ontology involving human-data assemblages. Digital media users are constantly generating data about themselves as they go about tracking steps, planning meals, managing finances, and seeking entertainment. All these actions contribute to their life experiences by shaping the advertisements websites show them, the insurance policies made available to them, the loans they qualify for, and—as the 2018 Cambridge Analytica scandal has made plain—even our political communities. Lupton, however, is less interested in the ways such data are used than she is in the way they are produced and discussed. In one striking example, a data analytics company ad depicts a comedian standing next to his doppelgänger alongside the copy, "If your Data Self looks good to lenders, you're more likely to be approved for credit."[1] It is these kinds of curious cultural moments—when data are personified in their relation to selfhood—that inspire Lupton's argument that "concepts of selfhood, identity and embodi-

1 Deborah Lupton, *Data Selves: More-than-Human Perspectives* (Cambridge: Polity Press, 2020), 49.

ment and how they are enacted with digital technologies as part of everyday life are central to understanding personal data experiences."[2]

A companion to Lupton's 2016 monograph, *The Quantified Self, Data Selves* takes up a feminist new materialist lens to name the ontology of the data we produce with our bodies and marks the ways these data contribute to and constitute—at least partially—our selves, at both social and ontological levels (although skepticism about the stability of selfhood is one of the book's strongest characteristics). Lupton is both a sociologist and a cultural critic, and her ability to unite science and technology studies, media studies, and social science strengthens her argument. While a number of monographs have emerged in recent years implicating the self with media technologies—John Cheney-Lippold's *We Are Data: Algorithms and the Making of Our Digital Selves* (2017) comes to mind—what makes *Data Selves* so unique and uniquely perceptive are Lupton's qualitative sociological studies, which provide valuable perspectives in combination with her examples from art and pop culture. Conducted between 2015 and 2018, these five studies consist of interviews with Australians who participate in data-generating practices of self-knowledge, such as tracking a pregnancy through an app or recording cycling trips with a GoPro. The testimonies of her subjects—who, across the five studies, represent a wide range of ages and class backgrounds—provide singular insight into people's motivations for data-making, which range from enthusiasm at finding others who share their experiences to a drive to "manage change or chaos."[3] Lupton argues that, regardless of people's reasons for creating such data or whether they are even aware that they are, human-generated data "challenge the ontological boundaries between the binary oppositions of Self/Other, nature/culture, human/nonhuman and living/dead."[4] In focusing on the human body and the ways in which it produces data, Lupton responds to what she identifies as a lack of attention to the "fleshy, intuitive and sensory dimensions" of the human-data relationship.[5] Moreover, she situates such dynamics in the realm of material media studies, a move that may seem surprising considering the seeming immateriality of both data and affect. Using specific examples from her studies, she defends the claim that data come to matter when they produce material effects and affects. In order to more fully understand personal data experiences, Lupton contends, scholars ought to pay more attention to the way concepts of selfhood, identity, and embodiment are influenced and indeed constructed by data. The fact that human-generated data have such strong powers of agency justifies their designation as not only components of human selfhood but also data selves in their own right.

Data Selves is organized into five chapters, including the introduction. Chapter 2, "More-than-Human Perspectives," provides an overview of the diverse theoretical insights that inform Lupton's analysis. Karen Barad's influence is made explicit in this section; Lupton observes that attempts

2 Lupton, 12.
3 Lupton, 82.
4 Lupton, 13.
5 Lupton, 75.

to impose meaning onto data represent "agential cuts" that "identif[y] the boundaries of a phenomenon . . . [making] meaning from the potentially infinite sources that are available."[6] These agential cuts in the data produced from, about, and by us reveal how information technologies "work fundamentally to differentiate certain aspects of embodied practices and properties from others . . . render[ing] them more visible than other bodily attributes"[7]—for example, steps taken, pulse rate, or energy intake. Donna Haraway also appears in this chapter, adding another layer to Lupton's critique of humanism. She takes seriously Haraway's move away from posthumanism and toward a new theoretical identity as a "compost-ist," examining the affective and ontological implications of considering data as if they were human remains. Like remains, data can be "reliquaries of our humanity, testaments to our lived experiences and unique identity," with the potential to "decompose" and disperse into the environment over time.[8] This proves an immensely fruitful perspective to elucidate the powers that non-living data exert over humans. Indeed, Lupton uses the term "'lively data' . . . to characterize and explain the vitality of human-data assemblages."[9]

This theoretical chapter provides backbone for the provocative insights of the chapters that follow. In chapter 3, Lupton explores materializations of data, attending to contemporary artworks that seek to better visualize and understand it, such as the dystopian speculative fiction series *Black Mirror* (Channel 4, 2011–2014; Netflix, 2016–2019) and the OkCupid-based fiber artwork *Felt Personality* (Laurie Frick, 2019). Chapters 4 and 5 deal with her sociological research, with chapter 4 exploring the epistemological aspects of self-tracking and chapter 5 gesturing toward its ethical implications. Lupton's theoretical insights might not necessarily feel new to cultural critics, but her introduction of this sociological element alongside art criticism feels novel and rewarding. It is satisfying to see these theories borne out in the testimonies of subjects who have unexpected experiences with their own data—like "Damon," a self-tracking cyclist who is sometimes "surprise[ed] when you actually measure [performance] versus how you feel. . . . I found it's good having the watch as well to validate that feeling versus reality," indicating that he has a self-disciplining and self-verifying relationship to his data.[10] While Lupton may not robustly theorize the connections between visual culture, art, and the self-trackers she studies, their juxtaposition offers a more textured vision of the role data plays in the construction of the self.

Lupton cites ethnographers, sociologists, philosophers, literary critics, anthropologists, cultural geographers, and information scientists as part of her multidisciplinary analysis. Indeed, one of the great successes of this text is its scholarly diversity; it draws together surprising and divergent viewpoints to fully illustrate how data selves operate. Among the most important for Lupton is affect theory, which she reads through the perspective of "data

6 Lupton, 28.
7 Lupton, 29.
8 Lupton, 40.
9 Lupton, 5.
10 Lupton, 88.

sense" to understand the way data interact with bodies. One poignant section sees her explore the affective responses that data visualization and physicalization produce in people. When people meet the "anxiety-inspiring qualities and privacy implications" of the data gathered from their bodies, they experience strong affective bodily responses such as distress—exemplified in the 2017 project *Persuasive Anxiety* in which participants interfaced with three intrusive, "controversial" self-tracking artifacts over six months.[11] Thus, Lupton demonstrates with elegance the completeness of the loop between human bodies and data, confirming their place in an assemblage together.

A theoretically dense and provocative text, *Data Selves* leaves many of its arguments' implications murky. Lupton's engagement with ethics seems to fall short in places, stopping at a criticism of Enlightenment autonomy and mastery. For instance, she often gestures toward the potential political or ethical ramifications of the datafication of the self, mostly having to do with privacy. "The affective responses that data physicalizations [i.e., visualizations] can evoke," she writes, "may lead people to engage more actively, including at the political level, in challenges to violations of their personal data privacy and security."[12] Without a theory of the political or of data aesthetics, however, it is left to the reader to discern what that engagement might look like. The thorny issue of digital privacy, treated in chapter 5, feels especially unresolved; knowing that voluntary data-tracking is both a practice of self-actualization and easily exploited by corporate interests, Lupton fails to deliver a fully conclusive argument about its ethical ramifications. Despite this shortcoming, *Data Selves* nevertheless puts forward a thorough and complete theory of human-data entanglement. Its strength lies in its breadth and ambition, uniting a variety of fields of study to produce nuanced views that will be fruitful for readers from both humanistic and social-scientific disciplines. Ultimately, Lupton's monograph represents a thoughtful and novel exploration of media-human ontology, rich with diverse examples, which will benefit undergraduates, graduate students, and scholars alike.

Bren Ram is a doctoral student in the Department of English and Diluvial Houston Predoctoral Fellow at Rice University, where she studies the intersection of risk and ecology.

11 Lupton, 67.
12 Lupton, 70.

Reviewed by Weixian Pan

Radiant Infrastructures: Media, Environment, and Cultures of Uncertainty

by Rahul Mukherjee.
Duke University Press.
2020. 288 pages.
$99.95 hardcover; $26.95 paper; also available in e-book.

In *Radiant Infrastructures: Media, Environment, and Cultures of Uncertainty*, Rahul Mukherjee presents a compelling investigation into the multiple environmentalisms of contemporary India. He convincingly argues for the crucial role of media and mediation in constituting perceptions and publics around infrastructures capable of emitting radiant energies that are difficult to perceive, comprehend, and control. Mukherjee uses invigorating ethnographic and analytical details to elaborate how the mediated and empirical traces of "radiance" contribute to conceptual debates on intermediality, infrastructural politics, public spheres, and human-nonhuman relationality.

The two radiant infrastructures investigated in this book—cell towers and nuclear power plants—are rarely paired in public debates, even though they both symbolize India's national aspiration to modernity and provoke uncertainty and fear around the health impacts of radiation. These two infrastructures emit different types of radiation (ionizing and non-ionizing, respectively), but more importantly, they are perceived as two separate problems affecting different social classes. While cell towers exist largely in urban areas and affect mainly urban middle-class citizens with techno-social lifestyles, nuclear plants are strategically built in rural areas and impact mostly lower-income populations of farmers and fishermen. By juxtaposing the differences and similarities of the two large-scale infrastructures, Mukherjee not only illustrates "how divided the social fabric of India is," and correspondingly a highly polarized media sphere, but also highlights the way media representation allows people to make sense of their contact with and exposure to the imperceptible radiation.[1]

Throughout the book, Mukherjee expertly demonstrates how different media coverages at the local and national levels help to concretize radiant energies through their material properties, discursive circulation, and ability to generate affective relations between people and techno-infrastructures. Mukherjee makes a convincing case that in order to understand the complex everyday encounters people have with controversial infrastructure, scholars and relevant stakeholders must attend to the intermedial forms and practices around radiant infrastructure that are shaped by class and power struggles and in turn construct radiation as a normality in life.[2]

One of Mukherjee's main concerns, which cuts across the entire book, is how media both shape the expert-layperson divide and help negotiate that divide when knowledge systems clash in environmental controversies. Mukherjee carefully assembles a broad spectrum of media texts, events, and discourses—including popular talk shows, investigative TV journalism, activist documentaries, institution-made energy advertisements, local newspapers, and neighborhood meetings—in order to illuminate persistent tensions between scientism and embodied knowledge. The former often relies on technical experts and forms of scientific knowledge such as evaluative reports, standardized threshold levels, and data sets. However, Mukherjee rightfully emphasizes the significance of laypeople's knowledge and experiences in environmental publics and vigorous debates around the uncertain health effects of radiant infrastructures. To put it differently, Mukherjee argues that scientific experts should take seriously forms of indigenous knowledge that they often dismiss as anecdotal evidence, rumors, or superstitions, because this knowledge also influences public perceptions of environmental uncertainties. Toward the end of the book's introduction, Mukherjee talks about one such anecdote, in which local residents distrust radiation detectors but regard the return of peacocks as a sign of normality. This story, in which nonhuman signs of security are valued more than scientific knowledge, attests to how in situations of uncertainty, "perceptions of technology are articulated using vernacular mythologies of the everyday."[3]

Epistemologically, Mukherjee contrasts and channels these two knowledge systems in order to rethink the political subjects and relations formed around radiant infrastructure. This theoretical goal engages with Partha Chatterjee's civil society–political society framework. Chatterjee contends that only a small group in Indian society have access to civil society, and the majority of the Indian population form a political relationship with the state through informal and quasi-legal access to social welfare, falling under the scope of "political society."[4] Mukherjee similarly acknowledges

1 Rahul Mukherjee, *Radiant Infrastructures: Media, Environment, and Cultures of Uncertainty* (Durham, NC: Duke University Press, 2020), 4.

2 Mukherjee, 33. He defines "intermediality" as "relations among media texts and forms covering a particular environmental controversy, as well as the interactions between the media technologies assembled to demonstrate radiation" (19).

3 Mukherjee, 25.

4 Partha Chatterjee, *The Politics of the Governed: Reflections on Popular Politics in Most of the World* (New York: Columbia University Press, 2004).

the insufficiency of civil structures when presumed avenues of civil participation and democratic decision-making became hard to obtain regarding environmental controversies in non-Western contexts such as India.[5] As a macro framework, "political society" helps to explain how, for example, the affected fishing communities around nuclear power plants seek political relationships with the Indian state despite not being recognized as citizens. However, Mukherjee's ethnographic engagements with local community and activist media practices also push to complicate "the neat divide between civil and political society."[6] He attends to the possible intersections between civil engagement and quasi-publics of non-citizens, we understand, because such clean-cut binary categorization is incapable of calibrating other social and cultural factors at work in India's quest for radiant energies.

Radiant Infrastructures begins with two analytical chapters that trace the environmental controversies around cell towers and nuclear reactors, respectively. Across these two chapters, Mukherjee convincingly establishes how intermedial practices are crucial for ordinary people to comprehend the varying hyper-visibility and invisibility of radiant infrastructures. In doing so, he manages to address the variety of human and nonhuman actors operating in the media ecology around radiation—from urban middle-class residents, talk show audiences, radiation-affected fishing villagers, and environmental activists to radiation detectors, microwave ovens, and aluminum foil. Mukherjee thus asserts that environmental publics are ontologically heterogeneous and are constituted by the intermedial relations across media texts and events and across human and nonhuman bodies.[7]

Chapter 1, "Debating Cell Towers," emphasizes the distribution of discourses around cell antenna radiation across media systems and among scientists, antiradiation activists, and television and newspaper audiences. In tracing this circulatory path, he vividly illustrates how mediation transforms the public perception of cell infrastructure. Imperceptible radiation from cell towers is rendered into beeping LED lights, flows across the urban lifestyle talk show *Living It Up* (CNN-IBN, 2006–2014), and infiltrates live presentations of microwave radiation levels at rooftop meetings, all of which spark more uncertainty and speculations. Stories about the health impact of cell towers' radiation move from the local community newspapers to national TV talk shows, shaping environmental debates across various spatial and social scales. Through mediation, then, radiation becomes not only a technical issue but a sociocultural concern with uncertainty at its core.[8]

Chapter 2, "Contested Nuclear Imaginaries," investigates how stakeholders around the Koodankulam nuclear plant strategically use representations to evoke environmental publics. Mukherjee skillfully reads across mediated texts and discourses produced by anti-nuclear activists, affected fishing communities, and institutions such as the Nuclear Power Corporation of India Limited (NPCIL) and pieces together highly contested imaginaries

5 Mukherjee, *Radiant Infrastructures*, 29.
6 Mukherjee, 188–189.
7 Mukherjee, 41.
8 Mukherjee, 54.

of nuclear energy in India—some see it as unregulated and risky, others as secured and promising. For example, a *National Geographic*–NPCIL advertisement embodies a promise for techno-modernity by constructing nuclear plants as the nation's energy future, "brightening millions of lives."[9] Countering such a utopic vision, anti-nuclear activists (including documentary filmmakers, photojournalists, and protesters) collectively paint and organize around a post-apocalyptic imaginary of nuclear fallout and the social abandonment of an affected population, one that is at times satirical, at other times spectacular. Mukherjee deliberately leaves the readers in this muddy ground, where he concludes that nuclear futures mediated from both sides need to be accounted for in order to negotiate the present of living in the shadow of nuclear energies.

Chapters 3, 4, and 5 merge the discussions of these two infrastructures to compare their tactics in shaping and sustaining environmental publics. Chapter 3, "Emissions," thinks through the polemic of transparency and secrecy by outlining various groups' attempts to control unregulated signal emission and contain radioactive radiance. Mukherjee argues that transparency, or the performance of transparency through visualization, more often than not conceals more than it reveals. In the chapter, he offers a timely reflection on how discourses of transparency can be mobilized by media and related institutions as a way to manage public knowledge of radiant infrastructure. This can take the form of exclusive TV reporting inside the Koodankulam Nuclear Plant done by journalist Pallava Bagla, whose insider knowledge of the plant is meant to assure the public of its safety. Or it can appear as Tarang Sanchar, an e-portal created by Indian telecom companies that can control how much antenna data to share with the public. Mukherjee sees "secrecy," rather than "transparency," at the center of institutional players' desire to regulate both the uncontained radiation and flow of radiant information. The notion of "secrecy," as he states, "draws its power not just from the content of what is kept secret but also from the way in which the secret is managed and organized."[10]

Chapter 4, "Exposures," shifts to various mediations of communities and bodies exposed to radiant infrastructure. Mukherjee analyzes testimonies of cancer patients who have lived in close proximity with the nuclear radiation for long periods of time. The patients' stories and irradiated bodies are mediated in lifestyle shows and documentary films such as R. P. Amudhan's *Radiation Stories Part I: Manavalakurichi* (2010) and Shri Prakash's *Buddha Weeps in Jadugoda* (1999). In his close reading of the two documentaries, Mukherjee demonstrates the affective and embodied qualities of the environmental effects of radiant infrastructure. At the molecular level, human bodies absorb, store, and interact with radiant energies, but these often unwanted techno-intimacies, he argues, need to be visualized through technologies such as CT scans and electroencephalograms in order to be recognized in environmental public discourse.

At this point, the book has established material, discursive, and affective

9 Mukherjee, 93.
10 Mukherjee, 134.

resonances between cell towers and nuclear reactors, but avid readers might also note that the intermedial relays and flows of embodied experiences seldom move across the environmentalism of the poor and bourgeois. This feeling persists into the fifth and last chapter, "Styling Advocacy: Activism and Citizenship." Mukherjee elaborates how anti-nuclear and anti–cell antenna activists use contrasting "styles" of advocacy, drawing their own connections to Bollywood celebrities or aligning with the history of activism in India. These tactics of styling, he contends, point to the different political subjectivities engendered around controversial radiant infrastructure. Nevertheless, this argument seems to re-enforce how environmentalism in India is still structured by its divided social fabrics and media sphere, which Mukherjee challenges from the beginning of the book. Rather than seeing this as a flaw to the book's overall argument, Mukherjee instead suggests that intersections at the conceptual level are often difficult to perceive, let alone to put our fingers on, but they take a clearer shape in everyday contacts. For Mukherjee, thinking and writing about radiant energy is only the first step to joining the efforts of activists and local communities to build relationality across seemingly disparate publics and social spectrums. If so, that might help readers better understand why he concludes with a strange assemblage of speculative looks into the radiant futures.

It would be wrong to attribute the significance of this book solely to adding cultural specificity to existing studies on environmental crises and critical infrastructures. The book's energizing conceptualization of *radiance* puts it in conversation with the recent body of interdisciplinary scholarship around mediating energies, such as rare earth minerals, solar power, wind, carbon, and the sociotechnical relations generated by these energies.[11] Mukherjee is not simply present in this book as a distant observer. He often stands in alliance with the communities affected daily by radiations, and at other times he converses with concerned scientists, filmmakers, and activists to show the intersections of their mediation and opinions around radiant infrastructures. This book will be compelling for a wide range of readers, as it offers an invaluable framework for thinking about environmental justice and critical infrastructure in Asia, from post-Fukushima Japan to China's accelerated adoption of 5G cellular infrastructures and Southeast Asia's energy crisis.

Weixian Pan is an Assistant Professor of Interactive Media Arts at New York University, Shanghai. Her current book project examines how media transforms the materiality and imaginary of geological, riverine and oceanic environments, a process corresponding to China's geopolitical desires.

11 See Nicole Starosielski, "Beyond the Sun: Embedded Solarities and Agricultural Practice," *South Atlantic Quarterly* 120, no. 1 (January 2021): 13–24; Anne Pasek, "Managing Carbon and Data Flows: Fungible Forms of Mediation in the Cloud," *Culture Machine* 18 (April 2019): 1–15; and Cymene Howe, *Ecologics: Wind and Power in the Anthropocene* (Durham, NC: Duke University Press, 2019).